W9-CKE-324

WORKING IN A
24/7 ECONOMY

WORKING IN A 24/7 ECONOMY

CHALLENGES FOR AMERICAN FAMILIES

HARRIET B. PRESSER

RUSSELL SAGE FOUNDATION | NEW YORK

The Russell Sage Foundation

Library of Congress Cataloging-in-Publication Data

Presser, Harriet B.
  Working in a 24/7 economy : challenges for American families / Harriet Presser.
      p. cm.
  Includes bibliographical references and index.
  ISBN 0-87154-670-1
    1. Work and family—United States.   2. Hours of labor—United States.
  3. Hours of labor, Flexible—United States.   4. Child care—United States.
  5. Quality of work life—United States.   I. Title: Work in a twenty-four/seven economy.   II. Title.
  HD4904.25.P74   2003
  331.25—dc21   2003047051

Text design by Suzanne Nichols.

RUSSELL SAGE FOUNDATION
112 East 64th Street, New York, New York 10021
10 9 8 7 6 5 4 3 2 1

In loving memory of my mother, Rose Jabish

Contents

About the Author

HARRIET B. PRESSER is Distinguished University Professor in the Department of Sociology at the University of Maryland.

Preface

My interest in the study of nonstandard work schedules began with a serendipitous finding over twenty years ago. In 1980, I was analyzing data for a conference paper on child care arrangements among employed women—then a little-researched topic.[1] To my surprise, I found that about one-seventh of all employed American women (married and single) with preschool-age children reported that the father was the primary child care provider when the mothers were at work (Presser 1982). I wondered how this could be, given that most fathers are employed full time. I speculated that many dual-earner married couples may include spouses working different shifts and sharing child care responsibilities—and that the ratio of father care would be even higher, looking specifically at dual earners. Unfortunately, the data set for the paper on child care I was preparing (the June 1977 Current Population Survey) did not include questions on work schedules that would permit me to test this hypothesis.

However, the May 1980 Current Population Survey, which did not have any child care information, did have national data on work schedules. In collaboration with my (then) graduate student, Virginia Cain, I examined the work shifts of both spouses among dual-earner couples with preschool-age children. Again, I was greatly surprised: One-third of all such couples in the United States were "split-shift" couples, one spouse working in the daytime and the other mostly in the evenings, nights, or on a regularly rotating schedule (Presser and Cain 1983). One would never have guessed this high prevalence from the existing literature on either mothers' or fathers' employment; indeed, I do not recall ever having read about such a work pattern among couples.

Yet, the notion of people working nonstandard hours and weekends was not new to me. I grew up in a resort town with parents in the cocktail lounge business who both worked evenings and weekends, and when their marriage ended, my mother continued to work this late schedule as well as a daytime job, so that she could support three children. (After we were grown, she became a hotel owner, and living in the hotel, was on call around the clock.) I always felt our family's lack of time together was rare. But after seeing the 1980 CPS statistics, I realized that families in which at least one spouse was working late shifts was not uncommon, just not visible to the public's—or scholar's—eye. (The phrase "24/7" had not yet become common parlance.)

Single mothers sharing child care with grandmothers is also a phenomenon in which I had personal experience. After my own marriage ended, and prior to going to graduate school, I worked part-time in the early evening as a restaurant hostess while my mother cared for my daughter, Sheryl—then a toddler. This experience stimulated my interest in the 1980s to study "split-shifting" between mothers and grandmothers; I found that one-third of all grandmothers who provide child care for their preschool-aged grandchildren were otherwise employed (Presser 1989).

I also began to explore the overall prevalence of nonstandard work schedules for the country as a whole, focusing on the particular groups of people and family types that were most likely to engage in such employment and on what the social consequences of working nonstandard times were, particularly with regard to family life. A key problem was the paucity of existing data. Fortunately, based on my early findings, several of those conducting large-scale work or family surveys were willing to add questions about *which* hours people work, as well as how many. The Bureau of Labor Statistics, which had been asking about specific work hours in certain May supplements of the Current Population Survey questions, agreed to expand their questions to include which *days* people work (not just how many) and their reasons for working nonstandard shifts. This book draws on data from two major surveys with detailed data on work schedules: the May 1997 Current Population Survey and two waves of the National Survey of Families and Households. Both surveys are described in the chapters to follow.

Financial support for conducting this research came from several sources for which I am most grateful: a grant from the William T. Grant Foundation, a year's visiting scholarship at the Russell Sage Foundation, and training funds for graduate students from the William and Flora Hewlett Foundation. Also, one of the book chapters was drafted during a month's stay at the Rockefeller Foundation's Bellagio Study and Conference Center.

I am also deeply grateful to several graduate students who assisted me with the data analysis for this book: Soumya Alva, Rose Kreider, Kei Nomaguchi, and Lijuan Wu. Their programming expertise and dedication to the task were invaluable. I also thank Barbara Bergmann for as-

tutely reviewing two of the chapters, as well as three anonymous re-
viewers who provided extremely helpful comments. I benefited greatly
from copyediting by Cindy Buck and editorial supervision by Suzanne
Nichols.

Special thanks go to my partner, Phil Corfman, who not only read
and commented on all chapters, but provided sustained encouragement
during the entire writing process.

1

Introduction

I**N THE** United States, two-fifths of all employed Americans work
mostly at nonstandard times—in the evening, at night, on a rotating
shift, or during the weekend. Although much attention has been
given to the *number* of hours Americans work (Schor 1991; Robinson
and Godbey 1997), the issue of *which* hours—or days—Americans work
has generally gone unnoticed by researchers and policymakers alike. Yet
the pervasiveness of nonstandard work schedules is a significant social
phenomenon, with important implications for the health and well-being
of individuals and their families and for the implementation of social
policies.

How did these high levels of nonstandard work schedules come
about? The practice of working evenings and nights has been around at
least as long as midwives have been employed for childbirth, an event
that can occur at any hour. Policies encouraging late-hour employment
go back at least to Roman times, when city deliveries of goods by horse-
drawn vehicles were restricted to the night hours to reduce daytime traffic congestion (Scherrer 1981). Regulations against night work during
the Middle Ages may have stalled an emerging trend, as Jeffrey Scherrer
has argued, but by the nineteenth century the growth of large cities, the
increasing complexity of the division of labor that accompanied the industrial revolution, and the introduction of artificial lighting were providing strong motivation to expand economic activity around the clock.
Reflecting on the early part of the twentieth century, Amos Hawley
(1950) wrote that periodicity was giving way to continuity, and the diurnal cycle, while still predominant, was becoming a twenty-four-hour cycle. A few decades later, Murray Melbin (1978, 3) offered the intriguing
notion of night as frontier, seeing the "expansion into the dark hours [as]
a continuation of the geographic migration across the face of the earth."
Both scholars viewed the growth of shift work in the United States—
that is, work schedules that deviated from regular daytime hours—as a
demonstration of this trend. Today the new phrase "24/7" has taken
hold in our everyday language to denote around-the-clock availability,

and the demand for such availability is increasingly evidenced in labor market activity as well as in our interpersonal relations.

This book does not focus on the precise trend in nonstandard work schedules among employed Americans over the decades because it cannot be rigorously assessed, owing to lack of comparable data.[1] It focuses, rather, on the challenges to various aspects of family functioning posed by today's high levels of nonstandard work schedules. In looking at these challenges, we will see that the prevalence of nonstandard work schedules has produced a new "home-time" family structure for many Americans, particularly the working poor: spouses often are not at home together in the evening or at night, and parents are often not home at such times with their children. What does this new temporal structure mean for the nature and stability of family life, including the care of children? Do scholars and policymakers need to reconceptualize the family to take into account the temporal diversity at home generated by temporal diversity at work? A key objective of this book is to address these questions with empirical data and to document in some detail the characteristics of persons in different family situations who work nonstandard work schedules and the factors that may encourage this decision.

We will see that the consequences of working nonstandard schedules often differ for men and for women, and for families with and without children. While there are some positive consequences relating to more gender equality in housework and increased parental time with children, and some individuals may find other advantages to such schedules, there are negative social consequences such as higher marital instability and complex child care patterns that give cause for concern.

It should be noted at the outset that in this book nonstandard work schedules are defined as those in which the *most hours* employed are within a fixed daytime/weekday period. We will focus on the prevalence and impact of nonstandard work *shifts* in the evening or at night, on a fixed or rotating basis, or otherwise variable schedules, and of weekend employment. This is a perspective distinct from a focus on the total number of hours worked or on flextime; these aspects of employment timing have received far more attention. These three aspects, of course, are not mutually exclusive: people working either day or nonday shifts may work short or long hours or may vary the specific hours they work within a narrow range of starting and ending times. Moreover, people who work day shifts may start their jobs in the very early hours of the morning or end their work in the early evening but still be designated as daytime workers, given the focus here on the shift on which American workers spend *most* of their hours. This focus is important because it best differentiates the temporally "deviant" workers from others. (A focus on *some* but not necessarily *most* of the hours worked clearly would lead to much higher prevalence rates for nonstandard work shifts than shown here.)

Correspondingly, American society as a whole is moving toward a 24/7 economy at the same time as there is a growing diversity in the number of hours people work (Smith 1986; U.S. Department of Labor 2002a), more flextime (U.S. Department of Labor 1998), and a trend toward employment during the "fringe times" of the traditional nine-to-five workday (Hamermesh 1999a). Also, there have been significant changes in the nature of employer-employee relations; these bonds have weakened with the rise of temporary and contract work, even though such workers represent a small proportion of the labor force (Clinton 1997; Kalleberg 2000). Interestingly, these trends have occurred even as there has been little change in the average number of hours worked each week—an increase of just 1.1 hours between 1976 and 2001 (Rones, Ilg, and Gardner 1997; U.S. Department of Labor 2002a).[2]

It is important in setting the stage for the current study that we understand factors at the societal level that may be driving the demand for employment at nonstandard times. In particular, it is relevant to consider the impact of changing societal conditions at the macro level on the timing of labor force activity, and by extension, on individual and family well-being.

The Growing Demand for Employment at Nonstandard Times

As portrayed in figure 1.1, at the macro level there are at least three interrelated factors that increase the demand for Americans to work late or rotating shifts and weekends: the changing economy, changing demography, and changing technology.

An important aspect of the changing economy is the growth of the service sector, with its high prevalence of nonstandard schedules relative to the goods-producing sector. In the 1960s the number of employees in manufacturing greatly exceeded the number in service industries, whereas by 2000 the percentage was over twice as high in services as in manufacturing (Meisenheimer 1998; Department of Labor 2002b).[3] During the same period women's labor force participation almost doubled, from about one-third to two-thirds of all women (U.S. Department of Commerce 1975, 2002). The interaction between the growth of women's employment and the growth of the service sector is highly relevant. It is generally acknowledged that women increasingly entered the

FIGURE 1.1   *The Movement Toward a 24/7 Economy and Its Consequences*

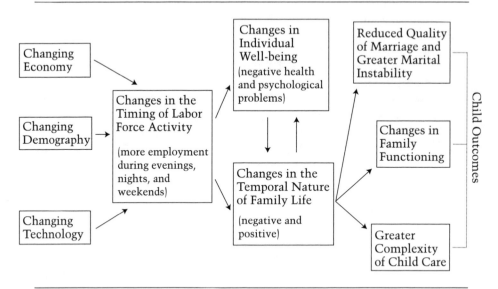

Source: Author's configuration.

labor force because of the growing demand for employees in the service occupations that are disproportionately female, such as clerical and sales (Oppenheimer 1970; Goldin 1990). But the influence goes in the other direction as well: women's increasing labor force participation contributed to the growth of the service economy. For example, the decline in full-time homemaking has generated an increase in the extent to which family members eat out and purchase other homemaking services. Moreover, women's increasing daytime labor force participation has generated a demand for services during nondaytime hours and weekends, since women are increasingly less able to shop during the day or to be home for daytime service workers—at least not on weekdays.

Demographic changes have also contributed to a growing demand for late-shift and weekend employment. One relevant change is the postponement of marriage by almost three years since 1960 for both women and men; by 1998 the median ages at first marriage were 25.0 and 27.7, respectively (U.S. Department of Commerce 1960, 1998).[4] This change, along with the rise in real family income resulting from the growth of two-earner couples, has increased the demand for recreation and entertainment during evenings, nights, and weekends.[5] Further, the aging of the population—from 9.2 percent age sixty-five and over in

4

1960 to 12.4 percent in 2000 (U.S. Department of Commerce 1975, table 3; 2002, table 11)—has increased the demand for medical services over a twenty-four-hour day, seven days a week.

Finally, technological change, along with reduced costs, has moved us to a global twenty-four-hour economy. Frances Cairncross (1997) has written about the "death of distance" due to such changes. But global low-cost technological change is also encouraging what might be termed the "death of diurnal time." The ability to be "on call" at all hours of the day and night to others around the world at low cost generates a need to be so available. For example, the rise of multinational corporations and the use of computers, faxes, and other forms of instant communication increase the demand for branch offices in different locations to operate at the same time corporate headquarters is open. Similarly, international financial markets are expanding their hours of operation, and overnight mailing companies require round-the-clock workers, all days of the week.[6]

With a watchful eye, one can see many anecdotal reflections of these trends in the mass media. For example, it was reported in the *New York Times* on November 1, 1998, that United Parcel Service (UPS) found it difficult to fill its midnight-to-3:00 A.M. shift in Louisville, Kentucky, its busiest package-processing hub. As an incentive, it offered free tuition at three of the local colleges, with the city and UPS splitting the cost. Moreover, UPS and the city built a dormitory with rooms to rent to these late-night employees, "with special soundproofing, heavy blinds and more classrooms, and offering shuttle bus service between the job, the dormitory and classes."

There are also many indications in the media that financial markets are expanding their services around the clock. On June 16, 1999, the *New York Times* carried Nasdaq's announcement that it would extend its trading hours in the United States. U.S. institutions specializing in foreign exchange and interest rate derivatives with trading hubs in different parts of the world, such as Fleet Global Markets, whose website boasts of its "real time, 24-hour transaction services and counseling for our customers, as well as 24-hour monitoring."

Although the global markets are contributing to the demand for nonstandard work schedules, most of the demand for employment during late hours in the United States, as we will see, is for jobs in low-paying occupations in local markets, such as around-the-clock nursing attendance, food services, and recreation and entertainment.[7] Technology may change the way some local services are being dispensed, as exemplified by the 24/7 availability of local librarians via the Internet to assist Maryland residents, as reported in the *Washington Post* on March 17, 2003. In assessing the impact of demand for around-the-clock services, it is important to distinguish among consumers, employers, and employees. Whereas, generally, consumers may benefit from the 24/7 availability of services, and employers may benefit from 24/7 capital utilization, many employees may find late-hour employment far from desirable.

The focus of this book is on employees. The data presented here will show that most people who work nonstandard hours report that they do so primarily because it is a job requirement rather than for personal reasons. Pay differentials for working late hours are not common; the amounts when provided tend to be small, and such differentials are rarely reported as a primary motivating factor. The fact that a disproportionate number of those working nonstandard work schedules have low incomes adds an important economic stressor to the physical, psychological, and social stressors affecting their lives.

Although this book analyzes microlevel data, a critical outcome at the macro level is work-time inequality among employed Americans. This issue is closely tied to income inequality. Indeed, as Daniel Hamermesh has shown (1999b), when taking into account nonpecuniary aspects of employment, such as late hours and accident rates, one finds that labor force inequalities based solely on income are understated.[8]

Responding to Demand

Figure 1.1 is a dynamic model that views employees responding to growing demand by increasingly working late hours and weekends, work schedules that in turn alter individual well-being and the temporal nature of family life and consequently child outcomes. In this book, given the data limitations, we necessarily take a more static view, with two major objectives.

The first objective is to provide a better understanding of the distinctive characteristics of those who respond to the demand for employment at nonstandard times, why they work such schedules, and the family context in which this occurs (chapters 2 and 3). The second objective is to assess some of the consequences of nonstandard work schedules for the family—namely, the quality and stability of marriages, various aspects of family functioning, how children are cared for when parents are at the workplace, and the misfit between work hours and child care for many low-educated mothers (chapters 4 through 8). (Although figure 1.1 points to the very important issue of the potential consequences of diverse family work schedules for child well-being, this cannot be assessed with the data sources used here.)

To address the first objective, the analyses rely on the May 1997 CPS, a nationally representative sample of over fifty thousand households described in some detail in chapter 2. The large numbers of employed persons in the CPS provide a rare opportunity to examine detailed occupations in relation to work schedules. Also, the CPS is the only national data source on employees' reasons for working late or rotating hours. We will see that employment during nonstandard hours and days is most evident for those who are young, single, less-educated, and black. However, with one-fifth of all employed Americans working something other than a fixed daytime schedule and one-third working weekends, employment during nonstandard hours and days is pervasive among all subgroups. Moreover, the ratios are higher when married couples rather than individuals are the unit of analysis because either spouse can work such nonstandard schedules. As we shall see, one-fourth of two-earner married couples include at least one spouse (rarely both) who works a schedule other than a fixed daytime shift. This ratio increases to one-third when couples have children. The younger the age of spouses, the lower their education, and the larger the number of children, the higher the ratio. Moreover, the ratio is higher among blacks than whites. Using education as a proxy for income, it is clear that "split-shift" couples are most prevalent among the working poor.

How unique is the United States? Although there is a problem of comparability between countries as well as within the United States over time, I offer a rough comparison of the CPS data with Labour Force Survey (LFS) data for a number of European countries to demonstrate that the United States is not alone in the widespread prevalence of nonstandard schedules (chapter 2).

Family Consequences

To address the second objective of this book—better understanding of the consequences of nonstandard work schedules for American families—I draw on the National Survey of Families and Households (NSFH). The first wave of the NSFH was conducted in 1987 to 1988 and the second in 1992 to 1994. The nationally representative sample in this survey comprises about thirteen thousand main respondents in the first wave and approximately ten thousand in the second wave and is further described in chapter 4.

Each of the chapters on the family consequences of nonstandard work schedules (chapters 4 through 7) reviews the literature dealing with the subject of that chapter, from marital quality and stability to family functioning and child care. There is little research to draw on that directly links these topics to work shifts or weekend employment, since there are few studies designed with this main purpose. An important exception is the classic study conducted in the early 1960s by Paul

Mott and his colleagues (1965), which intensively investigated the social, psychological, and physical effects of shift work on a sample of white, male, blue-collar workers in continuous-process industries in the east-central part of the United States. Even though it discussed family life from a traditional perspective (ignoring the employment status of the wife entirely), this 1965 study represented a significant step forward in our knowledge of the social aspects of shift work—at least for one important subgroup of American society—and no comparable in-depth study of shift work in the United States has since been conducted. Of special significance in this study is the detail it paid to the type of shift, with evening, night, and rotating shifts often showing differing outcomes. As we will see, the type of shift worked remains an important contingency in assessing family outcomes—even though, at times, we cannot assess this for particular subgroups because the sample size is too small.

Overall, we will see that the timing of labor force activity affects the temporal nature of family life in both positive and negative ways, and that negative consequences appear to be more likely, at least among the consequences considered. Moreover, short-term advantages may be offset by long-term disadvantages. For example, whatever financial and psychological benefits result from the greater participation of employed fathers in child care during the hours mothers are employed (and the fathers are not) may be offset by the greater risk of marital dissolution when parents work at night. Nonstandard work schedules are also associated with a lower quality of intact marriages. As for specific aspects of family functioning, we will see that among dual-earner couples, when either spouse works a nonday shift, husbands participate more in traditionally female household tasks. The findings with regard to parent-child interaction are mixed, depending on the type of interaction, type of shift, and gender of parent. We will also see that child care arrangements are more complex when parents work nonstandard schedules. Relying on CPS data, we will also look at what this complexity implies for the ability of low-educated mothers, who are especially likely to work late hours and weekends, to hold on to their jobs and not move on and off of welfare.

Moving Forward

The overarching theme of this book is that nonstandard work schedules not only are highly prevalent among American families but also generate a level of complexity in family functioning that needs greater attention. Because the findings are based on secondary analyses of two national data sets not specifically designed to study work schedules in depth, they are therefore far from definitive. Nevertheless, a significant social phenomenon is unfolding that merits our attention, and the fact that our data sources on this issue are so limited should be of concern. Chapter 9, in addition to summing up, addresses some serious gaps in our knowledge while calling for an expanded research agenda and offers some policy alternatives while calling for more public discourse.

A Note About Health

An important gap in our knowledge that should be kept in mind throughout this book is the fact that we cannot assess the role of health factors linked to shift work that undoubtedly have ramifications for family functioning. Moreover, the desire of many shift workers to be in sync temporally with their family when not on the job has health implications. There are no national data sources that would permit us to address this interrelationship,[9] but a large body of research attests to the negative health consequences for individuals who work nights and rotating shifts. The greater health risk associated with very late or changing work hours stems from changes to an individual's circadian rhythms, which are linked to such biological functions as body temperature, hormone levels, and sleep. Behaviorally, there is evidence of greater gastrointestinal disorders, higher rates of cardiovascular disease, breast cancer, miscarriage, preterm birth, and low birthweight (U.S. Congress 1991; Boggild and Knutsson 1999; Wedderburn 2000; Schernhammer et al. 2001). The increased risk can be substantial. For example, a review of studies on cardiovascular disease suggests a 40 percent greater risk among shift workers (Boggild and Knutsson 1999). Chronic sleep deprivation and the resulting fatigue and stress are viewed as a major problem for job productivity (Tepas and Price 2001).

The negative social outcomes of late or rotating schedules may well be a consequence of the interaction among social, psychological, and physiological stressors. Research indicates that memory, reaction time, manual dexterity, and subjective feelings of alertness vary over the course of the day and are altered by changes in circadian rhythms and chronic sleep deprivation. How these factors affect job performance depends on the type of job (how much vigilance, physical activity, and cognition are required), the specific work hours, motivational factors, and the adaptability of the individual. It is not coincidental that the major performance disasters at Chernobyl and Seven Mile Island and aboard the Exxon *Valdez* were all late-night events; each of these disasters was linked to the fatigue of workers (U.S. Congress 1991).

The chapters that follow demonstrate the need to acknowledge the challenges that American families face as we move toward a 24/7 economy. These challenges become evident from the descriptive data that demonstrate the pervasiveness of late work shifts and weekend employment for family members as well as single individuals, and for parents as well as nonparents—raising questions as to why Americans, particularly those with children, have responded to the demand for employment at nonstandard times in such large numbers. The statistical analyses presented allow us to assess some of the consequences of this work schedule decision on family functioning, after adjusting for the possible effects of other social and economic factors on family life. Challenges to the family emerge here as well, and one wonders whether Americans are aware of the tradeoffs they are making in working such schedules. Clearly, the more we learn from research, the more informed the public will be. Let us begin with a detailed look at who works nonstandard schedules and why.

2

Who Works Nonstandard Schedules and Why

ARE THOSE who work nonstandard schedules like most other employed Americans, or do they differ as a group in their job, family, and background characteristics? The answer to this question is important in that it will give us some insight into where the demand for such workers lies (largely reflected by the workers' job characteristics) and who is responsive to such demand (largely reflected by workers' family and background characteristics). If people who work nonstandard schedules tend to be those who are relatively disadvantaged in the labor force in terms of family and background characteristics (for example, they are inexperienced owing to age, not highly educated, or of minority status), then working nonstandard schedules might reflect their lack of options and thus add to their disadvantage—assuming they do not like being out of sync with family and friends, do not like altering their circadian rhythms, or have other negative reasons for wanting to avoid such schedules.

On the other hand, some workers may prefer late-night or weekend employment. In spite of the social or health costs, they may see certain advantages in such work: there is often less supervision on the job; the job may be especially interesting despite the hours; they may enjoy a strong sense of community with coworkers both off and on the job because they are out of sync with others; there may be child care advantages, a pay premium, or better commuting; or they may simply like to work late and sleep for large parts of the day.[1]

The data limitations in exploring this issue stem from there being only one question on a national survey about the reasons Americans work other than a regular day shift, and no question as to why they work weekends. Moreover, there is no question asking those on nonstandard schedules whether they would prefer to work a standard one.[2] Individuals may take a combination of factors, both pro and con, into consideration when deciding whether to accept (or stay in) a job that requires nonstandard times of employment, and we do not have the data to assess the trade-offs they are making. Nevertheless, it is revealing to examine the characteristics of those working nonstandard schedules and the main reason they give for doing so.

We will see that although nonstandard work schedules are pervasive among all Americans, there are notable differences by work schedule status in job, family, and demographic characteristics. Moreover, most people who work nonstandard hours give as their main reason for doing so job-constraining rather than personal-familial considerations. Within each of the major occupations that employ many nonday and weekend workers, we will see little evidence of financial benefit for working such schedules.

The analysis to follow is done first at a bivariate level with extensive descriptive detail, which is missing in the literature. This description is followed by a multivariate analysis that addresses the question of whether certain family and background characteristics matter after adjusting for differences in job characteristics. Given the still highly sex-segregated labor market (Reskin and Roos 1990) and the persistence of gender differences in the division of labor in the home (Bianchi et al. 2000), both types of analysis are done separately for men and women.

In assessing the findings in this chapter, and throughout the book, it is important to keep in mind the distinction noted in chapter 1—that the issue of working nonstandard times is different from that of having flexible work hours or days ("flextime"). Schedules involving nonday shifts and weekend employment are usually set by employers and often are viewed as contrary to the employee's interests.[3] Indeed, Karl Hinrichs (1991, 36) calls the standardized work schedule "one of the major achievements of the working class" and considers the trend toward greater diversity a setback in many ways for employees and the unions that represent them. In contrast, the practice of flexibility in work schedules (for example, the option of changing the starting and ending hours of employment by a few hours), although instituted by employers, reflects employees'—not employers'—preferences and is invariably viewed positively by employees.

How different is the overall prevalence of nonstandard work schedules in the United States from what we find in European countries, where a greater proportion of the labor force are union members? A comparison of the United States with selected European countries addresses this issue and considers the extent to which parental status makes a difference in these countries.

We begin with a brief discussion of the data source for the United States and the definitions of the work schedule measures to be used.

Data Source: The May 1997
Current Population Survey

This chapter and the next, as well as chapter 8, are based on an analysis of the May 1997 Current Population Survey (CPS). The CPS is a nationally representative monthly survey of about fifty thousand households conducted by the U.S. Bureau of the Census for the Bureau of Labor Statistics (BLS), primarily to estimate the extent of unemployment in the nation.[4] In May of selected years since 1973, the CPS has included a supplement with questions on work schedules, although the questions on specific work hours are not comparable over time, and the specific workdays were not asked until 1991.[5] The May 1997 CPS provides the most recent, publicly available national data on work schedule behavior.[6]

I drew a subsample of those age eighteen and over who held at least one job for the week prior to the interview and whose principal job was in a nonagricultural occupation. I included both the self-employed and wage and salary workers, and part-time as well as full-time workers. The total number of cases fitting this description with values on all the work schedule variables is 48,672, representing about 116.6 million persons. The sample size becomes smaller when additional variables are considered in multivariate regression analyses, since there are missing values on these variables.

The percentages reported are weighted for national representativeness. However, the number of cases reported refers to the unweighted sample.

Work Schedule Measures

Throughout the book I consider two temporal dimensions of nonstandard work schedules: whether employed on nonstandard *shifts*, relating to specific hours on the job, and whether employed on nonstandard *days.* For the May 1997 CPS data, these hours and days relate to the principal job for the 7.6 percent who hold more than one job.

The May 1997 CPS included questions on the specific hours work began and ended most days in the week prior to the interview and a question in which the respondent self-identified his or her usual work shift. Since self-reported shifts are not explicitly defined as to the beginning and ending times that constitute a shift, and individuals working similar hours may report their shift differently (for example, what one calls an "evening" shift another calls a "night" shift), I prefer to define shifts utilizing the specific hours worked.[7] Two exceptions are the self-designation of being a rotator, which I use to distinguish between those who periodically change shifts from those on a fixed schedule, and the self-designation of having an irregular schedule determined by the employer, when the respondent so reports and does not provide answers to the questions on the time that work generally began and ended.[8]

It is important to emphasize that work schedules as used in this book refer to when people work *most* of their hours. Accordingly, people who work mostly in the day but also in the evening or night are considered here to be daytime workers. This also means that if we were to include the hours of a second job for those with multiple jobs, it would make little difference in the designation of work shifts, since the principal job is the one in which those persons spend most hours during the reference week. For example, a person who works one job from 9:00 A.M. to 5:00 P.M. and another job 7:00 P.M. to midnight would be classified as working a day shift even if the hours of both jobs are included—since most hours worked are during the daytime.

I have chosen to focus on "most" rather than "some" hours in defining work shifts because doing so more sharply differentiates people who organize their lives around one predominant work schedule. However, throughout the study it is important to remember that the prevalence rates for nonstandard hours would be much higher if those working "some" late hours were included as nonstandard workers.

In determining what constitutes a specific work shift, I have modified the definition used by the Bureau of Labor Statistics (Hedges and Sekscenski 1979; U.S. Department of Labor 1981) to include the "hours vary" category used in 1997:[9]

Fixed day: At least half the hours worked most days in the prior week fell between 8:00 A.M. and 4:00 P.M.

Fixed evening: At least half the hours worked most days in the prior week fell between 4:00 P.M. and midnight.

Fixed night: At least half the hours worked most days in the prior week fell between midnight and 8:00 A.M.

Rotating: Schedules changed periodically from days to evenings or nights.

Hours vary: An irregular schedule that cannot be classified in any of the above categories.

I define persons as working *nonstandard hours* when they worked other than fixed-day schedules the previous week, and as working *nonday hours* when they worked evenings, nights, or rotating schedules. (The latter grouping underestimates the extent of nonday employment, since some of those in the excluded "hours vary" group undoubtedly were working evenings or nights.)

The specific days of the week worked were asked for the principal job, although no reference to the last week or the usual week was included in the question.[10] However, this question was asked after other questions relating to the usual week. The workdays are categorized by specific weekday or weekend combinations. Those who worked *nonstandard days* are defined as working on Saturday and/or Sunday. This designation may include people who worked either standard or nonstandard hours.

The Prevalence of Nonstandard Work Schedules

The standard workweek in the United States is generally considered to be thirty-five to forty hours, five days a week, Monday through Friday. An implicit assumption is that these hours are worked mostly during daytime hours. This definition of the daytime standard workweek describes only a minority of employed Americans—29.1 percent. For employed men, the proportion is 26.5 percent, for employed women 32.8 percent.[11] When we omit the condition of working thirty-five to forty hours a week and consider all of those who regularly work during the daytime, all five days from Monday to Friday, for any number of hours, the proportion of all employed Americans increases to only 54.4 percent—a bare majority.

Putting aside the notion of a standard workweek and considering work hours and days separately, and in selective combinations, we see in table 2.1 some striking national estimates for 1997. Looking down column 1, we see that one-fifth of all employed Americans did not work a fixed daytime schedule on their principal job. Two-fifths of those employed did not work five days a week, Monday through Friday.

Part-time workers, those working fewer than thirty-five hours a week on all jobs, are distinguished in table 2.1 from full-timers working thirty-five to forty hours and more than forty hours. We see that part-timers were more likely than both kinds of full-timers to work nonstandard hours on their principal job. But it was both part-timers and the full-timers who worked more than forty hours a week who were most likely to work weekends. However, these long-hour full-timers had similar work shifts on their principal job as those who worked thirty-five to forty hours. (As we will see in table 2.6, fewer than 8 percent of all those employed had two or more jobs, and these work hours may have been concentrated in the late hours or weekends.)

Although the labor force is highly segregated by gender, with men and women having very different occupational distributions, gender differences in work schedules among all those employed in 1997 were not

TABLE 2.1   The Work Schedules of Employed Americans Age Eighteen and Over, by Gender and Number of Hours Employed

Work Schedules	Total				Males				Females			
	Total	Less Than 35 Hours	Thirty-Five to Forty Hours	Greater Than 40 Hours	Total	Less Than 35 Hours	Thirty-Five to Forty Hours	Greater Than 40 Hours	Total	Less Than 35 Hours	Thirty-Five to Forty Hours	Greater Than 40 Hours
Hours												
Fixed day	80.1%	70.4%	83.2%	82.9%	78.9%	67.5%	80.7%	81.4%	81.4%	72.0%	85.6%	86.3%
Fixed evening	8.1	14.4	6.7	5.8	8.1	15.2	7.6	6.2	8.1	14.0	5.8	5.0
Fixed night	4.1	3.7	4.7	3.7	4.5	4.5	5.3	3.8	3.7	3.3	4.1	3.6
Hours vary	4.2	7.7	2.5	4.0	4.4	8.5	2.8	4.4	3.9	7.2	2.3	2.9
Rotating[a]	3.6	3.8	2.9	3.6	4.1	4.4	3.6	4.2	2.8	3.5	2.2	2.2
Number	49,570	11,201	21,153	17,119	25,916	3,800	10,457	11,610	23,654	7,401	10,696	5,509
Days												
Weekday only, five days	60.3%	42.4%	74.1%	55.2%	59.7%	45.6%	73.2%	52.2%	61.1%	40.6%	75.1%	61.6%
Weekday only, less than five days	8.0	22.9	4.4	2.6	5.3	16.1	4.5	2.4	11.0	26.6	4.2	3.2
Seven days	7.9	8.0	4.7	11.5	8.7	9.5	4.6	12.0	6.9	7.2	4.7	10.6

Weekday and weekend, less than seven days	23.1	24.3	16.8	30.5	25.7	26.2	17.7	33.2	20.1	23.3	15.8	24.5
Weekend only, one or two days	0.7	2.4	0.1	0.2	0.5	2.6	0.1	0.2	0.9	2.2	0.1	0.1
Number	50,275	10,771	20,859	16,968	26,167	3,635	10,300	11,502	24,108	7,136	10,559	5,466
Combination												
Fixed day, weekday only, five days	54.4%	36.5%	67.0%	50.3%	52.9%	38.6%	64.9%	46.9%	56.2%	35.3%	69.2%	57.8%
Fixed day, weekday only, less than five days	6.1	17.9	3.5	2.0	3.9	11.9	3.4	1.7	8.6	21.2	3.5	2.6
Rotators or hours vary and weekend[a]	5.3	7.2	3.6	5.8	5.9	8.6	4.0	6.6	4.5	6.5	3.1	4.1
All others	34.2	38.4	26.0	41.9	37.2	40.9	27.7	44.8	30.7	37.0	24.2	35.5
Number	48,672	10,765	20,849	16,964	25,469	3,631	10,291	11,499	23,203	7,134	10,558	5,465

Source: May 1997 CPS.

Notes: The total number of cases is more than the sum of those working less than thirty-five, thirty-five to forty, and more than forty hours because of missing data on the number of hours worked in the last week on all jobs. Also, differences in the number of cases by type of work schedule are due to missing data for these variables. All percentages are weighted for national representativeness; the number of cases reports unweighted samples for each category. Work schedules refer to the principal job; total hours refer to all jobs. Percentages may not add exactly to 100.0 because of rounding.

[a]This includes seventy-four individuals designated as twenty-four-hour workers (for example, those always on call).

great. With regard to work *hours,* men were somewhat more likely than women to work other than fixed daytime schedules (21.1 percent and 18.6 percent, respectively). The gender difference is seen specifically in the higher percentages of men than women working fixed nights and variable and rotating hours. There is no gender difference in the prevalence of evening work (both 8.1 percent). Among part-time workers of both sexes, substantial proportions worked evenings (15.2 percent of men and 14.0 percent of women). Part-time workers are the subgroup showing the highest percentages with variable hours.

As for work*days,* men were only slightly more likely than women to work during nonstandard times—that is, other than a five-day workweek, Monday through Friday (40.3 percent and 38.9 percent, respectively). The distribution of nonstandard workdays varied considerably, however, by gender. In particular, men were more likely than women to work weekends (34.9 percent and 27.9 percent, respectively). Women were more likely than men to work weekdays but fewer than five days a week (11.0 percent versus 5.3 percent). For both men and women, those working less as well as more than thirty-five to forty hours were most likely to work weekends. Very few employed Americans, men or women, worked weekends only—and understandably, almost all were part-timers.

When work hours and days are combined, table 2.1 shows the figure cited earlier—that only 54.4 percent of employed Americans worked Monday through Friday, five days a week, on a fixed day schedule. Their counterparts are the 45.6 percent who did not work such a schedule— 47.1 percent of men and 43.8 percent of women. It is those who worked thirty-five to forty hours who conform most to a fixed, daytime, weekday-only schedule: 67.0 percent. This is followed by only 50.3 percent of those working more than forty hours and only 36.5 percent of those working less than thirty-five hours.

Reasons for Working
Nonstandard Hours

As noted in chapter 1, the demand for employment during nonstandard hours is driven by many factors. But given the demand, why do people take these jobs? Do they prefer them to fixed daytime jobs for personal reasons, or are they constrained by the nature of the job to accept nonstandard hours?

The May 1997 CPS included a question for respondents (wage and salary earners only, not the self-employed) who reported they did not work a regular daytime schedule on their reason for working nonstandard hours.[12] (There was no equivalent question for working nonstandard days.) The distribution of reasons is shown in table 2.2.

TABLE 2.2   Distribution of Main Reason Reported for Working Nonstandard Hours, Wage and Salary Earners, by Gender and Age of Youngest Child

Main Reason	Total	Male				Female			
		Total Male	No Child	Youngest Child Less than Five	Youngest Child Five to Thirteen	Total Female	No Child	Youngest Child Less than Five	Youngest Child Five to Thirteen
Personal-familial reasons	25.3%	18.9%	19.5%	20.3%	13.2%	34.2%	29.0%	49.3%	42.8%
Better child care arrangements	5.7	2.0	0.6	7.6	3.9	10.7	2.4	35.3	24.5
Better arrangements for care of family members	3.1	1.4	0.8	3.3	2.4	5.5	3.7	8.5	10.8
More time for school	10.8	9.4	12.4	2.5	0.1	12.7	17.3	2.5	2.1
Easier commute	0.6	0.9	0.8	0.9	1.0	0.3	0.4	0.0	0.3
Better pay	5.1	5.2	4.9	6.0	5.8	5.0	5.3	2.9	5.1
Job constraining reasons	62.6	68.8	67.9	69.7	73.4	54.2	57.7	43.0	49.2
Could not get any other job	6.3	6.2	6.4	6.3	5.0	6.4	5.2	10.4	8.1
Mandated by employer	10.8	12.9	12.5	12.0	16.5	8.0	8.6	5.4	7.8
Nature of the job	45.5	49.7	49.0	51.4	52.0	39.8	43.9	27.2	33.4
Other reason	11.5	11.7	12.0	9.6	12.9	11.2	12.8	7.2	7.9
No response/don't know	0.5	0.6	0.7	0.5	0.5	0.5	0.5	0.5	0.2
Number	7,587	4,261	3,095	637	529	3,326	2,311	505	510

Source: May 1997 CPS.
Notes: Percentages are weighted; numbers of cases are unweighted. Sample excludes those cases with missing data on shift status in the previous week and those self-employed.

We see that over three-fifths (62.6 percent) of wage and salary earners working nonstandard hours gave a reason that relates to the constraints of the job: they could not get any other job, the hours were mandated by the employer, or the nature of the job required nonstandard hours. Being able to make better child care arrangements by working nonstandard hours, a personal-familial reason more directly reflecting preference, was mentioned by only 5.7 percent. This low percentage is due in part to the fact that almost three-fourths (71.3 percent) of those working nonstandard hours did not have children under the age of fourteen living with them. Yet even when we limit our consideration to those with children this age, we find that a minority of mothers working nonstandard hours (35.3 percent of those whose youngest child is under age five and 24.5 percent of those whose youngest is school-aged) and far fewer fathers working nonstandard hours—7.6 percent and 3.9 percent, respectively—did so primarily to facilitate child care—even though, as shown in chapter 7, most fathers working nonstandard schedules in fact provide such care. When family caregiving is broadened to include family members other than children, the percentage working nonstandard hours mainly for caregiving reasons increases substantially for women but not for men. The highest proportion is found for mothers of children under age five, with a combined percentage of 43.8 percent working nonstandard hours for caregiving reasons; while substantial, this proportion is still a minority. These findings are consistent with analyses of the May 1985 and 1991 CPS (Presser 1989a, 1995b). Better pay and an easier commute were reasons given only by a small minority of those working nonstandard hours, with somewhat higher percentages (particularly among those without children) saying that their late shifts allowed time for school. (Students who reported this reason were especially likely to be young.)

Given the importance of job-related reasons for working nonstandard hours, it is relevant to ask: What are these jobs? And what is the economic status of those who hold them?

The Occupations and Earnings of Workers with Nonstandard Schedules

The top ten occupations of those working nonstandard schedules are cashiers, truck drivers, commodities sales workers in retail and personal services, waiters and waitresses, cooks, janitors and cleaners, sales supervisors and proprietors, registered nurses, food serving and lodging managers, and the category of nursing aides, orderlies, and attendants.

TABLE 2.3   *The Top Ten Occupations of Workers with*
              Nonstandard Schedules

Rank			Percentage of All Nonstandard Hours Workers	Percentage of All Weekend Workers
Nonday/ Hours Vary	Weekends	Occupations		
1	3	Cashiers	4.7	4.4
2	5	Truck drivers	4.1	3
3	2	Sales workers, retail and personal services, commodities	3.4	4.5
4	7	Waiters and waitresses	3.3	2.4
5	4	Cooks	3.2	3.2
6	10	Janitors and cleaners	3.1	1.5
7	1	Supervisors and propri- etors, sales occupa- tions	2.8	7
8	9	Registered nurses	2.8	2.2
9	6	Managers, food serving and lodging	2.6	2.8
10	8	Nursing aides, order- lies, and attendants	2.5	2.3
		Sum, top 10 occupa- tions	32.5	33.3
		Total, all occupations	100.0	100.0
		Number	9,728	16,048

Source: May 1997 CPS.
Note: Percentages are weighted; numbers of cases are unweighted.

We see in table 2.3 that these occupations rank in the top ten for both nonstandard hours (nonday and varying) and weekends, although the rankings differ for the two types of schedules. Altogether, these top ten occupations include about one-third of all nonstandard workers, whether considering hours or weekends. Indeed, these are in large part the same workers, as 73.3 percent of those working nonstandard hours in the top ten occupations also work weekends.

An interesting aspect of these top ten occupations is that they are all service-sector jobs that serve the local community, with the exception of truck drivers. In other words, most of those working nonstandard schedules are not producing services for the global economy. Thus, we cannot attribute the schedules of a large part of our 24/7 labor force to technological advances that connect us with the rest of the world.

Another notable aspect of the top ten occupations is that they are, for the most part, low-paying occupations. We do not have earnings data for the total May 1997 CPS sample, only for a subgroup of wage and salary earners in the Outgoing Rotation Group (months 4 and 8 in the CPS). Tables 2.4 and 2.5 present earnings data for this subgroup: the medians and the means adjusted for age and education, since we have seen that those who work nonstandard schedules are younger and less educated than others; such differences contribute to the earnings difference. The adjustment (which cannot be done for medians) allows us to consider pay differences by work schedule status after removing these human capital differences. (See appendix table A2.1 for details on unadjusted means.)

Looking first at the median hourly earnings for all wage and salary earners, we see that it was relatively low for those working nonday or variable hours—$8.00, as compared with $9.50 for those working fixed days.[13] Those working weekends were also paid less per hour ($7.60) than those working only weekdays ($10.00). Thus, despite the fact that nonstandard schedules may be undesirable for most workers, they are not as a group rewarded with higher hourly pay. This is the case when comparing the adjusted means as well, although the pay difference is smaller: $.49 an hour more for those working standard rather than nonstandard days, and $.99 an hour more when working on weekdays rather than weekends. These differences are statistically significant.

When looking at earnings differences within specific occupations by work schedule status, the number of cases decreases (see appendix table A2.1) and thus statistical significance is harder to attain. (Also, the small number of cases precludes a more detailed analysis by gender.) But we can see in tables 2.4 and 2.5 that similar or lower pay of those working nonstandard schedules is evident for most of these top ten occupations. The adjusted means are significantly lower only for weekend work among janitors and cleaners, and near-significantly lower for weekend work among sales supervisors and proprietors. We see higher (but not statistically significant) adjusted means for cashiers, waiters and waitresses, and registered nurses who work nonstandard hours. (The higher earnings among waiters and waitresses may be due to the higher tips earned serving dinner rather than earlier meals.)

The only notable higher earnings for weekend employment (again, not statistically significant) are for registered nurses. The higher earnings of nurses may be due in part to the fact that a relatively high percentage are union members, and union membership is linked to pay differentials (King and Williams 1985). However, several of the other occupations in this listing have similarly high union membership and do not show higher earnings for working nonstandard schedules.[14] Again, the precise figures for each occupation should be interpreted with caution, given the small number of cases.

TABLE 2.4   Median and Adjusted Mean Hourly Earnings of Top Ten Occupations of Wage and Salary Earners, by Work Shift

Rank Nonday/ Hours Vary	Top Ten Occupations	Median Hours			Adjusted Mean Hours[a]		
		Nonday/ Hours Vary (a)	Fixed Day (b)	Difference (a)-(b) (c)	Nonday/ Hours Vary (d)	Fixed Day (e)	Difference (d)-(e) (f)
1	Cashiers	5.75	6.06	−0.31	7.24	6.75	0.49
2	Truck drivers	9.50	10.00	−0.50	10.51	10.57	−0.06
3	Sales workers, retail and personal services, commodities	6.02	6.28	−0.26	6.89	7.01	−0.12
4	Waiters and waitresses	4.25	4.25	0.00	4.52	3.98	0.54
5	Cooks	6.00	6.00	0.00	6.18	6.52	−0.34
6	Janitors and cleaners	7.02	7.00	0.02	7.55	7.79	−0.23
7	Supervisors and proprietors, sales occupations	8.27	9.10	−0.83	8.68	9.95	−1.27[+]
8	Registered nurses	18.64	17.00	1.64	18.55	16.82	1.73[+]
9	Managers, food serving and lodging	7.00	8.34	−1.34	8.36	9.70	−1.34
10	Nursing aides, orderlies, and attendants	6.25	7.44	−1.19	8.04	8.04	0.00
	All wage and salary earners	8.00	9.50	−1.50	10.31	10.80	−0.49**

Source: May 1997 CPS, outgoing sample.
Notes: Medians and means are weighted. Sample excludes self-employed and those with zero earnings. For number of cases in each occupation and unadjusted means, see table A2.1. Earnings exclude overtime. For
Significant test for means only: [+] p = <.10; * p = <.05; ** p = <.01; *** p = <.001.
[a]Adjusted for differences in education and age.

TABLE 2.5 Medians and Adjusted Mean Hourly Earnings of Top Ten Occupations of Wage and Salary Earners, by Whether Work Weekends

Rank Weekends	Top Ten Occupations	Median Hours			Adjusted Mean Hours[a]		
		Weekends (a)	Weekdays only (b)	Difference (a)-(b) (c)	Weekends (a)	Weekdays only (b)	Difference (a)-(b) (c)
1	Supervisors and proprietors, sales occupations	8.27	11.00	−2.73	9.14	10.22	−1.08[+]
2	Sales workers, retail and personal services, commodities	6.00	6.50	−0.50	6.81	7.15	−0.34
3	Cashiers	6.00	6.00	0.00	7.06	6.95	0.11
4	Cooks	6.00	5.80	0.20	6.35	6.54	−0.18
5	Truck drivers	10.00	10.00	0.00	9.84	10.73	−0.90
6	Managers, food serving, and lodging	8.00	8.25	−0.25	9.10	8.98	0.12
7	Waiters and waitresses	4.00	4.25	−0.25	4.29	4.59	−0.30
8	Nursing aides, orderlies, and attendants	7.00	7.50	−0.50	7.76	8.46	−0.70
9	Registered nurses	18.64	17.00	1.64	18.22	16.90	1.32
10	Janitors and cleaners	6.00	8.00	−2.00	6.93	8.25	−1.32**
	All wage and salary earners	7.60	10.00	−2.40	10.02	11.01	−0.99***

Source: May 1997 CPS, outgoing sample.
Notes: Medians and means are weighted. Sample excludes self-employed and those with zero earnings. Earnings exclude overtime. For number of cases in each occupation and unadjusted means see table A2.1.
Significant test for means only: [+]p = <.10; [*]p = <.05; [**]p = <.01; [***]p = <.001.
[a]Adjusted for differences in education and age.

The hourly rates reported here do not include overtime rates, which may be higher. Those who work nonstandard schedules are about twice as likely to work overtime as those who work standard schedules (not shown in tables). Among those working nonstandard hours, 11.4 percent had overtime weekly pay, as compared with 6.8 percent for those working standard hours. Among weekend workers, the figure is 12.1 percent, as compared with 6.1 percent for weekday workers only. This finding is consistent with the earlier one in table 2.1 (which includes the self-employed): those who worked more than forty hours a week were much more likely to work weekends. Many of these weekend workers were undoubtedly compensating for their low hourly pay.

The lack of higher hourly pay among those working nonstandard schedules may seem to run counter to economic theory, which suggests that jobs at presumably undesirable times require higher pay to entice workers to take them, particularly in a tight labor market.[15] However, as suggested by the fact that only 5.1 percent gave better pay as the main reason for working nonstandard hours (table 2.2), pay differentials are not common and, when available, not substantial. Even for males in manufacturing, who are most likely to get them, the shift premium is generally less than 10 percent higher than that of daytime workers (Kostiuk 1990). Among registered nurses (mostly female), the shift premium is estimated to be 4 percent for evenings and 11.6 percent for nights (Schumacher and Hirsch 1997).

Subgroup Differences in the Likelihood of Nonstandard Work Schedules: Bivariate Analysis

Whereas we have focused thus far on those who work nonstandard schedules and considered how they cluster with regard to occupation, another approach is to focus on the occupations and consider which ones are most likely to include people who work nonstandard schedules. Indeed, we can go beyond occupation and include other job characteristics, as well as family and background characteristics. Essentially we are asking: Which subgroups of Americans are most likely to work nonstandard schedules? A descriptive bivariate analysis that addresses this question is followed by a multivariate analysis that considers whether the family and background characteristics shown to be associated with working a nonstandard schedule still matter after taking into account differences in job characteristics.

Job Characteristics

We would expect that, insofar as employment at nonstandard times is driven by the demand for workers in certain sectors of the economy, people holding certain jobs in these sectors will be most likely to work nonstandard times. As noted in chapter 1, the service sector is of special interest in this regard, and we have seen that many of those working nonstandard schedules have service occupations. But many of those working *standard* schedules have service occupations as well. So now we ask: To what extent are those in service occupations—and industries—more likely to work nonstandard schedules relative to other occupations and industries? And given that the service sector is highly varied (Meisenheimer 1998), which service occupations and industries are most likely to include people who work nonstandard schedules?

Occupation Table 2.6 shows the bivariate relationship between occupation and nonstandard work schedules for all those employed and for men and women separately. Occupation is shown for eight broad groupings and in detail when there were at least three hundred persons in the full sample. Although not shown in this table (see appendix table A2.2), seven of the eight broad occupational groupings are similar in size, the exception being the small number in technical and related support. Men and women, however, show different occupational distributions, the most extreme contrasts being that women are far more concentrated in administrative support occupations than men, and men are much more concentrated in precision production, craft, and repair occupations than women.

Work Hours As previously noted, 19.9 percent of employed Americans work nonstandard hours, either nonday shifts or hours too variable to classify. Accordingly, we consider occupations to be "high" on nonstandard work hours when the percentages working such schedules exceed this percentage. As expected, very high percentages are evident in service occupations: 37.2 percent of these workers, or over one in three, work nondays or variable hours. Operatives, fabricators, and laborers also notably exceed the average: 28.6 percent, or over one in four, work nonstandard hours. All of the other occupational groups are near or below the average. The lowest percentage is for those employed in executive, administrative, and managerial occupations: only one in ten (10.3 percent) work nonday or variable hours.

Although service occupations as a group are the strongest contributors relative to other groups to the overall high prevalence of nonstandard work schedules, there is considerable variation among detailed occupations *within* the other occupational groups. For example, in the executive, administrative, and managerial occupations, employment during nonstandard hours is very high among managers for food and lodging establishments (41.5 percent) but exceedingly low for administrators in education (4.0 percent). In the professional specialty occupations, the high prevalence of nonstandard work hours for registered nurses (35.5 percent) may be contrasted to the prevalence of such hours for another heavily female-dominated professional occupation, elementary school teachers, among whom there is the lowest prevalence of such employment (3.0 percent) for all the detailed occupations listed in table 2.5. In their shift status, registered nurses look more like nursing aides, orderlies, and attendants (service occupations) than like teachers: 36.6 percent in these supportive nursing positions work nonstandard hours. Among sales occupations, it is cashiers who predominate, with 43.4 percent working nonstandard hours, compared with only 6.8 percent of sales representatives for mining, manufacturing, and wholesale (all three grouped as a detailed occupation in the census codes). Among operatives, fabricators, and laborers, 45.9 percent of stock handlers and baggers work nonstandard hours, but only 6.7 percent of construction workers do so.

These differences within occupational groups point to the importance of industry, to be discussed shortly. They also point to the difference in the type of client the occupation serves: meeting the caregiving needs of the ill clearly cannot be done within the daytime temporal boundaries that can be set for educating young children. The need for daylight is also constraining on work hours for occupations such as construction workers.

Overall, it is difficult to generalize about the concentration of shift workers in the occupational hierarchy other than to say that they are heavily concentrated among service workers. All of the service occupations listed in table 2.6 (and these are the large ones) are high on nonstandard work hours relative to the average of 29.9 percent. Waiters and waitresses are the highest of all the detailed occupations listed: combined, over two-thirds (61.8 percent) worked nonstandard hours. Although women were more likely than men to hold service jobs (17.0 percent and 10.0 percent, respectively), when men held such jobs, they were more likely than women to work nonstandard hours (47.8 percent and 30.4 percent, respectively). This pattern is reflected in most of the detailed occupations listed.

Weekend Work   There is a strong correlation between nonstandard hours and nonstandard days. Two-thirds (60.0 percent) of those working nondaytime or variable days also worked weekends, compared with one-

TABLE 2.6   *Percentage of Employed Americans Age Eighteen*
and Over Who Work Nondays or Hours Vary and Who
Work Weekends on Their Principal Job, by Occupation
and Gender

Occupation	Percentage Nonday Shift/Hours Vary			Percentage Weekend		
	Total	Male	Female	Total	Male	Female
Executive, adminis-trative, and manage-rial occupations	10.3	11.1	9.3	28.0	33.5	21.4
Administrators, education	4.0	3.2	4.5	12.4	16.3	10.0
Managers, food and lodging establish-ments	41.5	49.1	32.7	75.0	79.9	69.3
Accountants and auditors	5.6	6.3	5.1	11.8	17.8	7.9
Other executives, administrative, managerial	8.0	8.2	7.7	26.0	31.0	19.3
Professional specialty occupations	14.1	12.0	15.8	27.1	30.8	24.1
Engineers	5.2	5.4	2.8	14.5	15.1	8.2
Computer systems analysts and scientists	5.5	4.8	7.0	13.8	17.3	6.2
Registered nurses	35.5	46.5	34.9	42.3	66.7	40.8
Elementary school teachers	3.0	3.1	3.0	14.9	14.8	14.9
Secondary school teachers	3.9	2.3	5.0	18.8	20.1	17.9
Social workers	17.0	18.6	16.3	16.7	23.1	13.9
Lawyers and judges	5.7	6.5	3.7	34.4	40.9	18.0
Other professional specialty	16.9	17.5	16.4	32.4	40.0	25.4
Technical and related support	21.5	23.8	19.5	24.4	24.8	24.1
Sales occupations	22.5	17.3	28.0	52.8	52.5	53.1
Supervisors and proprietors, sales	14.5	13.4	16.2	58.1	61.4	53.0
Real estate sales	20.8	20.5	21.1	65.0	63.8	66.4
Sales representa-tives: mining, manufacturing, wholesale	6.8	5.9	10.1	25.4	28.8	14.4
Cashiers	43.4	52.7	41.0	67.2	74.5	65.5
Other sales	24.1	18.8	29.3	46.6	46.1	47.1

TABLE 2.6   *Continued*

Occupation	Percentage Nonday Shift/Hours Vary			Percentage Weekend		
	Total	Male	Female	Total	Male	Female
Administrative support occupations	12.5	20.8	10.4	16.2	26.2	13.7
Secretaries, stenographers, and typists	4.9	–*	4.8	6.9	–*	6.8
Receptionists	13.6	–*	13.8	14.3	–*	14.5
Bookkeepers, accounting, auditing clerks	9.8	13.6	9.5	14.1	21.3	13.5
Investigators and adjusters, not insurance	12.1	14.1	11.5	19.7	26.8	17.4
Other administrative support	15.7	22.0	13.0	19.9	26.7	17.0
Service occupations	37.2	47.8	30.4	49.8	55.7	46.1
Waiters and waitresses	61.8	70.9	59.5	77.6	84.0	76.1
Cooks, including short-order	37.3	50.5	22.9	62.4	75.1	48.8
Nursing aides, orderlies, and attendants	36.6	37.3	36.5	52.1	50.7	52.2
Janitors and cleaners	35.2	33.9	37.6	27.2	28.4	25.2
Other service	34.4	51.5	23.9	48.4	59.6	41.8
Precision production, craft, and repair occupations	13.9	13.3	19.3	27.0	27.4	22.6
Automobile mechanics	7.8	7.4	–*	34.4	34.5	–*
Carpenters	7.6	7.5	–*	21.2	21.0	–*
Supervisors, production	23.7	24.4	21.2	25.2	27.5	16.0
Other precision production, craft, repair	14.0	13.5	18.9	27.4	27.7	23.9
Operators, fabricators, and laborers	28.6	29.5	26.0	29.9	32.7	21.3
Assemblers	23.6	22.8	24.5	15.4	17.3	13.1
Truck drivers, light and heavy	31.0	31.0	32.2	39.0	38.7	42.4
Construction laborers	6.7	6.1	13.6	21.4	20.2	36.4

TABLE 2.6   *Continued*

Occupation	Percentage Nonday Shift/Hours Vary			Percentage Weekend		
	Total	Male	Female	Total	Male	Female
Stock handlers and baggers	45.9	50.9	35.0	60.1	63.8	52.3
Laborers, except construction	23.1	22.3	26.1	24.3	24.9	21.7
Other operators, fabricators	29.5	31.2	25.4	27.9	31.8	18.9
Number	51,411	25,916	23,654	51,411	26,167	24,108

Source: May 1997 CPS.
Notes: Categories are based on full sample; occupations with over three hundred or more adults before attrition due to missing cases for the other variables are specified. To calculate the approximate number of cases in each cell, see table A2.2. Some cases in the total have missing data on work schedules, and thus excluded in the subcategories.
*Base fewer than twenty sample cases.

fourth (24.8 percent) of those working days (figures not shown in table). Nevertheless, certain occupations show distinctively high or low levels in one type of schedule and not the other. As may be seen in table 2.6, service occupations are generally high on both, but sales occupations are higher than service occupations in weekend employment (52.8 percent and 49.8 percent, respectively) but much lower—specifically among males—in nonstandard hours of employment. This contrast can be seen with regard to the detailed occupations as well; for example, whereas only 14.5 percent of sales supervisors and proprietors worked nonstandard hours, 58.1 percent worked weekends. This is also evident in other occupational groups; for example, among lawyers and judges, only 5.7 percent had nonday or variable shifts, but 34.4 percent worked weekends. At the lower end of the occupational hierarchy, while only 6.7 percent of construction laborers worked other than fixed daytime shifts, 21.4 percent worked weekends. Waiters and waitresses, the occupation (among all those listed) with the highest prevalence of nonday employment, is also the occupation with the highest prevalence of weekend employment (77.6 percent). The lowest level of weekend employment is among secretaries, stenographers, and typists (6.9 percent).

Industry   In addition to occupation, work schedules differ by other job characteristics, as shown in table 2.7. (For percentage distribution of all the variables in table 2.7, separately by gender, see appendix table A2.3). A key job characteristic is industry.

I have grouped industries into the six major categories derived by Joachim Singlemann and Marta Tienda (1985); this grouping differentiates four service sectors—distributive, producer, social, and personal—in addition to the extractive and transformative sectors.[16] This differentiation of service sectors is important, since some sectors reflect a 24/7 demand more than others. For example, I expect the prevalence of nonstandard work hours and days to be highest in the personal services industry (two-fifths of such jobs are in eating and drinking places) and lowest in the producer services (more than one-third of such jobs are in banking and insurance).

Work Hours   The bivariate relationships on work hours support this expectation. Over 35 percent of those employed in personal services worked mostly nonday shifts or variable hours, in contrast to 12.4 percent in producer services, with distributive and social services and the extractive and transformative industries in between. Gender differences are not substantial except for extractive and social service industries, in which men were much more likely than women to work nonstandard hours.

Weekend Work   Personal services also ranks highest on weekend work, with three-fifths (60.5 percent) so employed. Distributive services (primarily because of the influence of retail trade and transportation) and extractive industries (which include agriculture, forestry, fishing, and mining) also exceed the average on weekend work (44.8 percent and 42.2 percent, respectively). The other three industrial sectors are relatively low (percentages in the low twenties). Gender differences in weekend employment are minimal for personal and distributive services, but men were more likely than women to work weekends in the other industrial groupings.

Other Job Characteristics   The industrial *class of worker,* whether a worker is a multiple job holder, and whether he or she is employed part- or full-time (all jobs combined) are additional relevant job characteristics included in the May CPS. Briefly, those employed in the private sector, those who held more than one job, and those who worked part-time were more likely to work nonstandard *hours and days* than their counterparts. The one exception is the self-employed, who were especially likely (52.0 percent) to work weekends or variable days—far more than wage and salary earners in private industry (31.5 percent).

Although government workers are relatively low on working non-

TABLE 2.7   *Percentage of Employed Americans Age Eighteen and Over Who Work Nondays or Hours Vary and Who Work Weekends on Their Principal Job, by Selected Variables and Gender*

Selected Variables	Percentage Nonday Shift/Hours Vary			Percentage Weekend		
	Total	Male	Female	Total	Male	Female
Selected job characteristics						
Industry						
Extractive	19.1	22.3	11.6	42.2	46.9	31.2
Transformative	16.0	15.7	16.6	21.5	24.1	14.2
Distributive services	23.9	23.5	24.6	44.8	45.8	43.5
Producer services	12.4	14.3	10.6	23.1	29.4	17.5
Social services	16.9	21.6	14.7	24.0	31.1	20.6
Personal services	35.4	37.0	33.9	60.5	62.9	58.3
Class of worker						
Private industry	20.9	21.5	20.1	31.5	33.4	29.5
Government	15.1	21.4	10.4	19.5	25.7	15.0
Self-employed	17.7	15.5	21.7	52.0	56.0	45.1
Multiple job holder						
Has one paid job	19.5	20.5	18.4	31.9	35.3	28.2
Has more than one paid job	21.3	23.2	19.2	32.5	36.7	27.9
Part-time and/or full-time						
One to thirty-four hours per week	28.9	31.6	27.5	34.4	37.5	32.8
Thirty-five to ninety-nine hours per week	16.7	18.6	14.1	31.1	35.0	25.8
Family characteristics						
Marital status						
Married, spouse present	16.4	17.4	15.2	29.4	33.8	24.1
Other	24.6	26.5	22.8	35.9	38.3	33.6
Number of children under age five						
Zero	19.5	20.8	18.0	31.8	35.3	28.1
One	20.2	20.5	19.9	32.8	37.0	28.1
Two or more	22.1	19.2	26.5	32.8	33.9	31.1

TABLE 2.7   *Continued*

Selected Variables	Percentage Nonday Shift/Hours Vary			Percentage Weekend		
	Total	Male	Female	Total	Male	Female
Number of children age five to thirteen						
One	17.6	19.2	16.1	29.6	34.1	25.4
Two or more	17.2	16.3	18.1	31.2	35.4	26.6
Number of children under age fourteen						
Zero	20.3	21.8	18.7	32.4	35.6	28.8
One	17.1	18.1	16.2	30.3	34.6	26.4
Two	18.6	18.3	18.8	30.2	34.0	26.1
Three or more	20.1	18.6	22.1	34.6	37.9	30.4
Demographic characteristics						
Age						
Eighteen to twenty-nine	28.7	29.2	28.2	37.8	39.3	36.3
Thirty to forty-four	17.3	18.7	15.7	29.9	34.2	25.3
Forty-five and older	16.3	17.4	15.0	30.4	34.4	25.9
Race-Ethnicity						
Non-Hispanic white	18.8	19.7	17.9	31.9	35.5	27.8
Non-Hispanic black	24.4	28.1	21.4	29.9	32.9	27.5
Hispanic	21.2	22.8	19.1	31.9	34.6	28.4
Other	20.9	21.7	20.1	36.7	38.7	34.4
Education completed (years)						
Less than twelve	26.2	23.8	29.6	36.8	36.4	37.4
Twelve	21.2	23.8	18.4	32.6	36.0	29.1
Thirteen to fifteen	22.5	24.5	20.6	34.3	38.9	29.9
Sixteen	13.4	13.5	13.3	26.0	29.6	22.1
Seventeen and more	9.8	9.7	10.0	28.4	33.4	21.4
Number	51,411	25,916	23,654	51,411	26,167	24,108

Source: May 1997 CPS.
Notes: To calculate the approximate number of cases in each cell, see table A2.3. Some cases in the total have missing data on work schedules, and thus excluded in the subcategories.

standard hours and days, these workers show the largest gender difference of all these other job characteristics. About twice as many men as women in government jobs worked nonday shifts or variable hours (21.4 percent and 10.4 percent, respectively), and about 70 percent more men than women worked weekends (25.7 percent and 15.0 percent, respectively).

Family Characteristics

The availability, or supply, of workers during nonstandard hours and days may be facilitated or constrained by their *marital status* and *the number and age of their children.* Insofar as workers can exercise their preference (that is, find alternative acceptable jobs with differing schedules), married persons, particularly those without children, may wish to maximize overlapping work hours (if both spouses are employed) and synchronize their social life with others more so than the unmarried, and this preference can be more readily achieved by spouses working during the daytime and on fixed weekdays. However, those with children may wish to work when their spouse, mother, or other potential caregiver is not employed, to provide quality child care at minimal cost, and this preference requires non-overlapping schedules.[17]

The middle of table 2.7 shows that those who were not married (single, separated, divorced, or widowed) were more likely to work nonday or variable hours (24.6 percent) and weekends (35.9 percent) than those who were married with a spouse present (16.4 percent and 29.4 percent, respectively). This relationship holds for both men and women.

Whereas the presence and number of preschool-aged children (under five) is linked to a *greater* likelihood that women—but not men—will work nonstandard hours, the presence and number of school-aged children (ages five to thirteen, young enough generally to require after-school supervision) is associated with a *lower* prevalence of nonstandard hours, particularly for men.[18] As we will see from the multivariate analysis, when controlling for the age of the parent and other factors, these relationships change. As for weekend employment, the bivariate analysis shows no clear relationship to presence and age of children for either gender.

Background Characteristics

An individual's *age* and *educational attainment* reflect human capital, or the experience and training that person may have had in the labor market. To the extent that working nonstandard hours and weekends is undesirable, and the individual is not self-employed, having more tenure and greater skills may serve to minimize employment at such times. We see in the lower part of table 2.7 that there is a negative relationship between age and working nonstandard schedules, the substantial difference being between those younger than thirty and those thirty and over. This difference holds for both men and women. Educational attainment is also negatively associated with nonstandard work schedules. Here the critical difference is between those who are college graduates (sixteen or more years of schooling) and those with less education. Those who are not high school graduates show the highest proportions working nonstandard hours (26.2 percent) and weekends (36.8 percent). These patterns obtain for both men and women.

Race and ethnicity, separate from issues of human capital, may reflect discrimination in the labor market. Accordingly, to the extent that working nonstandard schedules is undesirable, minority groups may be more likely than the white non-Hispanic majority to work nonstandard schedules. The combined variable of race-ethnicity in table 2.7 shows that non-Hispanic whites were least likely to work nonstandard hours (18.8 percent) and non-Hispanic blacks were most likely (24.4 percent), with Hispanics (black and white) and "others" in between. ("Other" includes American Indian, Aleut, Eskimo, Asian, Pacific Islander, and all other ethnic groups; they are grouped because of their small numbers in the sample.) Weekend employment was least characteristic of non-Hispanic blacks, however, and most characteristic of "others," which may be related to the relatively high levels of self-employment for some of these groups in businesses that are typically open seven days a week (for example, Korean groceries and Chinese restaurants).

In a separate analysis published elsewhere (Presser forthcoming), also based on the 1997 CPS, I considered the extent to which the racial-ethnic differences in nonstandard work schedules are due to differences in occupational distributions. Differences in human capital and discrimination may limit the occupational choices of minorities, but one may nevertheless ask: If non-Hispanic blacks and Hispanics had the same occupational structure as non-Hispanic whites, how much less would their work schedules differ? It was found that, for both men and women, the difference between non-Hispanic blacks and non-Hispanic whites would be reduced by more than half. And when comparing Hispanics, both men and women, with non-Hispanic whites, Hispanics would actually have lower prevalences in nonstandard work schedules than non-Hispanic whites. Thus, it is the difference in occupational decisions (resulting from either necessity or choice) that largely explains these ethnic differences in nonstandard work hours.

In sum, based on this bivariate analysis, we can say that the job characteristics that are most likely to encourage nonstandard work schedules, in terms of both hours and days of employment, are having a service occupation, being in a personal service industry, holding more than one job, and working part-time. In addition, being a wage or salary earner in the private sector enhances the likelihood of working nonstandard hours, and being self-employed encourages weekend employment. The family characteristics most highly positively associated with working nonstandard hours and days are being unmarried and, among women, having preschool-aged children. As for background characteristics, being young and less-educated is positively linked to nonstandard work schedules, as is being a non-Hispanic black.

Family and Background
Characteristics and Nonstandard
Work Schedules:
Multivariate Analysis

An underlying assumption in this analysis is that the number of jobs at nonstandard times is driven by demand. Employers create such jobs, and employees fill them. (For the self-employed, of course, they are one and the same.) As we have seen, there is variation in the family and demographic characteristics of those who respond to this demand. This variation suggests a greater or lesser disposition among certain subgroups to accept such jobs, as well as the differential availability of alternative job options. Although we cannot analytically assess the relative influence of preference and availability with these data, we can assess the importance of certain family and background characteristics when we adjust for differences in the job and other family and background characteristics of individuals. The question then becomes: Assuming that workers have similar job and other characteristics, how do certain family and background characteristics affect the likelihood they will work nonstandard schedules?

To answer this question, I present logistic regressions in which the coefficients are recalculated as odds ratios of working nonstandard schedules. A ratio of one means equal likelihood with the designated reference category; less than one means less likelihood, and more than one greater likelihood. The regressions in table 2.8 are done separately for men and women. For both genders, there are three models of nonstandard schedules, each with a different dependent variable: (a) nonstandard hours, (b) weekends, and (c) the combination of nonstandard hours and weekends. Odds ratios are shown for each of the family and background characteristics previously discussed, controlling for the others, as well as for job characteristics (occupation, industry, class of worker, whether multiple job holder, and whether employed full- or part-time).

Family Characteristics

In the multivariate models, as in the bivariate analysis, *marital status* is related to a nonstandard work schedule; being married (with spouse present) significantly decreases the odds of working nonstandard hours and weekends compared with being unmarried, for both men and women. This is true of the combination of both work schedules as well.

I have combined the presence and age of children into a single variable, *parental status,* to allow for the possibility that it is the combination of the two that may be relevant because of the different child-rearing demands and child care needs generated by the various combinations. In other words, it may be that having one child under age five and a school-aged child may have a different influence on an individual's work schedule than having two children under age five, or that having one child under age five may have a different influence than having one child between the ages of five and thirteen. By "influence" I mean constraining as well as encouraging effects: some parents may want to be home in the evenings and at night because they have children, while others may see the economic and other possible gains in working split shifts with spouses or other relatives as offsetting some of the negative effects. As we saw earlier in the chapter, among parents working nonstandard hours, being able to make better child care arrangements was the primary reason reported by a substantial minority of mothers, but a reason far less frequently cited by fathers.

Although we cannot address child care preferences with this data set, we can ask: How relevant are the presence and age of children in determining the likelihood that a parent will work a nonstandard work schedule when we adjust for differences in job, background, and other family characteristics, including the parent's age?[19] And are there differences by parent's gender, given the different reasons mothers and fathers give for working nonstandard hours?

The regression reported in table 2.8 shows that children significantly depressed the likelihood of working nonstandard hours for mothers only, and only for mothers with one child who was either under age five or between the ages of five and thirteen. For women with one child age five to thirteen there were significantly lower odds of working a combination of nonstandard hours and weekends relative to women without children.

For men, parental status shows a different relationship to nonstan-

TABLE 2.8   *Odds Ratios of Employed American Men and Women Age Eighteen and Over Working Nonstandard Schedules in Their Principal Job, for Selected Family and Background Characteristics, Controlling for Job Characteristics*

| | Types of Nonstandard Work Schedule | | | | | |
| | Men | | | Women | | |
Independent Variables	Nonday or Hours Vary (a)	Weekend (b)	Both (a) and (b)	Nonday or Hours Vary (a)	Weekend (b)	Both (a) and (b)
Family characteristics						
Marital status						
Married, spouse present	0.78*** (0.04)	0.89*** (0.04)	0.85*** (0.04)	0.77*** (0.04)	0.70*** (0.04)	0.72*** (0.03)
Parental status						
No child under age fourteen	1.00	1.00	1.00	1.00	1.00	1.00
One child under age five only	1.08 (0.08)	1.23** (0.07)	1.18** (0.07)	0.84* (0.08)	0.96 (0.07)	0.91 (0.07)
Two or more children under age five but no children age five to thirteen	1.19 (0.11)	1.03 (0.10)	1.05 (0.09)	1.14 (0.13)	1.09 (0.12)	1.11 (0.12)
One child age five to thirteen only	1.02 (0.07)	1.05 (0.06)	1.09 (0.05)	0.75*** (0.07)	0.9 (0.06)	0.83*** (0.05)
Two or more children age five to thirteen but no child under age five	0.96 (0.07)	1.12 (0.06)	1.07 (0.06)	0.97 (0.07)	1.06 (0.07)	1.05 (0.06)
Two or more children, at least one under age five and at least one age five to thirteen	1.31*** (0.07)	1.20** (0.06)	1.25*** (0.06)	0.99 (0.08)	0.90 (0.07)	1.00 (0.07)
Background characteristics						
Age (years)						
Eighteen to twenty-nine	1.23*** (0.05)	1.15*** (0.04)	1.22*** (0.04)	1.79*** (0.05)	1.23*** (0.05)	1.40*** (0.04)
Thirty to forty-four	1.02 (0.04)	1.04 (0.04)	1.04 (0.04)	1.12* (0.05)	1.01 (0.04)	1.04 (0.04)
Forty-five and older	1.00	1.00	1.00	1.00	1.00	1.00
Education completed (years)						
Less than twelve	1.00	1.00	1.00	1.00	1.00	1.00

TABLE 2.8   *Continued*

| | Types of Nonstandard Work Schedule | | | | | |
| | Men | | | Women | | |
Independent Variables	Nonday or Hours Vary (a)	Weekend (b)	Both (a) and (b)	Nonday or Hours Vary (a)	Weekend (b)	Both (a) and (b)
Twelve	0.83***	1.03	0.91*	1.26***	1.11	1.20***
	(0.05)	(0.05)	(0.05)	(0.06)	(0.06)	(0.06)
Thirteen to fifteen	1.10*	1.09*	1.06	1.16***	1.14**	1.14***
	(0.04)	(0.04)	(0.04)	(0.05)	(0.04)	(0.04)
Sixteen	0.75***	0.77***	0.75***	0.93	0.86**	0.87**
	(0.06)	(0.05)	(0.05)	(0.06)	(0.06)	(0.05)
Seventeen or more	0.59**	0.92	0.83**	0.97	1.12	1.11
	(0.09)	(0.07)	(0.06)	(0.10)	(0.08)	(0.07)
Race-ethnicity						
Non-Hispanic white	1.00	1.00	1.00	1.00	1.00	1.00
Non-Hispanic black	1.05	0.86**	0.96	1.15**	0.94	1.02
	(0.05)	(0.05)	(0.05)	(0.06)	(0.05)	(0.05)
Hispanic	0.84**	0.83***	0.87**	0.80***	0.87*	0.88*
	(0.06)	(0.05)	(0.05)	(0.07)	(0.06)	(0.06)
Other	0.92	1.03	1.11	1.10	1.37***	1.37***
	(0.08)	(0.07)	(0.07)	(0.09)	(0.08)	(0.08)

Source: May 1997 CPS.
Note: All regression models control for the following job characteristics: occupation, industry, class of worker, whether multiple job holder, and whether employed full- or part-time. Numbers in parentheses are standard errors.
*p = <.05; **p = <.01; ***p = <.001.

dard work schedules. The effect of children on nonstandard work hours was positive for fathers, not negative, and the odds of working such hours were significantly greater only when there was one child only under age five and a second (or more) child(ren) between the ages of five to thirteen. Weekend employment, or the combination of nonstandard hours and weekends, was significantly more likely both for these fathers and for fathers with only one child under age five (and no older children).

Although the expected difference by gender in the effect of children is observed, the reasons for the particular pattern of difference are unclear. Among all respondents with children in the household, men were more likely than women to be married and to have a non-employed spouse fully available to care for their children than women; this division of labor might have made nonstandard work schedules less demanding for these men when they were home from their jobs. But when

TABLE 2.9   *Odds Ratios of Working Nonstandard Schedules in Their Principal Job for Employed Married Men and Women Who Have Employed Spouses, by Parental Status*

| | Types of Nonstandard Work Schedule | | | | | |
| | Men | | | Women | | |
Parental Status	Nonday or Hours Vary (a)	Weekend (b)	Both (a) and (b)	Nonday or Hours Vary (a)	Weekend (b)	Both (a) and (b)
No child under age fourteen	1.00	1.00	1.00	1.00	1.00	1.00
One child under age five only	1.17 (0.11)	1.19* (0.09)	1.17 (0.13)	1.03 (0.12)	0.93 (0.10)	1.02 (0.16)
Two or more children under age five but no children age five to thirteen	1.16 (0.16)	0.98 (0.14)	1.20 (0.20)	1.46** (0.16)	1.12 (0.15)	1.66** (0.19)
One child age five to thirteen only	1.08 (0.08)	1.08 (0.07)	1.00 (0.11)	0.83* (0.09)	1.07 (0.08)	0.91 (0.13)
Two or more children age five to thirteen but no child under age five	1.03 (0.09)	1.08 (0.07)	1.01 (0.12)	1.16 (0.10)	1.08 (0.09)	1.16 (0.13)
Two or more children, at least one under age five, and at least one age five to thirteen	1.23* (0.10)	1.21* (0.08)	1.31* (0.12)	1.27* (0.10)	1.09 (0.09)	1.18 (0.14)

Source: May 1997 CPS.
Note: All regression models control for the following job characteristics: occupation, industry, class of worker, whether multiple job holder, and whether employed full- or part-time, as well as for marital status, age, completed education, and race-ethnicity. Numbers in parentheses are standard errors.
*p = <.05; **p = <.01; ***p = <.001.

doing the regressions separately for married couples with an employed spouse (table 2.9), similar positive relationships obtain for men, diminishing the salience of this explanation. Interestingly, for women in dual-earner households there were some significant *positive* effects of children on nonstandard work hours for particular family types of two or more children, in contrast to the overall negative effects for all women, although having one child between the ages of five and thirteen had a negative effect here as well.[20] But overall, when restricting the analysis to employed married individuals with an employed spouse, gender differences are less evident. (The employed married men and women in this analysis were not married to one another but had an employed spouse.)

The relationship between parental status and nonstandard work schedules clearly needs further study, using more extensive data on child care preferences and employment choices. Only then can we get a good sense of how children of various numbers and ages affect the decision to work nonstandard hours, net of other determining factors.

Background Characteristics

Age maintains its negative relationship to nonstandard work schedules in a multivariate context, for both men and women. This is the case for both nonstandard hours and weekend employment. In table 2.8 we see that men age eighteen to twenty-nine were 23 percent more likely to work nonstandard hours than men age forty-five or over, whereas there was minimal difference between men age thirty to forty-four and men age forty-five and over. For women, there was a significant difference between all age groups, and being young more strongly enhanced their likelihood of working nonstandard hours than it did for men: the odds were 79 percent greater comparing eighteen- to twenty-nine-year-old women with those age forty-five and over, and 12 percent greater when comparing thirty- to forty-four-year-olds with those age forty-five and over. Weekend employment for both men and women was most likely for those age eighteen to twenty-nine; the likelihood for those age thirty to forty-four was roughly equivalent to that for those age forty-five and over.

Education, a key indicator of human capital, does not show a linear relationship to nonstandard work schedules. Men with less than a high school degree, compared with high school graduates, were significantly less likely to work nonstandard hours (.8), and those with some college were significantly more likely (1.1). However, college graduates (those with both sixteen years of schooling and seventeen or more) were significantly less likely to work nonstandard hours. The relationship differs for women: both those with less than a high school degree and those with some college (thirteen to fifteen years of schooling) were significantly more likely to work nonstandard hours than high school graduates, and there was no significant difference between high school graduates and college graduates (sixteen years) and higher (seventeen years or more).

The relationship between education and weekend employment was the same for both men and women. Both those with some college and college graduates were significantly less likely to work nonstandard hours compared with high school graduates; the other educational levels show no significant difference. As for the combination of nonstandard hours and weekend employment, there are gender differences again. For men, those at the bottom and top educational levels were least likely to work such combinations relative to high school graduates. For women, those with less than a high school degree and those with some college were significantly more likely to work such combinations, with college graduates (sixteen years) being significantly less likely.

In a multivariate context, *race-ethnicity* differences between non-Hispanic whites and blacks were not significant with regard to nonstandard work hours for men, but they were for women. Black women were 1.15 times as likely to work nonstandard hours as white women. For both men and women, Hispanics were significantly less likely than non-Hispanic whites to work such hours (.84 for men and .80 for women). These findings are consistent with those reported earlier in this chapter on the substantial effect of ethnic differences in occupational composition on levels of employment at nonstandard hours. In the logistic regression we cannot use all the detailed occupations used for standardization, but the regression adjusts for other job as well as family characteristics. This analysis does not explain all of the difference in work shifts between black and white women, suggesting that discriminatory factors not tapped in this model may also be important. Why Hispanics were least likely to work nonstandard hours with these controls remains an open question.

We see gender differences in the relationship between race-ethnicity and weekend employment as well. Non-Hispanic black men and Hispanic men were significantly less likely than non-Hispanic white men to work weekends when controlling for the other variables in the model. No difference is shown between black and non-Hispanic white women, but Hispanic women were significantly less likely to work weekends, and non-Hispanic "other" women were significantly more likely, relative to non-Hispanic whites. When considering the combination of nonstandard hours and weekend employment among men and women, it is Hispanics who showed the only significant difference from non-Hispanic whites, being .87 times as likely to work such schedules; for women, only, the "other" group was significantly different, being 1.37 times as likely to work this combination as non-Hispanic white women.

Overall, then, when controlling for differences in job and other characteristics, each of the family and background characteristics seem to influence the decision to work nonstandard schedules. But except for marital status and age, the nature of this influence is altered in a multi-variate analysis that adjusts for differences in job and other family and background characteristics. Moreover, except for marital status and age, the nature of this influence is different by gender. Why this is so merits further study, as elaborated in the chapter's summary.

Future Job Growth and
Nonstandard Work Schedules

Given the widespread prevalence of nonstandard work schedules in 1997, what should we expect in the years ahead?[21] Job growth projections for the future suggest that the number of people working such schedules will increase in the decades ahead—and that this growth will disproportionately involve more women and, to a lesser extent, more blacks and Hispanics.

Table 2.10 shows the top ten occupations in 2000 that, according to the Bureau of Labor Statistics, are projected to have the largest job growth between 2000 and 2010 (Hecker 2001, table 4). Using the May 1997 CPS data, I have calculated the percentage of workers in these top growth occupations who worked nonstandard schedules. As specified in the table's notes, the occupations used by the BLS for job projections are based on the National Industry-Occupation Employment Matrix (NIOEM) and do not always correspond exactly with the CPS occupational classifications, and some regrouping was necessary. (It was not possible to identify customer service representatives in the CPS.)

We see that a disproportionately high percentage of workers in most of these occupations—namely, food preparation and serving workers, registered nurses, retail salespersons, cashiers, security guards, and waiters and waitresses—worked something other than a fixed day (far exceeding the average for all occupations of 19.9 percent). The same occupations that are disproportionately high on nonstandard hours are also disproportionately high on weekend employment.

The last three columns of table 2.10 also show, as of May 1997, the percentage of female, black, and Hispanic workers in these top growth occupations. These percentages can be compared with the percentages in all occupations for the respective groups shown in the column headings. When the percentages for specific occupations exceed those for all occupations, the subgroups fall disproportionately in those occupations.

TABLE 2.10 Top Projected Job Growth Occupations (from 2000 to 2010) and Their Work Schedule, Gender, and Race Characteristics

Job Growth Rank	Occupation[a]	Employment (Thousands)		Working Nonstandard Schedules, May 1997 CPS			Percentage of Group in Occupation, May 1997 CPS		
		2000	2010[b] (Projected)	Other Than Fixed Day (a)	Weekend (b)	(a) or (b) (c)	Female (All Occupations = 46.0)	Non-Hispanic Black (All Occupations = 10.5)	Hispanic (All Occupations = 9.8)
1	Food preparation and serving workers, including fast food[c]	2,206	2,879	45.8%	55.0%	68.0%	51.5%	11.8%	24.2%
2	Customer service representatives[d]	1,946	2,577	NA	NA	NA	NA	NA	NA
3	Registered nurses	2,194	2,755	34.6	42.9	55.1	94.5	7.5	3.2
4	Retail salespersons	4,109	4,619	32.2	62.9	70.6	55.3	7.7	8.7
5	Computer support specialists[e]	506	996	20.0	15.9	26.5	56.1	19.9	3.1

6	Cashiers, except gaming	3,325	3,799	50.4	71.0	80.1	77.2	15.6	12.3
7	Office clerks, general	2,705	3,135	16.2	15.7	23.5	76.3	13.6	8.9
8	Security guards[f]	1,106	1,497	57.0	55.8	73.9	22.8	19.4	13.0
9	Computer software engineers, applications[g]	380	760	5.2	13.5	16.9	31.5	6.6	2.4
10	Waiters and waitresses	1,983	2,347	65.1	79.0	89.5	78.8	3.1	12.6

Source: Author's compilation.

[a] The BLS occupational classifications for job projections are based on the National Industry-Occupation Employment Matrix (NIOEM) and do not always correspond exactly with the CPS occupational classifications, as noted below.

[b] Projections are derived by the Bureau of Labor Statistics (Hecker 2001, table 4).

[c] This category includes kitchen workers, food preparation, and "miscellaneous food preparation occupations" in the CPS.

[d] There is no separate classification in the CPS for this category.

[e] This category corresponds to "computer equipment operators" in the CPS.

[f] This category includes "guards and police, except public service" and "protective service occupations, n.e.c" in the CPS.

[g] This category includes "computer system analysts and scientists" and "operations and systems researchers and analysts" in the CPS.

Thus, we see that among these top growth occupations, those high on nonstandard work schedules are high on the percentage of female workers, the two exceptions being security guards and computer software engineers. The picture is more mixed for blacks and Hispanics, who are overly represented in the top growth occupations of food preparers and servers, cashiers, and security guards and, for Hispanics, waiters and waitresses, but underrepresented as registered nurses and, for blacks, as waiters and waitresses.[22]

If these projections are realized, employment at nonstandard times should increase in the near future, especially for women and minorities. The top ten job growth occupations detailed in table 2.10 represent 22.1 percent of the total increase of 22.2 million projected jobs between 2000 and 2010. This anticipated growth is "net" in that there also will be job decline in some occupations. However, the size of the declines in the top ten job-losing occupations are expected to be relatively small, representing in total only 778,000 jobs (Hecker 2001, table 5). Moreover, further analysis (not shown) indicates that most of these occupations do not show high levels of workers employed at nonstandard times. A notable exception is the occupation with the largest job loss projected, farmers and ranchers, whose nonday employment is very low but who have high employment (two-thirds) on weekends.

The speed at which Americans are moving toward a 24/7 economy cannot be assessed with the data available. Although I do not expect it to be dramatic or steadily upward, I would argue that this is the direction in which we are headed, and in some sectors of the economy we are there now. An important consideration that may affect the pace is the extent to which the recent slowdown in the economy, linked in part to the terrorist attacks on the United States on September 11, 2001, will disproportionately reduce activity in the travel, recreation, and restaurant industries, among others. If this slowdown affects the economy for some years to come, there may be a lull in the growth of nonstandard work schedules—especially among women and minorities—but I predict it would pick up again in subsequent years.

The U.S. Experience in Global Context

The United States is not alone in the high prevalence of nonstandard work schedules. Indeed, many countries seem to be following a similar course—even some European Union countries with national laws requiring substantial pay differentials—sometimes as much as 50 percent higher—for late-hour and weekend employment (reflecting the greater power of unions in determining labor practices in EU countries than in the United States; see Wedderburn 1991).

We cannot precisely compare levels of nonstandard hours in the United States with those of other countries because of differences in labor force surveys regarding sampling, work schedule definitions, and such. However, an analysis of data for various European Labour Force Surveys provided by Eurostat permits a rough comparison of selected European countries with the United States. It is rough primarily because the differences in the way work shifts are defined permit a more liberal inclusion of employees as nonday workers in Europe relative to the United States.[23] All of the surveys were conducted in 1997, and all of the samples (varying in size, but large) consist of persons age eighteen and over in nonagricultural occupations who are wage and salary earners. Further, for all surveys the work shifts refer to the principal job.

Figure 2.1 presents the percentages of those who usually worked nonday hours (evenings, nights, or rotating shifts) for thirteen European Union countries: Austria, Belgium, Denmark, Finland, France, Germany, Greece, Ireland, Italy, Luxembourg, the Netherlands, Sweden, and the United Kingdom; these percentages are shown for the total employed and for employed parents only.[24] The percentages of all those employed who worked nondays in these European countries range from a low of 9.7 percent for France to a high of 20.2 percent for Greece.[25] Other European countries on the high end are Denmark, Finland, and the United Kingdom, all of which are close to the 20.2 percent shown for the United States (restricted to wage and salary earners). Again, the definitions of work hours differ for the United States and European countries, the latter being more liberal; the use of similar definitions in the United States might make the percentage of nonstandard hours worked notably higher than in these European countries. But on the whole, it is evident that many Europeans are working what they refer to as "atypical" and rotating shifts. Moreover, as in the United States, European parents are participating fully in nonday employment. The percentages for employed parents differ only slightly from those for all employed.

With regard to weekend employment, there are fewer comparability problems between countries since the specification of whether an individual works Saturday or Sunday is more precise. Also, we have comparable weekend data for Portugal and Spain to add to data for the other European Union countries. Figure 2.2 shows the percentages of employees working Saturday and/or Sunday for the total and for parents only. (The large majority of employees in all countries who work weekends work on Saturday but not Sunday.)

We see that the prevalence of total employees working weekends among the European countries ranges from 11.4 percent for Belgium to

FIGURE 2.1   *Wage and Salary Earners Age Eighteen and Over in Nonagricultural Occupations Employed Nondays in the United States and Selected European Countries, 1997*

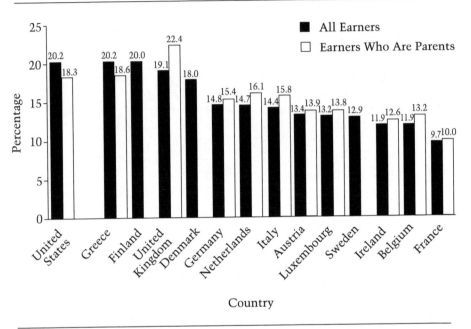

Sources: The May 1997 Current Population Survey for the United States; Eurostat for European countries.
Notes: In the CPS, working "nondays" is defined as working the most hours in the previous week during the evening, at night, or on a rotating shift that includes evenings and nights. Eurostat defines working "nondays" as "usually" working at least some hours in the evening, at night, or on a rotating shift that includes evenings and nights. The age range for children in the CPS is zero to thirteen; the Eurostat age range is zero to fourteen. For all countries, "work shift" refers to the principal job. Information about parental status in Finland, Denmark, and Sweden is not available.

33.1 percent for Italy. The prevalence in Italy exceeds that of the United States (29.3 percent). In ten of the other European countries, between one-fifth and one-fourth of all employees work weekends, attesting to the widespread prevalence of weekend employment in Europe. We also see in figure 2.2 that high proportions of parents work weekends; the percentage is very close to that for all those employed, and in some countries it is slightly more than for all employed. Again, Italy exceeds the United States, and the other countries have lower percentages

FIGURE 2.2   *Wage and Salary Earners Age Eighteen and Over*
in Nonagricultural Occupations Employed Weekends
in the United States and Selected European Countries,
1997

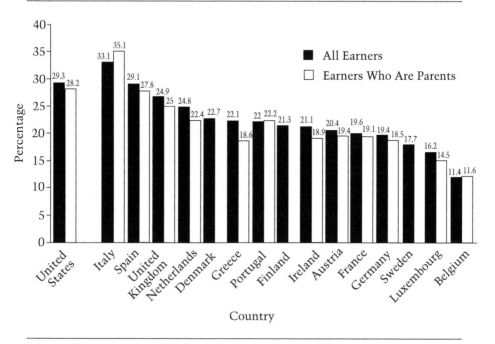

Source: The May 1997 Current Population Survey for the United States; Eurostat for European countries.
Notes: The CPS age range for children is zero to thirteen; the Eurostat age range is zero to fourteen. For all countries, weekend employment means working on Saturday, Sunday, or both and refers to the principal job.

of employed parents working weekends, but the percentages for most countries are around 20 percent or higher.

Summary

We have seen that employment during nonstandard hours and on weekends is widespread in the United States, among both men and women. Indeed, gender differences in the prevalence of nonstandard work schedules are minimal; rather, the differences are more marked when examining specific nonstandard work patterns.

Most of those working nonstandard schedules are serving the local economy in service-related occupations or industries, such as food preparation and service, health care, and the sale of commodities. Persons in these jobs are also likely to be low-paid workers who receive little if any additional pay to compensate for working nonstandard hours or weekends. Nevertheless, the primary reasons most of them give for working late, rotating, or variable hours are related to job demands, suggesting that many would prefer other schedules.

For the minority of those who give personal and familial reasons for working nonstandard times, there are offsetting compensations. It is mostly women who mention being able to care for children or other family members by working such schedules, as well as being able to combine schooling and employment. Also, although not tapped in this survey, many workers may prefer the reduced supervision typical of employment during late hours (U.S. Congress 1991), as well as other potential advantages noted at the start of this chapter. And the self-employed (for example, store owners), for whom I did not have earnings data or reasons for such schedules, may find it particularly beneficial financially to work weekends, despite the negative social aspects of being out of sync with others, thereby generating their high levels of such employment.

The bivariate analysis of the distribution of job, family, and background characteristics by nonstandard work schedules, separately for men and women, gives us a vivid picture of the subgroups in which those working nonstandard schedules concentrate, regardless of reason. This analysis goes beyond asking what those who work nonstandard schedules look like and examines the subgroups of job, family, and background characteristics from which these individuals are disproportionately drawn.

Whereas those in large service occupations were especially likely to work nonstandard schedules, nonstandard schedules were found to be pervasive throughout the occupational hierarchy. The bivariate analysis has also shown that generalizations regarding major occupational groups (for example, all sales occupations) can be misleading, since there is considerable variation by detailed occupation within these broad categories (for example, within sales, cashiers versus mining, manufacturing, and wholesale sales representatives). Moreover, while many occupations are high on both nonstandard work hours and weekend employment, there are also many occupations that are high on one but not the other. Further, there are some notable gender differences in nonstandard work schedules between occupations, and within occupations men are generally more likely to work nonstandard schedules than women. Yet, given the gendered nature of the occupational structure, the overall net result is that only slightly more men than women work a schedule other than fixed day shifts and weekends.

Nonstandard work schedules are especially common not only in certain occupations but in personal service industries, among workers who have more than one job, and among those who work part-time. Gender differences for these characteristics are not substantial, although men working in extractive and social service industries are much more likely than women to work nonstandard schedules.

The family characteristics that show high proportions working nonstandard schedules are being unmarried and, for women, having a pre-school-aged child. As for background characteristics, high proportions of nonstandard work schedules are found among those who are young, less-educated, and non-Hispanic black. These findings, along with those on hourly earnings, indicate that the most disadvantaged segments of the U.S. population, socially as well as economically, are those most likely to work nonstandard schedules, although many of the advantaged also work these schedules.

While the bivariate relationships tell us the subgroups in the United States that are disproportionately involved in nonstandard work schedules, they do not tell us whether specific group characteristics have an independent effect on the likelihood of working these schedules after adjusting for other group differences. We know that the nature of the jobs held by the individuals in these subgroups matters, and that these jobs are driven largely by demand. But what if we control for differences in job as well as other family and background characteristics? Would being married, having children, being young, being poorly educated, or being black or Hispanic matter? And would these characteristics matter for men in the same ways they matter for women?

The regression analysis to address this question showed that some of the associations noted in the bivariate analysis were similar after controlling for other differences: being single increased the likelihood of working nonstandard schedules for both sexes, and age had a negative influence for both. But for the other variables, the nature of the relationships with the additional controls changed and show very different patterns for men and women.

Specifically, in the regression analysis, fathers with at least two children, one under age five and the other between the ages of five and thirteen, are especially likely to work nonstandard schedules, whereas children do not encourage such work behavior among women. Rather, among women, having one child (only) of either age group significantly *decreases* the likelihood that they will work nonstandard hours relative to those who have no children, and having one child of school age (five to thirteen) *decreases* the likelihood that they will work weekends. When limiting the analysis to married respondents with an employed spouse, several of the parental status types showed positive effects on nonstandard work schedules, making the gender differences fewer. Overall, these findings suggest that the number and ages of children are important motivating factors for employment at nonstandard work times, net of job and other demographic and background characteristics, but why this is the case cannot be readily explained with the data on hand.

We have seen from the regression analysis that education is not linearly related to nonstandard hours, with the peak likelihood of working nonstandard hours occurring among men with thirteen to fifteen years of schooling and among women with twelve years. For weekend employment, the peak likelihood occurs among those with thirteen to fifteen years of schooling for both men and women. It would seem, then, that the relatively high levels of nonstandard work schedules among those with less than twelve years of schooling—evident in the bivariate analysis—can be attributed to differences in job, family, and other background characteristics.

The regression analysis also reveals the relevance of other factors in explaining the higher prevalence of nonstandard work schedules among minorities. In this analysis, the only minority more likely than non-Hispanic whites to work nonstandard hours is black women, and it is only women in the mixed "other" group who show a greater likelihood than non-Hispanic white women to work weekends. Minority men do not show any greater likelihood of working nonstandard schedules. The additional factors that might explain why black and "other" women remain highly likely to work nonstandard schedules after adjusting for various job, family, and other background characteristics merits further study. Perhaps these women have fewer options for jobs with standard work schedules because of discrimination.

Although the CPS provides highly reliable national data on the employment status of Americans and is a large enough sample to examine detailed occupations in relation to nonstandard work schedules, it is not a survey designed to study nonstandard work schedules in depth. We clearly need other data sources more targeted to this issue. It would be especially interesting to know the extent to which employees choose or decline certain occupational opportunities because of the hours or days they would be required to work. We also need to study how family members weigh the trade-offs between time together as a family and job demands, between personal health and economic needs, and the relevance of high occupational status in making these trade-offs. Although we will be looking at some of the family consequences of nonstandard work schedules in subsequent chapters, the National Survey of Families and Households, on which that analysis is based, also was not designed to consider such issues in depth.

The analysis of job growth and work schedules presented in this chapter suggests that not only will the future bring increases in the employment of women, but that more of them will be working nonstandard hours and days. The two-way relationship between women's daytime and nondaytime employment, discussed in chapter 1, is sure to continue, along with the aging of the population, the increasing demand for continuous twenty-four-hour medical care, and other demographic and technological changes.

To a lesser extent than for women, the job growth projections suggest that the employment of minorities in nonstandard schedules may also be on the rise in the near future. This could be interpreted as "good news" in that job opportunities for both women and minorities may increase as we move toward a 24/7 economy; but it could also be "bad news" in that the low pay of many of these new jobs will not facilitate the narrowing of the substantial gender and racial gaps in earnings in the United States (Blau 1998; Darity 1998).

The United States is not alone in having a high prevalence of employment at nonstandard times. Although the remaining chapters focus solely on the United States, for all countries experiencing such work schedule diversity, the increasing complexity of family life that it generates exceeds general conceptions. We next describe American families from this perspective in some detail.

Appendix

TABLE A2.1 *Unadjusted Mean Hourly Earnings of Top Ten Occupations of Wage and Salary Earners, by Shift Status and Whether Work Weekends*

Rank			Hours		Days	
Nonday/ Hours Vary	Weekends	Top ten occupations	Nonday/ Hours Vary	Fixed Day	Weekends	Weekdays Only
1	3	Cashiers	$6.93 (118)	$6.99 (120)	$6.95 (162)	$7.07 (82)
2	5	Truck drivers	$10.59 (38)	$10.45 (143)	$9.90 (49)	$10.66 (137)
3	2	Sales workers, re-tail and personal services, com-modities	$6.72 (65)	$7.03 (120)	$6.73 (114)	$7.15 (71)
4	7	Waiters and wait-resses	$4.48 (75)	$3.98 (37)	$4.27 (83)	$4.53 (23)
5	4	Cooks	$6.11 (63)	$6.49 (107)	$6.25 (107)	$6.55 (65)
6	10	Janitors and cleaners	$7.56 (56)	$7.75 (120)	$6.77 (52)	$8.26** (124)
7	1	Supervisors and proprietors, sales occupations	$8.64 (28)	$9.95+ (99)	$9.10 (66)	$10.28* (60)
8	9	Registered nurses	$18.11 (69)	$16.89 (103)	$17.98 (83)	$16.95 (84)
9	6	Managers, food serving and lodg-ing	$8.06 (20)	$9.41 (20)	$8.61 (26)	$9.07 (13)
10	8	Nursing aides, or-derlies, and at-tendants	$7.81 (52)	$8.08 (80)	$7.63 (73)	$8.46 (66)
		All wage and sal-ary earners	$9.77 (1,640)	$10.84*** (5,031)	$9.61 (2,033)	$11.03*** (4,704)

Source: May 1997 CPS, outgoing sample.
Notes: Means are weighted; unweighted number of cases are in parentheses; sample excludes self-employed and those with zero earnings. Earnings exclude overtime. Significance levels are: +p = <.10; *p = <.05; **p = <.01; ***p = <.001.

TABLE A2.2   *Distribution of Employed Americans Age Eighteen and Over, by Occupation and Gender*

Occupation	(n)	Total	Male	Female
Executive, administrative, and managerial occupations	7,674	14.9%	15.6%	14.3%
Administrators, education	331	0.6	0.5	0.8
Managers, food and lodging establishments	615	1.2	1.2	1.2
Accountants and auditors	675	1.3	1.0	1.7
Other executives, administrative, managerial	6,053	11.8	12.9	10.6
Professional specialty occupations	8,185	15.9	13.8	18.4
Engineers	818	1.6	2.8	0.3
Computer systems analysts and scientists	475	0.9	1.2	0.6
Registered nurses	877	1.7	0.2	3.4
Elementary school teachers	885	1.7	0.5	3.1
Secondary school teachers	548	1.1	0.8	1.3
Social workers	344	0.7	0.4	1.0
Lawyers and judges	395	0.8	1.1	0.5
Other professional specialty	3,843	7.5	6.8	8.2
Technical and related support	1,736	3.4	3.0	3.7
Sales occupations	6,163	12.0	11.6	12.5
Supervisors and proprietors, sales	1,980	3.9	4.5	3.2
Real estate sales	305	0.6	0.6	0.6
Sales representatives: mining, manufacturing, wholesale	539	1.0	1.5	0.5
Cashiers	1,043	2.0	0.8	3.4
Other sales	2,296	4.5	4.2	4.8
Administrative support occupations	7,656	14.9	5.6	24.8
Secretaries, stenographers, and typists	1,660	3.2	0.1	6.6
Receptionists	378	0.7	—[a]	1.5
Bookkeepers, accounting, auditing clerks	750	1.5	0.2	2.8
Investigators and adjusters, not insurance	409	0.8	0.4	1.2
Other administrative support	4,459	8.7	4.9	12.7
Service occupations	6,860	13.3	10.0	17.0
Waiters and waitresses	531	1.0	0.4	1.7
Cooks, including short-order	818	1.6	1.6	1.6
Nursing aides, orderlies, and attendants	724	1.4	0.3	2.6
Janitors and cleaners	930	1.8	2.2	1.4
Other service	3,857	7.5	5.5	9.7
Precision production, craft, and repair occupations	5,900	11.5	20.0	2.1
Automobile mechanics	330	0.6	1.2	—[a]
Carpenters	572	1.1	2.1	—[a]

TABLE A2.2   *Continued*

Occupation	(n)	Total	Male	Female
Supervisors, production	520	1.0	1.5	0.4
Other precision production, craft, repair	4,478	8.7	15.2	1.7
Operators, fabricators, and laborers	7,237	14.1	20.4	7.3
Assemblers	519	1.0	1.1	1.0
Truck drivers, light and heavy	1,260	2.5	4.5	0.2
Construction laborers	306	0.6	1.1	0.1
Stock handlers and baggers	348	0.7	0.9	0.4
Laborers, except construction	549	1.1	1.6	0.5
Other operators, fabricators	4,255	8.3	11.2	5.1
Total		85.1	84.4	85.8
Number	51,411		26,738	24,673

Source: May 1997 CPS.
Notes: Categories are based on full sample; occupations with three hundred or more adults before attrition due to missing cases for the other variables are specified.
ªBase fewer than twenty sample cases.

TABLE A2.3   *Distribution of Employed Americans Age Eighteen and Over, by Selected Variables and Gender*

Selected Variables	(n)	Total	Male	Female
Selected job characteristics				
Industry				
Extractive	621	1.2%	1.6%	0.8%
Transformative	12,318	24.0	34.0	13.1
Distributive services	10,956	21.3	23.8	18.6
Producer services	7,410	14.4	13.1	15.8
Social services	14,316	27.8	17.1	39.5
Personal services	5,790	11.3	10.3	12.3
Class of worker				
Private industry	37,755	73.4	73.9	72.9
Government	7,957	15.5	12.7	18.4
Self-employed	5,699	11.1	13.4	8.6
Multiple job holder				
Has one paid job	47,522	92.4	92.4	92.5
Has more than one paid job	3,889	7.6	7.6	7.5
Part-time and/or full-time				
One to thirty-four hours per week	11,247	22.7	14.7	31.3
Thirty-five to ninety-nine hours per week	38,396	77.3	85.3	68.7
Family characteristics				
Marital status				
Married, spouse present	31,036	60.4	63.4	57.1
Other	20,375	39.6	36.6	42.9
Number of children under age 5				
Zero	44,199	86.0	85.5	86.4
One	5,589	10.9	10.9	10.8
Two or more	1,623	3.2	3.6	2.7
Number of children age five to thirteen				
Zero	39,218	76.3	77.1	75.4
One	7,118	13.8	13.0	14.7
Two or more	5,075	9.9	9.9	9.9
Number of children under age fourteen				
Zero	35,365	68.8	69.5	68.0
One	7,622	14.8	13.7	16.1
Two	6,065	11.8	11.8	11.8
Three or more	2,359	4.6	5.0	4.2
Demographic characteristics				
Age				
Eighteen to twenty-nine	12,164	23.7	23.2	24.2
Thirty to forty-four	21,294	41.4	41.6	41.3
Forty-five and older	17,953	34.9	35.3	34.5

TABLE A2.3   *Continued*

Selected Variables	(n)	Total	Male	Female
Race-Ethnicity				
Non-Hispanic white	40,422	78.9	79.4	78.4
Non-Hispanic black	4,440	8.7	7.5	10.0
Hispanic	4,007	7.8	8.5	7.1
Other	2,345	4.6	4.6	4.5
Education completed (years)				
Less than twelve	5,297	10.3	11.7	8.8
Twelve	16,988	33.0	32.7	33.4
Thirteen to fifteen	14,988	29.2	27.2	31.2
Sixteen	9,501	18.5	18.4	18.6
Seventeen and more	4,637	9.0	10.0	7.9
Total		100.0	100.0	100.0
Number	51,411		26,738	24,673

Source: May 1997 CPS.
Note: Totals may not sum to 100.0 in general categories because of rounding.

3

The Temporal Structure
of American Families

A MERICAN families, like American work hours, are becoming more diverse. Indeed, the two trends go hand in hand. Dual-earner spouses (both employed) are now the predominant family type among married couples, even when children are young, and there are far more single employed parents with young children today than in previous decades. Employment at nonstandard hours and on weekends undoubtedly challenges such families, more so than traditional married couples with a single earner and a spouse at home full-time to respond to children's daytime and everyday demands.

In subsequent chapters, we will consider the consequences of non-standard work schedules for family life, taking into account different family types. But before doing so, it is important to gain a detailed understanding of the extent to which these different family types participate in late-hour and weekend work. As we will see, the temporal patterns of American families are complex and difficult to grasp—and that may account in part for why they are generally ignored. But it also seems that both policymakers and scholars are often unaware of this important aspect of work and family life.

This neglect of reality is reminiscent of the early 1970s, when the extent of women's employment was considered "one of America's best-kept national secrets" (Keller 1972, 274). Fortunately, this is no longer the case; it is now generally recognized that most women will be employed much of their lifetime, including during their child-rearing years. Moreover, both public discourse and social research give considerable attention to the problems of combining work and family when women (as well as men) are employed, especially the difficulties of juggling time. Such concepts as "the double shift" and "the time bind" have gained widespread popularity (Hochschild 1989, 1997).

These concepts tap the essential fact that time is a finite resource: the twenty-four-hour day is fixed. The demands of paid employment typically preclude participation at the same time in family caregiving or leisure. Although economists view the value of time in terms of money, time is not fungible, in the sense that one cannot work more hours to get more time for one's family or one's self.[1] There is a growing body of literature on how parents cope when they experience time constraints resulting from this lack of fungibility. But missing from most of this literature is any consideration of the additional temporal situation that many parents face: employment at nonstandard hours during this twenty-four-hour day adds a high degree of complexity to the juggling.

In this chapter, we consider all family types but focus on two that have been growing rapidly in the United States: dual-earner couples and single (nonmarried) mothers. As noted, dual-earner couples characterize the majority of married American couples today. We tend to think of them as couples in which both spouses leave for work during the day-time and return in the evening, if not before. For a substantial minority, however, one spouse is leaving for work while the other is returning, and this pattern is particularly common among couples with children and those of low income.

Single mothers are more likely than married mothers to work non-standard schedules, and they clearly merit our attention. As of 1999, one-third of all births to women in the United States were to nonmarried mothers (U.S. Department of Commerce 2001a). Although many of these mothers may cohabit with the child's father and/or eventually marry, many married mothers become separated or divorced. The net result in 2000 was that one-fourth of all parents with children under eighteen years of age were not married (Fields and Casper 2001, derived from table 2). Not only are single mothers more likely to be employed than married mothers, but among the employed they generally work more hours than married mothers (Cox and Presser 2000; Coverman and Kemp 1987).

Single mothers are also more likely to have a low income than married mothers, and the difficulties of juggling work and family are exacerbated when economic resources are minimal. This is true as well within each marital type. Accordingly, I compare the work schedules of both married and nonmarried mothers according to whether they have relatively high or low income for their family type and I consider whether the presence and age of children alter their work schedule behavior within these income groups.

To help explain the differences to be observed in work schedule behavior by marital status, it is useful to consider whether there are differences in the reasons that married and nonmarried mothers give for working late hours. Married mothers would seem to choose their work schedules for personal-familial rather than job constraining reasons more often than nonmarried mothers, given that they typically have better job opportunities (with higher human capital) and more family income (with earning husbands).

Better job opportunities are reflected in the different occupational compositions of married and nonmarried mothers. Since occupation is so closely linked to work schedule behavior (see chapter 2), it is relevant to ask whether married and nonmarried mothers would look much more similar in their work schedule behavior if they had the same occupational composition. As we will see, the answer is definitely yes.

The analyses for this chapter are based on the May 1997 CPS data described in chapter 2. Since the CPS collects information on all household members, I was able to construct a file of married couples that included data on both husbands and wives as well as the presence and age of children (biological, adopted, and step).

Dual-Earner Families

In the previous chapter, the prevalence of nonstandard work schedules was presented from an individual perspective. Here we take a couples perspective, giving special attention to dual-earner couples. Among such couples, either spouse may be "at risk" of working a nonstandard work schedule, and thus the prevalence of such schedules among couples is necessarily higher than among individuals. This is why, even if there were no change over time in the overall prevalence of nonstandard work schedules for individuals, its prevalence among families would rise as a consequence of the increase in dual-earner couples. As noted in chapter 1, married women's participation in the labor force has more than doubled since 1960. As of 2000, 53.5 percent of all married couples—30.2 million—were dual-earners; for married dual-earner couples with children under age six, the figure is 57.7 percent, or 6.8 million (U.S. Department of Commerce 2001b, table FG1).

To what extent are such dual-earner couples "split-shift" couples— that is, one spouse works fixed days and the other works evening, nights, rotating shifts, or highly variable hours? This question is examined both for all dual-earner couples and for the subset of those in which both spouses are employed full-time, that is, thirty-five hours or more per week. (The number of hours relates to the reference week.)[2]

Table 3.1 is a tabulation of husband's work shift by wife's work shift. We see that for 72.2 percent of dual-earner American couples, both the husband and the wife worked a fixed daytime schedule. This means that 27.8 percent of all dual-earner couples included at least one spouse who worked other than a fixed day. Only 1.4 percent of couples were those with both spouses similarly working an evening, night, or rotating shift, and for only 0.5 percent of couples did both spouses work variable

TABLE 3.1   *Distribution of Work Shift Patterns for Husbands and Wives of Dual-Earner Married Couples*

| Husband's Shift Status | Wife's Shift Status | | | | | Total (Number of Cases) |
	Fixed Day	Fixed Evening	Fixed Night	Rotating[a]	Hours Vary	
All Dual-Earners						
Fixed day	72.2%	4.2%	2.5%	1.6%	2.4%	83.0% (9,272)
Fixed evening	4.0	0.8	0.2	0.2	0.1	5.3 (582)
Fixed night	3.5	0.3	0.3	0.1	0.2	4.3 (451)
Rotating[a]	3.3	0.3	0.1	0.3	0.1	4.0 (459)
Hours vary	2.6	0.1	0.1	0.1	0.5	3.4 (401)
Total (Number of Cases)	85.5 (9,511)	5.7 (638)	3.3 (369)	2.2 (257)	3.3 (390)	100.0 (11,165)
Full-time dual-earners						
Fixed day	75.4	2.7	2.6	1.3	1.3	83.2 (5,755)
Fixed evening	4.0	0.7	0.2	0.1	0.1	5.0 (348)
Fixed night	3.7	0.3	0.3	0.1	0.04	4.4 (280)
Rotating[a]	3.5	0.1	0.1	0.3	0.1	4.1 (288)
Hours vary	2.5	0.1	0.2	0.1	0.5	3.3 (299)
Total (Number of Cases)	89.0 (6,124)	3.8 (265)	3.3 (230)	1.9 (135)	2.0 (146)	100.0 (6,900)

Source: May 1997 CPS.
Notes: Percentages are weighted; numbers of cases are not weighted. The sample of dual-earner couples was restricted to those who were both civilian adults over the age of eighteen, working for pay in non-agricultural occupations, and, except for rotators, working in the previous week (n = 11,248).
[a]The few cases in which husbands and wives reported working twenty-four hours (for example always on call) were included under rotating shift.

hours. Thus, we can characterize about one-fourth of all dual-earner couples in the United States as split-shift couples with spouses working very different schedules.

Limiting the analysis to only full-time dual-earner couples does not change the picture very much. As the bottom of table 3.1 shows, this limitation increases the percentage of such couples among whom both worked fixed days to 75.4 percent, leaving 24.6 percent with at least one spouse working other than a fixed day schedule—still about one-fourth.

Weekend employment by at least one spouse is characteristic of almost half of all dual-earner couples (44.5 percent) (not shown). This is broken down as follows: among 21.6 percent of these couples, only the husband worked weekends, among 11.6 percent only the wife did, and among 11.3 percent both spouses worked weekends. The greater likelihood of men than women working weekends is consistent with earlier findings (table 2.1) for all employed individuals. A similar pattern is evident when considering only full-time dual earners: 44.0 percent of such couples had at least one spouse working weekends; 22.1 percent had husbands only, 10.1 percent had wives only, and among 11.8 percent both spouses worked weekends. Thus, even though full-time dual-earner couples had more hours per week on the job that could spill over to weekends, they were not more likely than dual-earner couples with at least one part-timer to work Saturday and/or Sunday.

Individual spouses may, of course, work both nonstandard hours *and* weekends. This combined work pattern by at least one spouse characterized 15.5 percent of all dual-earner couples and 13.5 percent of full-time dual-earner couples. It is rare that both spouses worked this combined pattern.

Given the considerable diversity in work schedule behavior, with one or both spouses working nonstandard hours and/or weekends, a key question becomes: How prevalent are "traditional" dual-earner couples—both spouses working standard hours and weekdays only? The answer is that fewer than half were traditional: 45.7 percent of all dual-earner couples and 48.1 percent of full-time dual-earner couples. The converse, as shown in the fourth column in table 3.2, is that 54.3 percent of all dual-earner couples, 51.9 percent if both worked full-time, were couples with at least one spouse working nonstandard hours and/or weekends.

Presence and Age of Children

We observed in the previous chapter that from an individual perspective the relationship between the presence and age of children and nonstandard work schedules is complex. From a dual-earner-couple perspective,

TABLE 3.2   *Dual-Earner Couples with at Least One Spouse Working a Nonstandard Schedule, by Type of Schedule and by Presence and Age of Children Under Fourteen*

	With Spouse Working Nonstandard Hours	With Spouse Weekends	With Spouse Working Nonstandard Hours *and* Weekends	With Spouse Working Nonstandard Hours *and/or* Weekends
All dual-earners				
Total	27.8%	44.5%	15.5%	54.3%
	(11,165)	(10,908)	(10,903)	(10,903)
No child under	25.0	42.7	13.9	51.6
age fourteen	(6,001)	(5,877)	(5,874)	(5,874)
Child under age	31.1	46.5	17.4	57.3
fourteen	(5,164)	(5,031)	(5,029)	(5,029)
Child under age	34.7	48.6	19.9	59.8
five	(2,210)	(2,146)	(2,146)	(2,146)
Child age five to	30.6	46.4	16.9	57.4
thirteen	(4,015)	(3,908)	(3,906)	(3,906)
Full-time dual-earners				
Total	24.6	42.7	13.5	51.9
	(6,900)	(6,789)	(6,785)	(6,785)
No child under	23.0	42.2	12.8	50.6
age fourteen	(3,943)	(3,888)	(3,885)	(3,885)
Child under age	26.7	43.5	14.5	53.6
fourteen	(2,957)	(2,901)	(2,900)	(2,900)
Child under age	28.0	42.4	15.2	52.9
five	(1,203)	(1,177)	(1,177)	(1,177)
Child age five to	26.8	44.2	14.5	54.4
thirteen	(2,303)	(2,256)	(2,255)	(2,255)

Source: May 1997 CPS.
Note: Percentages are weighted; numbers of cases are not weighted. The numbers of cases for "child under age five" and "child age five to thirteen" total more than "child under age fourteen" because some couples have one or more children in both categories. The sample of dual-earner couples was restricted to those who were both civilian adults over the age of eighteen, working for pay in non-agricultural occupations, and, except for rotators, working in the previous week.

a clearer relationship is evident. Having children, and particularly children under the age of five, enhances the likelihood that at least one of the spouses will work a nonstandard schedule.

As may be seen in table 3.2, about one-third (34.7 percent) of couples with at least one child under age five worked nonstandard hours. Also, about one-half (48.6 percent) of couples with such young children worked weekends. Moreover, about one-fifth (19.9 percent) of dual-earner couples with such young children included a spouse who worked *both* nonstandard hours and weekends. Allowing for all three options, at least one spouse working nonstandard hours, weekends, or both, this characterized about three-fifths (59.8 percent) of dual-earner couples with children under age five—a strikingly high prevalence for couples with such young children.

The percentages are somewhat lower when the sample is limited to full-time dual-earner couples, but the same pattern by presence and age of children prevails. There is one exception: weekend employment was slightly less prevalent (rather than more) among those who had children under age five (42.4 percent) compared with those whose children were ages five to thirteen (44.2 percent).

Family Income

It is not only those families with children but those with low income who are most likely to experience nonstandard work schedules. The combination of having children *and* a low family income produces the highest prevalences.

Tables 3.3 and 3.4 show the percentages working nonstandard schedules among those with a family income of less than $50,000 and of $50,000 or more, respectively, by presence and age of children. In the under-$50,000 group (table 3.3), it is striking that in about two-fifths (41.7 percent) of dual-earner couples with children under age five, at least one spouse worked nonstandard hours, and at least one spouse in the majority (55.2 percent) of these couples worked weekends. In about one-fourth (24.6 percent), at least one spouse worked both nonstandard hours and weekends. Overall, at least one spouse worked nonstandard hours and/or weekends in over two-thirds (68.3 percent) of these low-income couples.

As may be seen in table 3.4, the percentages were lower for dual-earner couples with family incomes of $50,000 or more, particularly with regard to nonstandard hours (as distinct from weekend employment). In 28.4 percent of such families with children under age five, at least one spouse worked nonstandard hours, in contrast to 41.7 percent in families whose income was less than $50,000 (table 3.3). When limiting the sample to full-time dual-earner couples, a similar contrast obtains: 36.0 percent with at least one spouse working nonstandard hours when family income was less than $50,000, in contrast to 21.5 percent when family income was $50,000 or more.

Low-income dual-earner families with young children are thus not only working for less money but working at more nonstandard times. It

TABLE 3.3   *Dual-Earner Couples with Family Income of Less Than
$50,000 and with at Least One Spouse Working a
Nonstandard Schedule, by Type of Schedule and by
Presence and Age of Children Under Fourteen*

	With Spouse Working Nonstandard Hours	With Spouse Working Weekends	With Spouse Working Nonstandard Hours *and* Weekends	With Spouse Working Nonstandard Hours *and/or* Weekends
All dual-earners, family income less than $50,000				
Total	33.1%	48.6%	18.9%	59.7%
	(4,477)	(4,387)	(4,387)	(4,387)
No child under age fourteen	28.9	45.6	16.6	55.6
	(2,123)	(2,091)	(2,091)	(2,091)
Child under age fourteen	36.8	51.4	21.0	63.5
	(2,354)	(2,296)	(2,296)	(2,296)
Child under age five	41.7	55.2	24.6	68.3
	(1,085)	(1,055)	(1,055)	(1,055)
Child age five to thirteen	35.8	50.5	20.4	62.8
	(1,812)	(1,767)	(1,767)	(1,767)
Full-time dual-earners, family income less than $50,000				
Total	29.5	45.8	16.0	56.9
	(2,497)	(2,469)	(2,469)	(2,469)
No child under age fourteen	27.1	45.1	15.4	55.1
	(1,250)	(1,242)	(1,242)	(1,242)
Child under age fourteen	31.9	46.5	16.5	58.7
	(1,247)	(1,227)	(1,227)	(1,227)
Child under age five	36.0	47.0	18.8	60.8
	(545)	(534)	(534)	(534)
Child age five to thirteen	30.9	46.8	16.1	58.7
	(969)	(952)	(952)	(952)

Source: May 1997 CPS.

Note: Percentages are weighted; numbers of cases are not weighted. The numbers of cases for "child under age five" and "child age five to thirteen" total more than "child under age fourteen" because some couples have one or more children in both categories. The sample of dual-earner couples was restricted to those who were both civilian adults over the age of eighteen, working for pay in non-agricultural occupations, and, except for rotators, working in the previous week.

TABLE 3.4   *Dual-Earner Couples with Family Income of $50,000 or More and with at Least One Spouse Working a Nonstandard Schedule, by Type of Schedule and by Presence and Age of Children Under Fourteen*

	With Spouse Working Nonstandard Hours	With Spouse Working Weekends	With Spouse Working Nonstandard Hours *and* Weekends	With Spouse Working Nonstandard Hours *and/or* Weekends
All dual-earners, family income $50,000 or more				
Total	24.0%	41.5%	13.1%	50.2%
	(5,948)	(5,820)	(5,816)	(5,816)
No child under age fourteen	22.0	40.5	12.2	48.3
	(3,418)	(3,351)	(3,349)	(3,349)
Child under age fourteen	26.6	42.9	14.4	52.7
	(2,530)	(2,469)	(2,467)	(2,467)
Child under age five	28.4	42.8	15.6	52.6
	(1,021)	(993)	(993)	(993)
Child age five to thirteen	26.3	43.4	14.1	53.2
	(1,986)	(1,935)	(1,933)	(1,933)
Full-time dual-earners, family income $50,000 or more				
Total	21.4	40.9	12.0	48.7
	(3,909)	(3,847)	(3,844)	(3,844)
No child under age fourteen	20.2	40.4	11.5	47.6
	(2,386)	(2,352)	(2,350)	(2,350)
Child under age fourteen	23.3	41.5	12.8	50.5
	(1,523)	(1,495)	(1,494)	(1,494)
Child under age five	21.5	39.4	12.0	47.4
	(597)	(584)	(584)	(584)
Child age five to thirteen	24.2	42.4	13.4	51.5
	(1,186)	(1,162)	(1,161)	(1,161)

Source: May 1997 CPS.

Note: Percentages are weighted; numbers of cases are not weighted. The numbers of cases for "child under age five" and "child age five to thirteen" total more than "child under age fourteen" because some couples have one or more children in both categories. The sample of dual-earner couples was restricted to those who were both civilian adults over the age of eighteen, working for pay in non-agricultural occupations, and, except for rotators, working in the previous week.

may also be noted, however, that for both income groups a substantial proportion in all categories work nonstandard schedules. I shall address the question of what this means for family functioning in subsequent chapters.

Single-Mother Families

The temporal structure of American families is becoming more complex, not only because there are more dual-earner couples, with each spouse "at risk" of working a nonstandard schedule, but also because there are more single-mother families and single mothers are more likely to work nonstandard schedules than married mothers.

Differences by marital status as well as the presence of children can be seen in table 3.5. Not only were nonmarried women (single and separated) far more likely to work nonstandard hours and weekends than married women, but it is nonmarried women with children under age five who show the highest percentages of all: 25.3 percent worked nonstandard hours, 38.1 percent worked on weekends, 15.9 percent did both, and 46.0 percent did one or both. These are the women most in need of child care; not only are their children preschool-aged, but they are by definition without a husband—and usually without a partner—to share child care responsibilities by working "split shifts." As earlier research based on the 1984 National Longitudinal Survey of Labor Market Experience—Youth Cohort (NLSY) has shown (Presser 1989b), nonmarried mothers rely on grandmother care more than their married counterparts do, even though a high proportion of these grandmothers are otherwise employed.[3] In other words, many grandmothers and mothers, particularly when mothers are unmarried, are working "split shifts" and sharing child care in this way. We will address this issue in more depth in chapter 7.

When looking only at full-time employed women (table 3.6), the much higher prevalence of nonstandard work schedules among those not married is evident here as well. As for the presence of children, nonmarried women employed full-time with no children were similar to those with children under age five in terms of a high prevalence of employment during nonstandard hours (17.5 percent and 17.3 percent, respectively), yet both were much higher than their married counterparts (11.3 percent and 12.3 percent, respectively, a difference of 40 to 50 percent). With regard to weekend employment, nonmarried mothers with children under age five show the highest level of all full-time subgroups (34.1 percent) and have the highest levels for two combined nonstandard and weekend employment categories as well.

TABLE 3.5   *Employed Women Who Work Nonstandard Schedules, by Type of Schedule and by Marital Status and the Presence and Age of Children Under Fourteen*

	Working Nonstandard Hours	Working Weekends	Working Nonstandard Hours *and* Weekends	Working Nonstandard Hours *and/or* Weekends
Married, husband present				
Total	15.0%	23.6%	7.8%	30.4%
	(13,475)	(13,824)	(13,258)	(13,258)
No child under age fourteen	14.0	23.0	7.3	29.9
	(8,046)	(8,237)	(7,932)	(7,932)
Child under age fourteen	16.4	23.9	8.6	31.3
	(5,429)	(5,587)	(5,326)	(5,326)
Child under age five	19.0	25.0	9.8	33.4
	(2,310)	(2,430)	(2,259)	(2,259)
Child age five to thirteen	16.0	23.7	8.2	31.2
	(4,224)	(4,296)	(4,143)	(4,143)
All others				
Total	23.0	33.5	14.6	41.2
	(10,179)	(10,284)	(9,945)	(9,945)
No child under age fourteen	23.6	33.6	15.1	41.4
	(8,052)	(8,140)	(7,859)	(7,859)
Child under age fourteen	20.8	33.2	12.8	40.0
	(2,127)	(2,144)	(2,086)	(2,086)
Child under age five	25.3	38.1	15.9	46.0
	(820)	(832)	(799)	(799)
Child age five to thirteen	18.9	30.3	10.9	37.5
	(1,630)	(1,640)	(1,602)	(1,602)

Source: May 1997 CPS.
Note: Percentages are weighted; numbers of cases are not weighted. The numbers of cases for "child under age five" and "child age five to thirteen" total more than "child under age fourteen" because some couples have one or more children in both categories. The sample of dual-earner couples was restricted to those who were both civilian adults over the age of eighteen, working for pay in non-agricultural occupations, and, except for rotators, working in the previous week.

Reasons for Working Nonstandard Hours

The differences in prevalence among mothers by marital status and age of children raise the question of whether the reasons for working nonstandard schedules differ accordingly. Again, we have reported reasons

TABLE 3.6   *Full-Time Employed Women Who Work Nonstandard Schedules, by Type of Schedule and by Marital Status and the Presence and Age of Children Under Fourteen*

	Working Nonstandard Hours	Working Weekends	Working Nonstandard Hours *and* Weekends	Working Nonstandard Hours *and/or* Weekends
Married, husband present				
Total	11.6%	22.1%	5.9%	27.6%
	(9,022)	(8,933)	(8,932)	(8,932)
No child under	11.3	22.5	5.8	27.9
age fourteen	(5,649)	(5,596)	(5,596)	(5,596)
Child under age	12.2	21.4	6.2	27.1
fourteen	(3,373)	(3,337)	(3,336)	(3,336)
Child under age	12.3	19.4	5.7	25.7
five	(1,369)	(1,349)	(1,349)	(1,349)
Child age five to	12.5	22.3	6.5	28.1
thirteen	(2,634)	(2,606)	(2,605)	(2,605)
All others				
Total	17.2	29.7	10.7	36.0
	(7,183)	(7,092)	(7,091)	(7,091)
No child under	17.5	29.4	10.8	35.8
age fourteen	(5,696)	(5,619)	(5,618)	(5,618)
Child under age	15.9	30.9	10.3	36.5
fourteen	(1,487)	(1,473)	(1,473)	(1,473)
Child under age	17.3	34.1	11.6	40.0
five	(538)	(532)	(532)	(532)
Child age five to	14.9	28.8	9.2	34.3
thirteen	(1,148)	(1,138)	(1,138)	(1,138)

Source: May 1997 CPS.
Note: Percentages are weighted; numbers of cases are not weighted. The numbers of cases for "child under age five" and "child age five to thirteen" total more than "child under age fourteen" because some couples have one or more children in both categories. The sample of dual-earner couples was restricted to those who were both civilian adults over the age of eighteen, working for pay in non-agricultural occupations, and, except for rotators, working in the previous week.

with regard to employment during nonstandard hours, but not weekends, and only for wage and salary earners (not the self-employed).

We see in figures 3.1 and 3.2 that "better child care arrangement" is a reason cited more frequently by married than nonmarried mothers. The sharing of child care with other relatives is undoubtedly facilitated when mothers work hours that relatives do not, and this may be why many regard it as a better arrangement; moreover, the cost may be low

FIGURE 3.1   *Distribution of Main Reasons Reported by Married Women Wage and Salary Earners Working Nondays (Including Rotators) with Children Under Age Fourteen, by Age of Youngest Child*

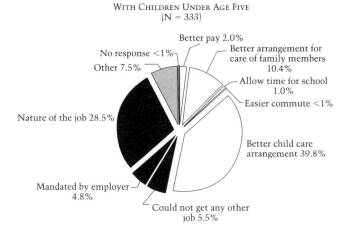

WITH CHILDREN UNDER AGE FIVE
(N = 333)

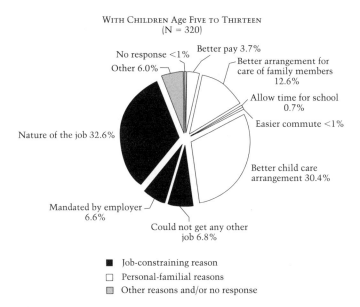

WITH CHILDREN AGE FIVE TO THIRTEEN
(N = 320)

■ Job-constraining reason
☐ Personal-familial reasons
▨ Other reasons and/or no response

Source: May 1997 CPS.
Note: Percentages are weighted; numbers of cases are not weighted. The sample excludes those who have missing data on the previous week of shift work, and those self employed.

FIGURE 3.2   *Distribution of Main Reasons Reported by*
Nonmarried Women Wage and Salary Earners
Working Nondays (Including Rotators) with Children
Under Age Fourteen, by Age of Youngest Child

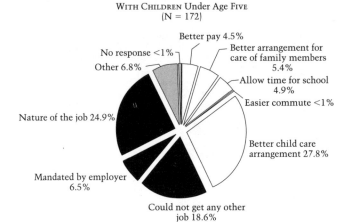

WITH CHILDREN Under Age FIVE
(N = 172)

Better pay 4.5%
No response <1%
Other 6.8%
Better arrangement for
care of family members
5.4%
Allow time for school
4.9%
Easier commute <1%
Nature of the job 24.9%
Better child care
arrangement 27.8%
Mandated by employer
6.5%
Could not get any other
job 18.6%

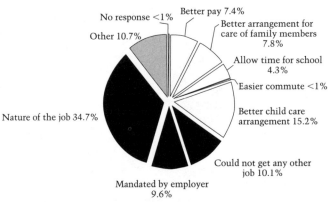

WITH CHILDREN Age FIVE TO THIRTEEN
(N = 190)

No response <1%   Better pay 7.4%
Other 10.7%
Better arrangement for
care of family members
7.8%
Allow time for school
4.3%
Easier commute <1%
Nature of the job 34.7%
Better child care
arrangement 15.2%
Could not get any other
job 10.1%
Mandated by employer
9.6%

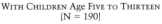

■ Job-constraining reason
☐ Personal-familial reasons
▨ Other reasons and/or no response

Source: May 1997 CPS.
Note: Percentages are weighted; numbers of cases are not weighted. The sample excludes
those who have missing data on the previous week of shift work, and those self employed.

(for further discussion, see chapter 7). Although grandparents and other relatives may help married as well as nonmarried mothers with child care, married mothers benefit from the greater availability of the child's father to share child care. This may explain why a higher percentage cited better child care arrangement as their reason for working nonstandard hours. Interestingly, married mothers also were much more likely than nonmarried mothers to report "better arrangements for care of family members." Unfortunately, we do not know the extent to which this involved elder care, spouse care, or other family care—an issue worthy of further study.

Nonmarried mothers were more likely than married mothers to report a job constraining reason for working nonstandard hours. It is the inability to get another job that shows the most substantial differentials: fully 18.6 percent of nonmarried mothers with children under age five, and 10.1 percent of nonmarried mothers whose youngest child was age five to thirteen, gave this reason; the figures for their married counterparts are 5.5 percent and 6.8 percent, respectively. This raises the question of the role of different occupational structures for married and nonmarried mothers in explaining the higher rates of nonstandard hours among the latter.

Standardizing on Occupation

To address this question, I standardized the occupational distributions of the two marital status groups to that of all mothers. The smaller the difference between the two groups in the percentages working nonstandard work schedules when given the same occupational distribution, the more relevant occupation is in explaining the differences in work schedule behavior.

The standardization process involves three steps. First, I grouped occupations into forty-five categories—thirty-five detailed occupations with at least fifty cases and ten broader occupational groups that combine the residuals. I then multiplied the proportion of all mothers in an occupation (without regard to marital status) by the nonstandard schedule rate of each marital status group of mothers in that occupation. This gives the percentage of each group of mothers who would have a specific occupation and would work a nonstandard schedule if that group had the same occupational distribution of all mothers. I did this separately for nonstandard hours and nonstandard days.

The results are shown in table 3.7. With regard to nonstandard hours, the difference between the actual percentages working nonstandard hours for married and nonmarried women is 4.4 percentage points. Giving these two groups the same occupational distribution gives them

TABLE 3.7   *Women Working Nonstandard Schedules Before and After Standardization on Occupational Distribution, by Marital Status*

	Married, Husband Present	All Others
Nonstandard hours		
Actual percentage	16.4%	20.8%
Standardized percentage	17.3	18.2
Weekends		
Actual percentage	23.7	32.8
Standardized percentage	25.0	29.9

Source: May 1997 CPS.
Note: Standardization is done by applying the occupational composition of all mothers to each of the two marital status categories.

standardized percentages that are roughly similar: a difference of only 0.9 of a percentage point. We may conclude that differences in the occupational distribution between married and nonmarried mothers largely explain the difference between them in work shifts. When we also consider that among those working nonstandard hours, nonmarried mothers were more likely than married mothers to say they did so because they could not get another job, it appears that nonmarried mothers are more constrained than married mothers in their ability to get jobs in occupations that do not require working late or rotating hours.

As for weekend employment, the standardization on occupation for the two marital groups cuts the difference in the percentage working Saturday and/or Sunday by almost one-half—from 9.1 to 4.9 percentage points. Thus, occupational differences are an important, but not sufficient, explanatory factor for this type of work schedule behavior.

Weekly Earnings

Given the relatively low occupational status of nonmarried women, we would expect their incomes to be low. It is more relevant to focus on the individual earnings of nonmarried women than on their family income (as we do for dual-earner couples), since most nonmarried women are not cohabiting.[4] The specific question here is whether nonstandard work schedules are more common among nonmarried women with relatively low earnings, as they are among dual-earner households with low family income. And how do the percentages vary by the presence and age of children?

As noted in chapter 2, we can obtain individual earnings data only for the subsample of CPS respondents who were in the Outgoing Rotating Group. I divided nonmarried women in this subsample into two earnings groups: those who earned over and under $400 a week; this figure was close to their median weekly amount.

The findings indicate that, overall, nonmarried women who earned less than $400 a week were substantially more likely to work nonstandard schedules than their counterparts who earned $400 or more a week. We see in table 3.8 that for all employed nonmarried women, 31.0 percent of those earning less than $400 a week worked nonstandard hours, compared with only 13.5 percent for higher earners. Also, 39.0 percent of the lower earners worked weekends, compared with 22.5 percent of the higher earners. Further, the combination of working nonstandard hours *and* weekends is 21.3 percent for the lower earners versus only 6.9 percent for the higher earners. Putting all of this together, close to half of all the lower earners (47.9 percent) worked nonstandard hours and/or weekends, as compared with slightly more than one-fourth (28.9 percent) of the higher earners.

Nonstandard work schedule behavior varied by presence and age of children more for the lower earners than the higher earners. Constituting the highest percentage of nonmarried mothers working nonstandard hours were those who earned less than $400 a week and had children under age five (34.6 percent). However, weekend employment was most common among the lower earners who had no children (39.9 percent), a few percentage points higher than for those with children under age five (37.2 percent).

When limiting the analysis to those employed full-time (table 3.9), the differences in nonstandard work schedule behavior by weekly earnings are somewhat smaller but remain substantial. Nonmarried mothers earning less than $400 a week were about twice as likely to work nonstandard hours (24.3 percent) as those earning $400 a week or more (12.6 percent). They were also much more likely to work weekends (34.8 percent and 22.7 percent, respectively) and to combine nonstandard hours and weekends (17.4 percent and 6.3 percent, respectively). Overall, about two-fifths (41.5 percent) of the low earners worked nonstandard hours and/or weekends, compared with fewer than one-third (28.9 percent) of the relatively high earners.

There was little variation by age and presence of children in work schedule behavior among full-time employed women. The more discriminating factor was weekly pay.

Discussion

Given this descriptive overview, what can be said about the evolving temporal structure of the American family? Our focus on the two family

TABLE 3.8   *Employed Nonmarried Women Who Work Nonstandard Schedules, by Type of Schedule, According to Weekly Earnings, and the Presence and Age of Children Under Fourteen*

	Working Nonstandard Hours	Working Weekends	Working Nonstandard Hours *and* Weekends	Working Nonstandard Hours *and/or* Weekends
Weekly earnings less than $400				
Total	31.0%	39.0%	21.3%	47.9%
	(1,389)	(1,338)	(1,337)	(1,337)
No child under age fourteen	31.5	39.9	22.4	48.4
	(1,065)	(1,023)	(1,022)	(1,022)
Child under age fourteen	29.5	36.4	18.0	46.4
	(324)	(315)	(315)	(315)
Child under age five	34.6	37.2	20.2	49.6
	(127)	(124)	(124)	(124)
Child age five to thirteen	28.4	33.7	16.8	43.9
	(244)	(236)	(236)	(236)
Weekly earnings $400 or more				
Total	13.5	22.5	6.9	28.9
	(1,018)	(1,009)	(1,009)	(1,009)
No child under age fourteen	14.0	22.1	7.2	28.7
	(850)	(844)	(844)	(844)
Child under age fourteen	11.0	24.4	5.5	29.6
	(168)	(165)	(165)	(165)
Child under age five	12.4	29.0	5.6	33.9
	(46)	(45)	(45)	(45)
Child age five to thirteen	10.5	22.9	4.6	28.9
	(139)	(137)	(137)	(137)

Source: Outgoing Rotation Group, May 1997 CPS.
Note: "Nonmarried" includes married but husband is not present, as well as separated, divorced, widowed, and never-married. Percentages are weighted; numbers of cases are not weighted. The numbers of cases for "child under age five" and "child age five to thirteen" total more than "child under age fourteen" because some couples have one or more children in both categories. The sample of dual-earner couples was restricted to those who were both civilian adults over the age of eighteen, working for pay in non-agricultural occupations, and, except for rotators, working in the previous week.

types that are on the rise, dual-earner and single-mother households, has revealed that nonstandard work schedules are pervasive for both.

Among dual-earner couples, the prevalence of nonstandard schedules is high for both those with children and those without. However, it is remarkably high for those with children under age five: over one-third

TABLE 3.9   *Full-Time Employed Nonmarried Women Who Work*
             Nonstandard Schedules, by Type of Schedule,
             According to Weekly Earnings, and the Presence and
             Age of Children Under Fourteen

	Working Nonstandard Hours	Working Weekends	Working Nonstandard Hours *and* Weekends	Working Nonstandard Hours *and/or* Weekends
Weekly earnings less than $400				
Total	24.3%	34.8%	17.4%	41.5%
	(807)	(794)	(794)	(794)
No child under age fourteen	24.1	35.3	17.9	41.3
	(617)	(605)	(605)	(605)
Child under age fourteen	24.9	33.1	16.0	42.1
	(190)	(189)	(189)	(189)
Child under age five	25.2	33.0	14.2	43.9
	(66)	(66)	(66)	(66)
Child age five to thirteen	23.4	31.1	16.1	38.4
	(145)	(144)	(144)	(144)
Weekly earnings $400 or more				
Total	12.6	22.7	6.3	28.9
	(923)	(915)	(915)	(915)
No child under age fourteen	13.1	21.7	6.3	28.4
	(773)	(767)	(767)	(767)
Child under age fourteen	10.3	27.3	6.1	31.6
	(150)	(148)	(148)	(148)
Child under age five	12.1	33.6	6.5	39.2
	(39)	(39)	(39)	(39)
Child age five to thirteen	10.0	25.5	5.2	30.5
	(125)	(123)	(123)	(123)

Source: Outgoing Rotation Group, May 1997 CPS.
Note: "Nonmarried" includes married but husband is not present, as well as separated, divorced, widowed, and never-married. Percentages are weighted; numbers of cases are not weighted. The numbers of cases for "child under age five" and "child age five to thirteen" total more than "child under age fourteen" because some couples have one or more children in both categories. The sample of dual-earner couples was restricted to those who were both civilian adults over the age of eighteen, working for pay in non-agricultural occupations, and, except for rotators, working in the previous week.

of such couples include a spouse who works nonstandard hours, and almost one-half include a spouse who works weekends. These ratios are even higher for those of relatively low family income (less than $50,000): over two-fifths and over one-half, respectively.

    Shifting from a couples' perspective to a comparison of mothers by marital status, we have seen that higher levels of nonstandard work schedules prevail among nonmarried mothers than among married mothers. Nonmarried mothers with children under age five show the highest levels: one-fourth work nonstandard hours, and close to two-fifths work weekends. Moreover, when breaking these percentages down further by earnings, it is nonmarried mothers with children under age five earning less than $400 a week who have the highest prevalence of nonstandard hours—over one-third—but it is those with no children who are most often working weekends (close to two-fifths); those with children under age five work only slightly less often on weekends.

We can infer from these findings that the home-time structure of many dual-parent households looks more like that of a one-parent household, particularly those with preschool-aged children and low family income. Also, many mother-only households may be mother-absent, in that the mother is often not at home, or at home but asleep during a child's waking hours, particularly those mothers with young children who earn less than $400 a week. Although there have certainly been both dual-earner and single-mother families in the past, the rising prevalence of these family types makes complex home-time structures of family life more widespread than ever before.

Why do women work a nonstandard schedule when it makes the temporal structure of their home life so complex? We have seen that the distribution of the main reasons differs by marital status. Married mothers more often than nonmarried mothers give personal reasons, relating often to family considerations such as the care of children. Nonmarried mothers more frequently than married mothers report job constraining reasons, the inability to get another job showing a marked difference by marital status. Whereas having a preschool-aged child enhances the extent to which both married and nonmarried mothers say that better child care arrangements are a main reason, having preschoolers rather than only school-aged children increases the extent to which nonmarried women say they could not get another job—but not married women. Nonmarried women with young children are themselves younger and less educated than their married counterparts, and thus their job opportunities may be more limited.

Taking a societal rather than a personal perspective, we have seen that the difference in the occupational distributions of married and nonmarried women is a critical explanatory factor. Applying the standardization procedure revealed that if nonmarried and married employed mothers were to have the same occupational distribution, they would have nonstandard schedules in very similar prevalences and would differ by only about five percentage points in the prevalence of their weekend employment.

Occupations are linked not only to work schedule behavior but to earnings, as shown in the previous chapter. Thus, although we have been looking at different earnings groups descriptively to assess how they differ in work schedule behavior, and we have observed that married and nonmarried women earn higher family and individual earnings, respectively, when they work standard schedules, earnings is clearly an outcome variable that is affected by the jobs people hold. In other words, those who are potentially low earners (for example, because of low education or minimal work experience) generally may be less employable in good daytime jobs, and those who work nonstandard schedules, particularly late hours, often may be paid less because of the nature of these jobs.

It is clear, then, that factors external to the family—namely, labor market demands for late-hour and weekend employment, along with the changing structure of American families—are dramatically altering the nature of time at home for millions of American families. What difference do these changes make in the quality and stability of marriages and family functioning? We turn now to this important issue in the chapters to follow.

4

The Quality and Stability of Marriages

I N THIS chapter, I begin with a consideration of married couples only and address the question: Do nonstandard work schedules affect the quality and stability of marriages? One might expect this to be the case, in that nonstandard work schedules reduce the amount of time spouses spend together, especially if they are both employed and working different shifts, and the amount of time spouses spend together would seem to enhance their bonding.

There is a body of literature on the effects of employment on marital quality and stability relevant to this issue. However, with few exceptions, this literature does not address the effects of shift work or weekend employment per se on marital outcomes. Moreover, the research on marital quality generally has been separate from research on marital instability (Glenn 1990), although the underlying assumption is that those in unhappy marriages are far more likely to divorce than those in happy marriages. (For support for this assumption, see Booth et al. 1985.)

With these limitations in mind, what do we know?

The Relevant Literature
Employment Effects

Interest in the possible negative effects of employment on marital quality and stability has generally been specific to the effects of *women's* employment. Such concern emanates from the rapid increase in the percentage of married women in the labor force, which doubled from 31.95 percent in 1960 to 62.0 percent in 2000 (U.S. Department of Commerce 1999, table 658; 2001, table 577). Most of what we know about the nature of this relationship focuses on the *number* of hours wives are employed, not *which* hours. The general finding is that the more hours women work outside the home, the greater the likelihood of marital discontent and divorce (Blair 1993), although there are findings to the contrary (Locksley 1980).[1]

Theodore Greenstein's (1995) review of the literature on the negative effect of women's employment on divorce summarizes two types of explanations: women's employment per se produces conflict (and thus divorce) because it counters traditional marriage norms and decreases husband's marital satisfaction; and women's employment facilitates divorce by making this alternative more attractive to couples already in conflict.

The first explanation posits an "absence effect" that makes the issue of time highly relevant: women are not at home enough hours to assume many of the traditional homemaking responsibilities, thus marital stress and conflict is generated. Glenna Spitze and Scott South (1985) spell out two processes by which women's greater time at the workplace could affect divorce: the perception (among women presumably) of greater gender inequities in the division of labor, and the decrease in marital interaction time. They note that empirically the evidence is mixed on the extent to which such factors lead to divorce; although these time-relevant factors may increase marital stress, it is not clear that they lead to higher rates of divorce.

The second explanation, whereby women's employment makes divorce more attractive when conflict already exists, focuses on money rather than time. There is a hypothesized "independence effect" for women (Ross and Sawhill 1975)—and, I would contend, a financially liberating effect for men—when employment earnings allow women to support themselves outside of marriage. Alternatively, women's earnings may increase the attractiveness of marriage for men, as women's marriage-specific assets and capital increase. As Greenstein (1990) notes, the findings with regard to both hypotheses are equivocal. His own research does not support an independence effect.

As noted earlier, this body of research focuses on the effect of women's employment on marital quality and instability, not men's. Moreover, though the absence-effect hypothesis deals with the important issue of reduced family time resulting from women's employment, it is limited in perspective because it ignores the possible relevance of *which* hours women work, as well as how many. Further, this hypothesis is silent about the possible relevance for marital quality and stability of men's absence from the home at particular times.

Nonstandard Work Schedule Effects

The existing literature on the effects of nonstandard work schedules on marital quality and instability is sparse and outdated. The one major study at the national level that focused on marital quality is that by Graham Staines and Joseph Pleck (1983). Their study was based on the 1977 U.S. Quality of Employment Survey (QES) and included an analysis of dual-earner couples. The authors found that for all married couples as well as dual-earner couples specifically, shift work was associated with difficulties in scheduling family activities; moreover, working weekends and variable days was linked with less time in family roles and higher levels of work-family conflict and family adjustment. Some of the negative family outcomes were reduced when a worker's control over his or her work schedule was taken into account.[2]

This study was an ambitious effort to explore the impact of work schedules on families, but it has methodological drawbacks. A critical one is that those working afternoon schedules were combined with evening and night workers, all of whom were categorized as shift workers. (Those working in the morning were classified among the day workers.) Also, the specific shifts and the gender of shift workers were not delineated. Moreover, the main respondents in the sample were eligible only if they worked at least twenty hours a week, but the number of hours of employment was not restricted for spouses. Furthermore, the QES is not a longitudinal survey, and thus the relationship between work schedules and subsequent divorce could not be analyzed.

The only other national study of employed Americans that considered the effects of shift work on marital quality was based on a 1980 survey with a follow-up component in 1983 (White and Keith 1990). Moreover, because the study was longitudinal in design, divorce outcomes could be studied. This was a telephone survey, and a simple question was asked as to whether the respondent's job or his or her spouse's job involved shift work. The researchers did not define the range of hours that constituted a shift nor the type of shift. Couples were identified as shift-work couples, but the gender of the shift-work spouse was not delineated.[3] The marital quality measures, however, were extensive. These included scales for marital happiness, marital interaction, marital disagreement, marital problems, sexual problems, and child-related problems. The authors concluded that marital happiness, sexual problems, and child-related problems were negatively affected by shift work, although the effects were of relatively low magnitude. They were surprised to find that the impact on marital interaction was not significant; they had expected this aspect of marital quality to be most affected by shift work. (This study included single- as well as dual-earner couples and did not differentiate between the two.) The longitudinal analysis revealed that among marriages that remained intact over the three-year period, entry into shift work significantly increased marital disagreements and quitting shift work significantly increased marital interaction and decreased child-related problems. Looking specifically at marital breakup, the investigators found that being a shift-work couple in

1980 significantly increased the likelihood of divorce by 1983—from 7 percent to 11 percent.

Neither of these two studies were designed to study shift work in depth; rather, they were secondary analyses of surveys undertaken for more general purposes. They are nevertheless distinctive in taking a national perspective on shift work and in considering the spouse's shift status as well as the respondent's. Another secondary analysis by Sampson Lee Blair (1993), based on the National Survey of Families and Households (the same data source as the present analysis), considered the effects of employment (and family) characteristics on various dimensions of marital quality for both husbands and wives, and it included shift status as one aspect of employment. The operational definition of "shift status" (a dichotomous variable) was not provided, but it was found to reduce marital quality significantly only when considering the issue of the frequency of quality time together (termed "daily contact").

Studies specifically designed to study shift work, while not national in scope, have suggested some negative family effects. As noted in chapter 1, the most extensive American study of this type, which dates back to the early 1960s (Mott et al. 1965), intensively investigates the social, psychological, and physical effects of shift work among a regional sample of white blue-collar workers employed in continuous-processing plants. Questionnaires were administered as well to the wives of married men. The authors discuss family life from a traditional perspective, however, ignoring the employment status of the wife entirely. (In 1965, when this book was published, 34.9 percent of all married women were employed; U.S. Department of Commerce 1999, table 658.) Analyzing three dimensions of marital quality, the investigators concluded that shift work led to "some reduction in marital happiness and an even greater reduction in the ability to coordinate family activities and to minimize strain and friction among family members" (Mott et al. 1965, 146).

There have been smaller qualitative studies relating the tensions of working late shifts to marital stress. These studies, also dated, have typically focused on husbands as shift workers and wives as homemakers. Husbands were found to have difficulty performing such traditional roles as protecting the family and being a sexual partner and companion (Banks 1956; Brown 1959; Maurice and Monteil 1965; Piotrkowksi 1979; Ulich 1957; Wyatt and Marriott 1953; Young and Willmott 1973); women were found to have difficulty in their traditional roles as well, typically expressed as problems with domestic routine, such as meal preparation, laundry, and child care (Banks 1956; Brown 1959).

Recent qualitative studies are rare. Lillian Rubin's (1994) study of

162 working-class and lower-middle-class families in the United States found that one-fifth included couples with spouses working different shifts. She discusses the pressures on time for both husbands and wives in such families and the lack of options when two-earner couples work different shifts, each caring for their children while the other is employed—a widespread phenomenon discussed elsewhere (Presser 1989a). Rubin (1994, 95) writes poignantly:

> If the arriving spouse gets home early enough, there may be an hour when both are there together. But with the pressures of the workday fresh for one and awaiting the other, and with children clamoring for parental attention, this isn't a promising moment for any serious conversation.

Similarly, Francine Deutsch's (1999, 177) study of thirty dual-earner couples working different shifts indicated that despite the benefit this allowed both spouses to rear their own children and have a joint income, "the loss of time together was a bitter pill. The physical separation symbolized a spiritual separation as well."

In sum, there is almost no rigorous research on the relationship between nonstandard work schedules and marital instability, and very little on the relationship between such schedules and marital quality. The existing data are dated and relate more to the effect on marital instability of wives' employment than that of wives' (or husbands') work schedules per se. In this chapter, I offer an updated, national analysis of the relationship between nonstandard work schedules and the quality and stability of marriages, give special attention to the relevance of spouse's gender, assess the extent to which marital quality is associated with gender-specific work shifts, and examine the relationship between marital quality and marital instability utilizing the longitudinal component of the survey.

General Hypotheses

The primary hypotheses are that nonstandard work schedules (1) reduce the quality of marriage and (2) increase the likelihood of marital instability. In the sections that follow, these hypotheses are considered with greater specificity by the specific work shift and weekend status, the gender of the spouse so employed, and, when the data permit, family type. Cross-tabular results are presented to provide important descriptive national data, followed by multivariate analyses in which the relevance of gender ideology for both husbands and wives is considered and a substantial number of control variables are introduced to assess the net effect of work schedules.

Before proceeding with separate analyses of the relationship between nonstandard work schedules and marital quality and marital instability, I provide some details about the national data source that permits such study.

Data Source

The data source for this chapter and the next three is the National Survey of Families and Households (NSFH). This survey has two waves. In wave 1, conducted from 1987 to 1988, a total of 13,007 men and women age nineteen and over were interviewed. This is a national probability sample. Minorities and households containing a single parent as well as other nontraditional families and recently married persons were oversampled so that there would be sufficient numbers for analysis. The appropriate weights are applied here to adjust for this oversampling, thereby producing reliable national estimates. The total response rate for wave 1 was 74 percent.

In addition to the interview at wave 1, all respondents completed a self-administered questionnaire. Married respondents' spouses also completed a self-administered questionnaire but were not interviewed. The response rate for this part of the study was about 80 percent. (For further details on the methodology of wave 1, see Sweet, Bumpass, and Call 1988.)

Wave 2 was conducted from 1992 to 1994. Of the 13,007 main respondents interviewed in wave 1, 10,007 (77 percent) were reinterviewed in wave 2. Moreover, interviews, in contrast to self-administered questionnaires, were conducted in wave 2 for both current spouses and former spouses of those whose marriages had ended by wave 2.[4]

In this chapter, the sample is limited to married couples. When examining the relationship of nonstandard work schedules to marital quality, the sample is married couples at wave 1. When looking at marital instability, the sample is married couples who participated at both waves 1 and 2.

Definitions of Variables
Work Schedules

The specific work shift and whether the respondent was employed on weekends are the primary independent variables for analysis in this and subsequent chapters. With regard to work shifts, both waves of the NSFH included detailed data for both respondents and spouses on the time work began and ended for each day of the week prior to the interview (reference week), and whether they worked a rotating schedule. These responses were used to derive a work shift measure that is similar to that used for the CPS data in the previous chapters. The only difference is that "hours vary" was not an option in the NSFH; respondents gave a full description of their hours and days of employment for the full week, and shift definitions were allocated accordingly:

Fixed day: At least half the hours worked most days in the prior week fell between 8:00 A.M. and 4:00 P.M.

Fixed evening: At least half the hours worked most days in the prior week fell between 4:00 P.M. and midnight.

Fixed night: At least half the hours worked most days in the prior week fell between midnight and 8:00 A.M.

Rotating: Schedules changed periodically from days to evenings or nights.

Weekend employment is defined as work performed on Saturday, Sunday, or both, whether or not the person was also employed during the week.

The usual shift and weekend schedules were used when the spouse had a job but was not at work during the reference week. The work hours and days refer to all jobs for those who held multiple jobs. "Nonstandard work hours" refers to nondaytime and rotating hours of employment; "nonstandard work weeks" refers to weekend employment.

Marital Quality

Main respondents and their spouses were asked the following questions relating to the quality of their marriages at both waves, although we focus here on responses at wave 1:

General marital unhappiness: "Taking things all together, how would you describe your marriage?" (Respondents were presented with a seven-point scale ranging from "very unhappy" to "very happy.")

Quality time: "During the past month, about how often did you and your husband/wife spend time alone with each other, talking or sharing an activity?" (Possible responses were "never," "about once a month," "two or three times a month," "about once a week," "two or three times a week," and "almost every day.")

Marital trouble: "During the past year, have you ever thought that your marriage might be in trouble?" (Possible responses were "yes" and "no.")

Chance of divorce: "It is always difficult to predict what will happen in a marriage, but realistically, what do you think the chances are that you and your husband/wife will eventually separate or divorce?" (Possible responses were "very low," "low," "about even," "high," and "very high.")

For this analysis, I classify a marriage as unhappy if one or both spouses reported a score of less than 5 on the general marital unhappiness scale; I classify a couple as not having quality time if one or both spouses reported time alone with each other as less than once a week; I consider the marriage in trouble if one or both spouses said it was; and I categorize the marriage as being at an even or higher chance of separation or divorce if one or both spouses responded accordingly. I use the response of either spouse (and not necessarily both) because the perspective is on the couple rather than the individual; moreover, this response helps offset any tendency to minimize marital problems to an interviewer.

Separation or Divorce

This variable was derived by considering whether a couple who were married at wave 1 had separated or divorced by wave 2. It represents a simple dichotomy ("yes"/"no"). Spouses who had divorced and remarried before wave 2 were coded as having divorced.

Gender Ideology Scale

Gender ideology is a control variable in the multivariate analyses that is of special interest, given its potential explanatory value, as noted in the literature review. A scale was derived to measure this, using responses to five statements in wave 1, separately for husbands and wives:

(1) It is much better for everyone if the man earns the main living and the woman takes care of the home.

(2) Preschool children are likely to suffer if their mother is employed.

(3) Parents should encourage just as much independence in their daughters as their sons.

(4) In a successful marriage, the partners must have freedom to do what they want individually.

(5) If a husband and wife both work full-time, they should share household tasks equally.

The responses to each statement were coded from 1 to 5, ranging from "strongly agree" to "strongly disagree." (Items 1 and 2 were reverse-coded.) Coded responses were then summed to obtain an overall score for each spouse. Scores could range from 5 to 25, with higher numbers indicating more egalitarian attitudes. The actual range of scores was from 6 to 25 for husbands and 8 to 25 for wives. Cronbach's alpha for the five items was .47 for husbands and .48 for wives. (This scale has been used in previous research; see, for example, Blair and Lichter 1991.)

Other Control Variables

The multivariate analyses also control for other variables that have been shown in previous research to be linked to either marital quality or marital instability. For marital quality, these control variables are: the number of hours the husband worked; the number of hours the wife worked; the husband's education; the wife's education; the number of times the husband had been married; the number of times the wife had been married; whether the husband had ever cohabited; whether the wife had ever cohabited; marital duration (in months); the difference in age between spouses; and whether the couple had children (including adopted and step) in the household younger than age nineteen. (This last variable is dropped as a control when separate regressions are done for those with and without children.) For the regressions on marital instability, in addition to all of these controls, the wife's age is added when the duration of marriage is expressed as a simple dichotomy (less than five years or five or more years), thereby minimizing the correlation.

Findings: Marital Quality

Returning to one of the major substantive issues of this chapter, are married couples who work nonday shifts more likely to report lower marital quality than those on fixed day shifts? Table 4.1 addresses this question, looking at the mean values for each of the four variables by shift status, for both single-earner couples and dual-earner couples, and specifying the gender of the nonday worker.

It is interesting to see in the top row of the table that in a substantial number of cases at least one spouse reported relatively low levels of marital quality for all four indicators. Among single-earner couples (of which 80 percent are male earners), close to one-third reported that their marriage was in trouble during the previous year, and more than one in ten reported a high chance of separation or divorce. Dual-earner couples show even lower marital quality than single-earner couples, with over one-third reporting that their marriage was in trouble and about one in seven indicating a high chance of separation or divorce.

As for the relationship between work shifts and marital quality, there is no clear relationship for single-earner couples. Comparing the means of single-earner husbands and wives working the day shift with the same gender employed nondays, we see that in some instances marriages with a single nonday earner were of higher quality than those with a day earner, and in other instances they were not. There are only three instances of statistical or near-statistical significance: couples with a single-earner husband on a rotating shift were generally *happier* than couples with a single-earner husband who worked days (p < .01); couples with a single-earner husband working nights had *more quality time* than couples with a single-earner husband who worked days (p < .10); and couples with a single-earner wife working a rotating shift were more likely to report that their marriage was in trouble than couples with a single-earner wife who worked days (p < .01). Thus, in these few single-earner cases, male nonday employment is associated with better-quality marriages, and female nonday employment is associated with poorer-quality marriages. These are not symmetric roles normatively: a marriage with a single-earner wife working nondays may be viewed from a traditional perspective as "double deviance," since the wife, not the husband, is the single earner, and she is not working during the daytime. (The impact of each spouse's gender ideology on this outcome will be considered shortly.)

Among dual-earner couples, the pattern was more generally one of greater marital dissatisfaction when either the husband or the wife worked a nonday shift compared with their both working days. This is evident for all the cases in which the means are statistically or near-statistically significantly different and for all but two of the other (nonsignificant) cases. When both spouses worked nondays (only 3.0 percent of all dual-earners), all four of the marital quality indicators showed low levels of marital quality at significant or near-significant levels.

With regard to weekend-work status, for single-earner couples the only significant association with marital quality is the higher proportion of couples (35.0 percent) who said their marriage was in trouble when the husband worked weekends relative to weekdays only (25.0 percent; p < .001). When the husband worked weekends rather than weekdays only, couples were also more likely to report an even or higher chance of divorce, but this relationship was only near-significant (p < .10). Interestingly, among dual-earner couples it is the wife's weekend employment and/or the couple's joint weekend employment that shows significantly higher levels of marital dissatisfaction (relative to both spouses working days). This is evident for all four indicators of marital quality. The husband's weekend employment while the wife was not employed shows little difference in marital quality levels compared with when both worked weekdays only.

Since single- and dual-earner couples differed in the availability of

TABLE 4.1 Means of Marital Quality Variables for Single- and Dual-Earner Married Couples, by Couple's Shift and Weekend Status

| | Single Earners | | | | | Dual-Earners | | | |
| | Marital Quality | | | | | Marital Quality | | | |
	Unhappy[a]	Talk Less Than Once a Week[b]	Marriage in Trouble[c]	Even or Higher Chance of Divorce[d]		Unhappy[a]	Talk Less Than Once a Week[b]	Marriage in Trouble[c]	Even or Higher Chance of Divorce[d]
All Married Total	0.17 (1,877)	0.26 (1,876)	0.29 (1,877)	0.11 (1,869)	All Married Total	0.17 (2,671)	0.30 (2,674)	0.37 (2,667)	0.15 (2,663)
Shift status									
Husband day	0.17 (1,125)	0.27 (1,124)	0.29 (1,125)	0.12 (1,121)	Both day	0.17 (1,576)	0.27 (1,577)	0.35 (1,574)	0.14 (1,574)
Husband evening	0.19 (83)	0.30 (83)	0.32 (83)	0.16 (83)	Husband evening, wife day	0.18 (87)	0.36+ (87)	0.44 (87)	0.16 (87)
Husband night	0.11 (51)	0.16+ (51)	0.32 (51)	0.13 (51)	Wife evening, husband day	0.25* (118)	0.34 (118)	0.46* (118)	0.20 (118)
Husband rotating	0.08** (104)	0.28 (104)	0.26 (104)	0.09 (103)	Husband night, wife day	0.13 (49)	0.35 (49)	0.43 (49)	0.24 (49)
Wife day	0.19 (288)	0.23 (288)	0.28 (288)	0.10 (285)	Wife night, husband day	0.20 (47)	0.38 (47)	0.38 (47)	0.24+ (47)

Wife evening	0.16 (17)	0.24 (17)	0.40 (17)	0.13 (17)	Husband rotating, wife day	0.18 (146)	0.39** (147)	0.36 (147)	0.12 (146)
Wife night	0.22 (9)	0.25 (9)	0.44 (9)	0.11 (9)	Wife rotating, husband day	0.21 (138)	0.36* (138)	0.41 (138)	0.22* (136)
Wife rotating	0.28 (28)	0.34 (28)	0.56** (28)	0.15 (28)	Both nonday	0.27+ (70)	0.45*** (71)	0.46+ (70)	0.25* (70)
Weekend status									
Husband works weekdays only	0.15 (816)	0.25 (815)	0.25 (816)	0.10 (815)	Neither work weekend	0.16 (1,059)	0.28 (1,059)	0.36 (1,055)	0.13 (1,056)
Husband works weekend	0.18 (493)	0.29 (493)	0.35*** (493)	0.14+ (490)	Husband works weekend	0.17 (553)	0.31 (555)	0.36 (555)	0.13 (554)
Wife works weekdays only	0.17 (238)	0.23 (238)	0.28 (238)	0.09 (236)	Wife works weekend	0.23** (356)	0.33* (357)	0.40 (357)	0.19** (356)
Wife works weekend	0.24 (103)	0.25 (103)	0.36 (103)	0.15 (102)	Both work weekend	0.19 (310)	0.33+ (310)	0.42* (310)	0.20** (308)

Source: NSFH, wave 1.

Notes: Statistical comparisons (t-tests) for single earners are day relative to each nonday shift for husbands and wives separately; for dual earners, each nonday shift pattern is compared to both day. Excluded are cases in which data for spouse are missing. Single- or dual-earner status is defined by current employment status. Weekend refers to Saturday and/or Sunday and includes those who also work weekdays.

Significant levels are: $^{+}p = < 0.10$; $^{*}p = < 0.05$; $^{**}p = < 0.01$; $^{***}p = < 0.001$.

Means and t-tests are weighted.

[a]Either or both husband and wife report unhappy.

[b]Either or both husband and wife report they talk less than once a week.

[c]Either or both husband and wife report they had thought their marriage had been in trouble.

[d]Either or both husband and wife report that the chance of divorce is even or higher.

the spouse when the earner was home, it is of interest to consider them separately. We turn now to the multivariate analysis.

Multivariate Analysis

To assess the relationship between nonstandard work schedules and marital quality net of other factors, logistic regressions were conducted for each of the four marital quality indicators. Odds ratios reported for the work schedule variables are net of the influence of the various control variables previously specified. (These odds ratios are calculated from the regression coefficient. For categorical variables, a ratio of one means a likelihood equal to the reference category; less than one means less likelihood, and more than one means greater likelihood.) The regressions are done for all single- and dual-earner couples and separately for couples with children (with the additional control of number of children). There are two models for each type of couple: one that excludes the gender ideologies of husbands and wives (model 1) and one that includes them (model 2). Accordingly, we can assess the extent to which these ideologies alter any observed relationships between nonstandard work schedules and marital quality.

Single-Earner Couples   Looking first at the model 1 columns for single-earner couples in table 4.2, we see that, with one exception, the nonstandard work shifts of husbands did not seem to affect the quality of marriages, as measured by the four indicators. In other words, the late shifts of men in a traditional family with only a male earner did not appear to interfere with the well-being of marriages. The near-significant exception was that general marital unhappiness may have been substantially *less* likely when the husband had a rotating schedule and the wife was not employed (odds ratio of .49). It may be that there were some special benefits to the marriage under these conditions, although more quality time did not seem to be one of them, since the odds on this indicator were more favorable to day workers (but not significant).

There were too few cases in this sample of the nontraditional single-earner family, in which it is the wife rather than the husband who is employed, to detail the type of nonday shift in the regressions. But with the nonday shifts grouped as one category, we see a significant difference in the odds of the marriage being in trouble (2.32 times more likely) relative to the traditional single-earner family with the husband employed during the day. Moreover, although not significant, when wives worked nondays, the odds were higher across the other three marital quality indicators. Further, when single-earner wives worked days, the odds were 1.48 times greater of reporting low-quality time relative

TABLE 4.2 Odds Ratios of Marital Quality of Employed, Single-Earner, Married Couples, by Shift and Weekend Status

Couple's Shift and Weekend Pattern of Employment	General Marital Unhappiness		Low-Quality Time		Marriage in Trouble		Even or Higher Chance of Divorce	
	Model 1	Model 2	Model 1	Model 2	Model 1	Model 2	Model 1	Model 2
Husband day	1.00	1.00	1.00	1.00	1.00	1.00	1.00	1.00
Husband evening	1.06	1.13	1.16	1.19	1.02	0.95	1.26	1.13
Husband night	0.41	0.43	0.56	0.61	0.81	0.83	0.83	0.70
Husband rotating	0.49+	0.42*	1.19	1.26	0.84	0.82	0.72	0.62
Wife day	1.28	1.24	1.48*	1.56*	1.26	1.24	1.14	1.11
Wife nonday[a]	1.10	1.12	1.58	1.62	2.32*	2.27*	1.81	1.72
Weekday only	1.00	1.00	1.00	1.00	1.00	1.00	1.00	1.00
Weekend	1.29	1.40*	1.02	1.06	1.31*	1.35*	1.19	1.21
Husband's gender ideology	—	0.99	—	1.02	—	1.01	—	1.03
Wife's gender ideology	—	1.07*	—	1.01	—	1.03	—	1.07+
Number of cases	1,487	1,363	1,487	1,363	1,487	1,363	1,481	1,359

Source: NSFH, wave 1.
Notes: "Weekend" refers to Saturday and/or Sunday and includes those who also work weekdays. Controls are: number of hours husband worked, number of hours wife worked, husband's education, wife's education, difference in age between spouses, marital duration (in months), number of times husband has been married, number of times wife has been married, whether they have children under age nineteen, whether husband cohabited, and whether wife cohabited.
[a]Evening, night, and rotating schedules are combined as "nonday" because of the small number of married women single-earners in these categories.
+p = < .10; *p = < .05.

to single-earner husbands who worked days, with higher (albeit insignificant) odds across the other three marital quality indicators as well.

Single-earner couples with a spouse working weekends (controlling for the work shift status of the employed husband or wife) had significantly higher odds that their marriage was in trouble (1.31 times greater) than couples with the single earner working weekdays only. Thus, among single-earner couples, it was both the daytime and nondaytime shifts of wives and weekend employment that posed a risk to the quality of the marriage.

The gendered nature of the negative effect of work shifts on marital quality raises the question of whether the gender ideologies of spouses are relevant. As previously noted, the combination of wife-only employment and nontraditional hours of such employment is a double source of gender deviance in the context of traditional views of appropriate gender behavior and thus may partly explain marital dissatisfaction among couples with such employment patterns.

As may be seen at the bottom of model 2, the more egalitarian a wife's gender ideology, the greater the odds of general unhappiness (1.07) and the greater the odds of an even or higher chance of divorce (1.07), each net of the effects of work schedule behavior and the various demographic controls in the model. (The husband's gender ideology shows no significant relationship.) But at issue here is what happens to the relationship between nonstandard work schedules and marital quality net of the effects of gender ideology and the various demographic variables.

We see in the columns for model 2 that when the wife had nonday employment and the gender ideologies of spouses are controlled, the odds of marital dissatisfaction for the three indicators are changed somewhat but remain high. Weekend employment continues to show higher odds of experiencing marital dissatisfaction relative to weekday employment only, general unhappiness now becoming as significant an outcome as a troubled marriage. We can conclude from these findings that the traditional gender ideologies of spouses do not substantially explain these relationships.

Does the presence of children matter for single-earner couples? Thus far we have considered children as a control factor in the regression and examined whether nonstandard work schedules affect marital quality adjusting for their effect (along with the other demographic controls). Now we look only at couples with children and consider whether the relationships between nonstandard work schedules and marital quality are different in this context (controlling for the number of children and other demographic factors).[5]

The model 1 regressions in table 4.3 show that for single-earner couples with children under age nineteen in the household, the odds of

TABLE 4.3   Odds Ratios of Marital Quality of Employed, Single-Earner, Married Couples with Children Under Age Nineteen, by Shift and Weekend Status

Couple's Shift and Weekend Pattern of Employment	General Marital Unhappiness		Low-Quality Time		Marriage in Trouble		Even or Higher Chance of Divorce	
	Model 1	Model 2	Model 1	Model 2	Model 1	Model 2	Model 1	Model 2
Husband day	1.00	1.00	1.00	1.00	1.00	1.00	1.00	1.00
Husband evening	0.92	0.93	1.35	1.31	1.21	1.11	1.35	1.17
Husband night	0.65	0.63	0.59	0.64	0.86	0.89	1.00	0.84
Husband rotating	0.40	0.29*	1.11	1.14	1.00	0.95	0.78	0.63
Wife day	1.15	1.19	1.05	1.29	0.91	0.98	0.89	0.87
Wife nonday[a]	3.09*	2.75*	2.95*	2.79+	4.20*	3.73*	2.52	2.43
Weekday only	1.00	1.00	1.00	1.00	1.00	1.00	1.00	1.00
Weekend	1.06	1.32	1.09	1.14	1.45*	1.56*	1.23	1.22
Husband's gender ideology	—	1.02	—	1.02	—	1.01	—	1.01
Wife's gender ideology	—	1.11*	—	1.03	—	1.05	—	1.11*
Number of cases	953	876	953	876	953	876	949	874

Source: NSFH, wave 1.

Notes: Weekend refers to Saturday and/or Sunday and may include those who also work weekdays. Controls are: number of hours husband worked, number of hours wife worked, husband's education, wife's education, difference in age between spouses, marital duration (in months), number of times husband has been married, number of times wife has been married, number of children under age nineteen, whether husband cohabited, and whether wife cohabited.

[a] Evening, night, and rotating schedules are combined as "nonday" because of the small number of married women single-earners in these categories.

+ p = < .10; * p = < .05.

marital dissatisfaction were more likely to be significant for women's nonday employment than in the preceding analysis for all single-earner couples. Greater dissatisfaction (relative to single-earner couples with the husband employed during the daytime) is the case for three of the four indicators of marital quality and is near-significant for the fourth, even though the sample sizes here are smaller than for all single-earner couples. Since many of these non-employed husbands may have been providing child care, either for preschoolers or after school, this situation further reinforces the nontraditional nature of gender roles and may take a toll on marital quality.[6]

On the other hand, when the analysis is limited to parents, the daytime employment of the wife among single-earner couples has no significant effect on marital quality (relative to the daytime employment of husbands who were the sole earner). This may be because when children were present, spousal quality time became a problem regardless of the gender of the employed spouse. The positive effect of the husband working a rotating shift for general marital happiness among all single-earner couples obtains when the analysis is limited to parents. The negative effects of a husband working weekends are also similar with this limitation. Further, the control for the gender ideologies of spouses (model 2 regressions) does not offer much explanatory value.

Thus, this analysis suggests that among single-earner couples with the wife employed, children condition the relationship between nonstandard work schedules and marital quality in a negative way by increasing marital dissatisfaction when the wife works nondays, and in a positive way by reducing the negative effect of the wife's daytime employment on marital quality (relative to husbands working days).

Dual-Earner Couples   When we focus on dual-earner couples, the analysis gets more complex, as both spouses have a work schedule we must consider. An examination of model 1 regressions in table 4.4, relating to all dual-earners (both with and without children), shows that the effect of shift work on marital quality depends on not only which spouse is working a particular shift but the indicator of marital quality.

With regard to general unhappiness, there is only one significant relationship with shift status: couples with both spouses working nondays were 1.98 times more likely to report unhappiness than couples with both spouses working days. (Their nonday shifts may have been different; for only 1.4 percent of all dual-earners were they the same.) With regard to weekend employment, general unhappiness was 1.52 times more likely to be reported when the wife (but not her husband) worked weekends.

Low-quality time is higher for all nonday work shift patterns relative to both spouses working days, but statistically significant only

TABLE 4.4   Odds Ratios of Marital Quality of Employed, Dual-Earner, Married Couples, by Shift and Weekend Status

Couple's Shift and Weekend Pattern of Employment	General Marital Unhappiness		Low-Quality Time		Marriage in Trouble		Even or Higher Chance of Divorce	
	Model 1	Model 2	Model 1	Model 2	Model 1	Model 2	Model 1	Model 2
Both day	1.00	1.00	1.00	1.00	1.00	1.00	1.00	1.00
Husband evening, wife day	1.02	1.14	1.28	1.07	1.04	1.15	1.13	1.26
Wife evening, husband day	1.51	1.46	1.25	1.34	1.71*	1.69*	1.48	1.46
Husband night, wife day	0.56	0.50	1.32	1.17	1.30	1.31	1.85	1.87
Wife night, husband day	1.01	1.03	1.45	1.44	0.95	0.95	1.52	1.63
Husband rotate, wife day	1.16	1.28	1.70**	1.70*	0.93	0.83	0.81	0.84
Wife rotate, husband day	1.20	1.22	1.70*	1.68*	1.30	1.30	1.51	1.44
Both nonday	1.98*	2.22*	2.00*	2.26*	1.60	1.70	1.62	1.79
Both weekdays only	1.00	1.00	1.00	1.00	1.00	1.00	1.00	1.00
Husband only weekend	1.26	1.29	1.05	1.03	1.09	1.11	0.99	1.03
Wife only weekend	1.52*	1.50*	0.90	0.87	1.09	1.11	1.30	1.31
Both weekend	1.20	12.21	0.79	0.78	1.14	1.07	1.41+	1.38
Husband's gender ideology	—	0.99	—	1.00	—	0.96+	—	0.99
Wife's gender ideology	—	1.05+	—	1.00	—	1.01	—	1.01+
Number of cases	2,040	1,916	2,042	1,918	2,039	1,916	2,035	1,911

Source: NSFH, wave 1.
Notes: Weekend refers to Saturday and/or Sunday and includes those who also work weekdays. Controls are: number of hours husband worked, number of hours wife worked, husband's education, wife's education, difference in age between spouses, marital duration (in months), number of times husband has been married, number of times wife has been married, whether they have children under age nineteen, whether husband cohabited, and whether wife cohabited.
+p = < .10; *p = < .05; **p = < .01.

when husbands or wives rotated (1.70 times higher for each pattern) or when both worked nondays (2.00 times higher). The weekend employment of either spouse seems to have no effect on quality time. The likelihood that a marriage would be in trouble is significantly higher (1.71 times) when the wife worked evenings and husband days, relative to both days, but shows no relationship to weekend employment. Although there are no significant relationships between nonstandard work shifts and the perceived chance of divorce, all nonday patterns except husband rotating and wife working days show higher odds on this chance relative to both working days. As for weekend employment, when both spouses were so employed, couples were more likely to perceive an even or higher chance of divorce relative to couples with both spouses working days, although the odds are only near significance (1.41 times higher).

The model 2 regressions, controlling for spouses' gender ideologies, show similar significant relationships. Again, such ideologies do not appear to be an important explanatory factor.

For dual-earner parents (table 4.5), the relationships are generally the same as for all dual-earners, although some statistically significant relationships change. For example, when the wife worked evenings and the husband worked days, the marriage was less likely to be in trouble. (Odds reduce from 1.71 and significant to 1.25 and not significant.) In contrast, the odds of the perception among dual-earner couples of an even or greater chance of divorce increase with children when the wife rotates and the husband works days (from 1.51 and not significant to 1.93 and significant). The additional controls for spouses' gender ideologies (model 2) again make little difference.

We may conclude from the analysis of dual-earner couples that nonstandard hours are associated with marital dissatisfaction but are specific to certain couple work schedule patterns and certain indicators of marital quality. The same is true for the conditioning aspect of the presence of children. The gender ideologies of the spouses are not especially relevant, either for all dual-earners or for dual-earners with children only.

The associations we have seen between nonstandard work schedules and attitudes about marital quality lead us to question whether, behaviorally, couples with such nonstandard work schedules are in fact more likely to experience marital disruption in the years to come.

Marital Instability

As previously noted, the NSFH collected data at two waves about five years apart. For the sample of married couples with at least one earner at

TABLE 4.5   Odds Ratios of Marital Quality of Employed, Dual-Earner, Married Couples with Children Under Age Nineteen, by Shift and Weekend Status

Couple's Shift and Weekend Pattern of Employment	General Marital Unhappiness		Low-Quality Time		Marriage in Trouble		Even or Higher Chance of Divorce	
	Model 1	Model 2	Model 1	Model 2	Model 1	Model 2	Model 1	Model 2
Both day	1.00	1.00	1.00	1.00	1.00	1.00	1.00	1.00
Husband evening, wife day	1.22	1.35	0.95	0.81	0.85	0.89	0.81	0.91
Wife evening, husband day	1.38	1.33	0.98	1.09	1.25	1.28	1.51	1.48
Husband night, wife day	0.46	0.40	1.26	1.10	1.94	2.04+	1.85	1.91
Wife night, husband day	0.96	0.97	1.30	1.32	0.88	0.87	1.66	1.82
Husband rotate, wife day	1.20	1.37	1.67*	1.68*	1.03	0.96	0.84	0.90
Wife rotate, husband day	1.73+	1.84*	1.79*	1.77*	1.16	1.14	1.93*	1.85+
Both nonday	2.73**	3.25**	2.32*	2.79**	1.67	1.76	1.33	1.60
Both weekdays only	1.00	1.00	1.00	1.00	1.00	1.00	1.00	1.00
Husband only weekend	1.20	1.20	0.98	0.94	1.04	1.04	0.96	1.01
Wife only weekend	1.63*	1.63*	0.99	0.94	1.19	1.22	1.27	1.26
Both weekend	1.30	1.28	0.76	0.74	1.10	1.07	1.22	1.13
Husband's gender ideology	—	0.95+	—	1.00	—	0.97	—	0.98
Wife's gender ideology	—	1.02	—	0.99	—	1.01	—	1.02
Number of cases	2,040	1,245	2,042	1,246	2,039	1,245	2,035	1,240

Source: NSFH, wave 1.
Notes: Weekend refers to Saturday and/or Sunday and includes those who also work weekdays. Controls are: number of hours husband worked, number of hours wife worked, husband's education, wife's education, difference in age between spouses, marital duration (in months), number of times husband has been married, number of times wife has been married, number of children under age nineteen, whether husband cohabited, and whether wife cohabited.
+p = < .10; *p = < .05; **p = < .01.

wave 1, 11.6 percent were separated or divorced at wave 2. Those who reported low-quality marriages were significantly more likely to experience marital instability than those who did not. For example, 31.2 percent of couples in which at least one spouse said there was an even or higher chance of divorce at wave 1 were no longer residing together at wave 2; this was the case for only 8.5 percent of those who said the chance was lower. The percentages were similar whether the couple at wave 1 were single- or dual-earner. Only a subgroup of these couples, however, worked nonstandard schedules.

In this section, we are interested in the direct relationship between nonstandard work schedules and marital instability, regardless of how spouses viewed their marital happiness or chance of divorce. We address this issue for all married couples with at least one earner, single- and dual-earner couples combined, because the reduced sample size due to attrition between wave 1 and wave 2 (15.2 percent for this subsample) results in some very small numbers in some of the nonday shifts.[7]

Table 4.6 presents three sets of logistic regressions: model 1 includes the employment, shift, and weekend status of both the husband and the wife as well as the demographic control variables;[8] model 2 adds the gender ideology of the husband and the wife as possible explanatory variables; and model 3 adds, along with gender ideology, the extent to which couples reported quality time together.[9]

Three samples were examined for each model: the total of all those married, regardless of marital duration; those married less than five years at wave 1; and those married five or more years at wave 1. The breakdown by duration of marriage is presented because this is a strong determinant of marital instability. (Many more marriages dissolve in the earlier than later years of marriage.)[10] It is important to consider whether recent marriages are more affected by work schedule behavior than marriages of longer duration.

Looking down the first column of model 1, we see that for the total sample, it is only the wives' fixed night shift that substantially increased the odds of separation or divorce between wave 1 and wave 2 (relative to day shifts). Although rotating shifts show higher odds when worked by wives than husbands, it is only fixed night shifts that show a significant relationship. The odds of marital disruption when wives worked fixed nights are 2.54 times higher than when wives worked fixed days. The odds when wives worked rotating shifts are 1.53 times higher than fixed days, but this relationship is not statistically significant. Weekend employment by either the husband or the wife does not show a relationship to marital instability.

When comparing the regression results for model 1 for those married less than five years and those married five or more years at wave 1, we see some interesting differences. Neither husbands' nor wives' work schedules are significant determinants of subsequent marital instability for couples married less than five years, although when husbands worked fixed nights, the odds are 2.18 times greater (but not significant) relative to husbands working fixed days. For couples married five years or more, the wife's work schedule is statistically significant: when the wife worked fixed nights, the couple was 2.69 times more likely to separate or divorce than when the wife worked fixed days.

Model 2 adds the additional controls of the husband's and the wife's gender ideology. As previously noted, Greenstein's (1995) research suggests that the gender ideology of wives partly explains the relationship between their employment and marital disruption. Thus, as we did for marital quality, we can ask whether the wife's—and the husband's— gender ideology also helps explain the relationship between employment schedules and marital disruption. In other words, if we removed the effect of both spouses holding more or less traditional views about gender roles, would this minimize the effect of night shifts on marital instability?

The results for model 2 suggest that traditional gender ideologies of either spouse do not explain the high odds of marital instability when the wife worked nights (more egalitarian equals more instability), either for the total sample or for only those married more than five years. Again, we are interested here in the gender ideology variables primarily as explanatory factors relating to work schedules. However, with regard to its direct effect on marital instability, it is interesting to see that only the wife's gender ideology, not the husband's, is significant (net of the effect of the other variables); this is evident for the total and for those married more than five years. The more egalitarian the wife, the more likely the marriage will be unstable. Whether this is because egalitarian wives are less likely than others to tolerate a bad marriage or that husbands are less happy with an egalitarian wife remains an open question.[11]

There is a further question: Is quality time together an important factor that explains the relationship observed between the wife's night shifts and marital instability? We see in model 3 that this control reduces the strength of the relationship, but it remains significant for the total (odds of 2.46) and becomes near-significant for couples married five or more years. Moreover, this control does not substantially reduce the strength of the relationship between the husband's night shift and marital instability for couples married less than five years (2.23, although still not significant). It thus appears that the frequency of quality time together, while significantly associated with marital instability, is not the sole or even primary explanatory factor for why night shifts are linked to marital instability. It may be the changing nature of family life

TABLE 4.6   Odds Ratios of Divorce or Separation at Wave 2 for Married Couples at Wave 1, by Employment, Shift, and Weekend Status

Employment Status	Model 1			Model 2			Model 3		
	Total	Married Less Than Five Years	Married Five or More Years	Total	Married Less Than Five Years	Married Five or More Years	Total	Married Less Than Five Years	Married Five or More Years
Husband									
Fixed days	1.00	1.00	1.00	1.00	1.00	1.00	1.00	1.00	1.00
Fixed evenings	1.06	1.05	1.03	0.97	0.78	1.06	0.96	0.79	1.05
Fixed nights	1.09	2.18	0.41	1.07	2.14	0.43	1.11	2.23	0.43
Rotating shifts	0.76	0.93	0.66	0.74	0.92	0.65	0.74	0.93	0.64
Not employed	1.00	1.06	1.12	0.99	1.07	1.12	0.96	1.06	1.07
Wife									
Fixed days	1.00	1.00	1.00	1.00	1.00	1.00	1.00	1.00	1.00
Fixed evenings	1.00	1.00	0.90	1.07	1.04	0.97	1.01	0.96	0.93
Fixed nights	2.54*	1.30	2.69*	2.66*	1.52	2.58*	2.46*	1.32	2.40+
Rotating shifts	1.53	1.25	1.78	1.64+	1.29	1.92+	1.59	1.28	1.81
Not employed	0.86	0.81	0.85	0.90	0.88	0.86	0.91	0.90	0.87

Husband worked weekends	0.93	1.19	0.77	0.97	1.37	0.78	0.97	1.35	0.80
Wife worked weekends	0.89	0.86	0.85	0.90	0.94	0.87	0.91	0.94	0.89
Gender ideology scale									
Husband	—	—	—	0.97	0.96	0.96	0.97	0.96	0.96
Wife	—	—	—	1.09**	1.06	1.10**	1.09**	1.07	1.10**
Quality time together									
Often	—	—	—	—	—	—	1.00	1.00	1.00
Occasionally	—	—	—	—	—	—	2.57***	2.23*	2.65***
Rarely	—	—	—	—	—	—	1.42*	1.38	1.42
Number of cases	3,001	980	2,021	2,806	920	1,886	2,806	920	1,886

Source: NSFH, Wave 1.

Notes: Controls are: number of hours husband worked in the previous week, number of hours wife worked in the previous week, husband's education, wife's education, difference in age between spouses, wife's age (for married-less-than-five years and married-more-than-five-years regressions only), marital duration (in months, for total regressions only), number of times husband has been married, number of times wife has been married, whether they have children under age nineteen, whether husband cohabited, and whether wife cohabited. The employed with shift unknown are missing values; the not employed are assigned mean values of number of hours worked for employed. Weekends refer to Saturday and/or Sunday, and include those who also work weekdays.

†p = < 0.10; *p = < 0.05; **p = < 0.01; ***p = < 0.001.

generated by different work schedules that is the critical issue. Unfortunately, we cannot directly test this possibility with these data.[12]

Again, testing for the relevance of the presence of children tells us whether this added complexity to family life is an important conditioning factor that enhances or decreases the effect of nonstandard work schedules on marital instability. Computing similar regressions separately for those with and without children reveals that nonstandard work schedules are not related to marital instability for couples without children (data not shown). For couples with children, however, there are some significant relationships, conditional upon the type of shift, the gender of the employed worker, and the duration of the marriage.

We see in model 1 of table 4.7 for couples with children that the husband's night work becomes a significant determinant when they were married less than five years at wave 1. Indeed, the odds in this instance are 6.18 times greater than for comparable husbands working days. Moreover, the odds remain high and significant even when controlling for spouses' gender ideologies (model 2) and for both gender ideologies and quality time together.

The wife's night and rotating shifts remain an important determinant of marital instability among couples with children, and some of these relationships become stronger. Although the relationships are significant for night shifts by the wife among couples with children who were married five years or more, the odds are substantially positive (but not significant, given the smaller numbers) for those married less than five years. In model 1, for example, the odds of separation or divorce when the wife worked nights and the couple had been married five or more years are 3.00 times greater than when the wife worked days ($p < .05$), and 2.86 times greater when the couple had been married less than five years (but $p = .42$). With regard to rotating shifts, significant relationships are evident only in models 2 and 3, and specifically for those married five years or more. There are no significant relationships for either wives' or husbands' weekend employment in any of the models.[13]

In sum, it appears that night and rotating shifts significantly increase the odds of marital instability, but only for couples with children. Gender and duration of marriage further condition this relationship.

Discussion

We have seen that nonstandard work schedules are associated with the quality and stability of marriages among American couples. The findings resulting from assessing the four dimensions of marital quality—general marital unhappiness, low-quality time, marriage in trouble, and perception of an even or greater chance of divorce—indicate that family type and the gender of the spouse working nonday shifts or weekends are highly relevant. Although there are also differences by which dimension of marital quality is being considered, some generalizations can be made.

Among single-earner couples, working nonday rather than day shifts is linked to a higher-quality marriage, providing it is the husband who is the single earner. But if the single earner is the wife working nondays, this is associated with a poorer-quality marriage. These findings suggest that the most traditional marriages (husband as sole provider) can better tolerate—and benefit from—nontraditional employment hours than the least traditional marriages (wife as sole provider). These findings obtain when looking specifically at couples with children. It may be that couples who chose both of these nontraditional work and family lifestyles are selective of those with poor-quality marriages. However, these outcomes remain after adjusting for the gender ideologies of both spouses, as well as for other spouse characteristics that could affect marital quality. Weekend employment shows significant negative effects on two indicators of marital quality, namely, general marital unhappiness and the perception of the marriage as being in trouble, both for all single-earner couples and for those with children.

Among dual-earner couples, there is evidence of lower marital quality when the husband or the wife worked a nonday schedule relative to when both worked days, but it is difficult to generalize given the variability by measure of marital quality and by which spouse worked a nonstandard schedule. The same is true when looking specifically at dual-earner couples with children. As for single-earner couples, the gender ideologies of the spouses do not appear to be an important factor in explaining significant relationships. For dual-earner couples both with and without children, weekend employment seems to have no effect on the quality of marriage.

Viewing marriages longitudinally, and combining single- and dual-earner couples, we have seen that nonstandard work schedules increase the likelihood of marital instability over a five-year period, but this is specific to certain conditions. Night and rotating shifts significantly increase the odds of separation or divorce, but only for couples with children. Gender and duration of marriage further condition this relationship. Among men with children who had been married less than five years at wave 1, working nights made separation or divorce more than six times more likely by the second interview, relative to working days. Among women with children married more than five years at wave 2, working nights increased by three times the likelihood of separation or divorce, and this might have had an effect (though not a statistically significant one) during the earlier years as well. Moreover, for mothers,

TABLE 4.7 Odds Ratios of Divorce or Separation at Wave 2 for Married Couples with Children Under Age Nineteen at Wave 1, by Employment Status

Employment Status	Model 1			Model 2			Model 3		
	Total	Married Less Than Five Years	Married Five or More Years	Total	Married Less Than Five Years	Married Five or More Years	Total	Married Less Than Five Years	Married Five or More Years
Husband									
Fixed days	1.00	1.00	1.00	1.00	1.00	1.00	1.00	1.00	1.00
Fixed evenings	1.15	0.86	1.31	1.16	0.69	1.33	1.20	0.75	1.37
Fixed nights	1.45	6.18**	0.43	1.46	7.07**	0.42	1.52	7.86**	0.43
Rotating shifts	0.85	1.07	0.77	0.83	0.92	0.77	0.83	0.92	0.77
Not employed	1.08	1.09	1.26	1.08	1.11	1.25	1.02	1.07	1.18
Wife									
Fixed days	1.00	1.00	1.00	1.00	1.00	1.00	1.00	1.00	1.00
Fixed evenings	0.91	0.73	0.84	0.99	0.76	0.94	0.94	0.71	0.91
Fixed nights	2.80*	2.86	3.00*	2.78*	4.80	2.73+	2.67*	4.33	2.67+
Rotating shifts	1.82+	1.08	2.05+	2.01*	1.11	2.32*	1.95*	1.12	2.21*
Not employed	0.85	0.84	0.78	0.83	0.95	0.73	0.84	0.98	0.73

Husband worked weekends	0.88	1.13	0.80	0.93	1.43	0.81	0.93	1.43	0.83
Wife worked weekends	0.91	1.28	0.79	0.91	1.55	0.79	0.92	1.56	0.81
Gender ideology scale									
Husband	—	—	0.93*	—	0.94	0.92*	0.94	0.95	0.92*
Wife	—	—	1.10**	—	1.11	1.12**	1.10	1.12+	1.12**
Quality time together									
Often	—	—	—	—	—	—	1.00	1.00	1.00
Occasionally	—	—	—	—	—	—	1.81	2.87*	1.54
Rarely	—	—	—	—	—	—	1.06	1.29	0.92
Number of cases	1,977	566	1,856	1,411	526	1,330	1,856	526	1,330

Source: NSFH, wave 1.

Notes: Controls are: number of hours husband worked in the previous week, number of hours wife worked in the previous week, husband's education, wife's education, difference in age between spouses, wife's age (for married-less-than-five-years and married-more-than-five-years regressions only), marital duration (in months, for total regressions only), number of times husband has been married, number of times wife has been married, number of children under age nineteen, whether husband cohabited, and whether wife cohabited. The employed with shift unknown are missing values; the not employed are assigned mean values of number of hours worked for employed. Weekends refer to Saturday and/or Sunday and include those who also work weekdays.

+p = < 0.10; *p = < 0.05; **p = < 0.01; ***p = < 0.001.

but not for fathers, rotating shifts doubled the odds of marital dissolution, specific to mothers married more than five years at wave 1.

Unfortunately, the NSFH does not include data on work schedules between the two waves of the study; a more refined analysis of work schedule behavior during this interval would be useful, as well as some knowledge of how long respondents had worked these schedules before the wave 1 survey. The NSFH results are nevertheless intriguing, and several unanswered questions remain.

First, the lack of significance of certain relationships is notable. The fact that nonstandard work schedules did not affect marital instability when couples had no children suggests that, in the absence of children, couples are fairly well able to cope with whatever stress such schedules generate. But when couples have children, nonstandard schedules complicate family life considerably, increasing the risk of separation and divorce relative to other couples with children.

This greater risk, however, does not apply to evening employment for either spouse, even though when one spouse works evenings the spouses typically are not together at dinner (see chapter 6) or for other social events those workdays, and fathers may be more involved in the care of their children when the mother is employed evenings. Rather, it is very late hours of employment, most of them past midnight, that seem to add special stress to marriages, but only when there are children. This holds for both men's and women's night work, but it is only women's, not men's, shift rotation that is associated with marital dissolution.

Both night work and shift rotation generally require that one spouse sleep during the daytime while the other does not. The difficulties of getting sufficient sleep when children are present might be a key factor in the marital tensions generated by being off-schedule with a spouse. As noted in chapter 1, the literature shows that physiological stress is greatest for night workers and rotators. When couples have children, this stress may be exacerbated, exacting a toll on the marriage. (It might also affect the well-being of children, regardless of marital outcome.) Interestingly, the NSFH data show that the frequency of sexual relations is not affected by night work (Presser 2000b).

It is notable that weekend employment, unlike night shifts, shows no relationship to marital instability, even among couples with children. This too suggests that physiological stress, combined with the social stress of working very late hours, is critical.

Reasons for the gender difference in the duration of marriage as a conditioning factor for marital instability cannot be adequately explored with these data. Again, only in the early years is night work associated with a higher rate of marital instability for men with children; for women with children this association holds throughout the life cycle but is significant only in the later years of marriage. Gender differences in the reasons for working these shifts might be relevant. We have seen from the CPS data that men report working late hours more because of job demands than for personal reasons. This could mean that employed men, early in marriage, are less likely than employed women to change their night shifts to days or evenings—or to stop paid employment— when the shift seems threatening to the marriage. This does not explain why night work for women late in marriage has a significant effect on marital dissolution. We clearly need data that would permit an in-depth analysis of reasons for night work (and other shifts), taking into account duration of shift as well as gender and duration of marriage.

Having seen that nonstandard work schedules may alter the quality and stability of marriages, what are the implications for family functioning? We turn next to this issue.

5

The Gender Division of Household Labor

A N ESSENTIAL aspect of family functioning is the performance of household tasks.[1] We have an abundance of data on the extent to which such tasks are gendered; that is, we know that wives spend far more hours per week than husbands cooking, washing dishes, cleaning the house, and washing and ironing clothes, and that husbands spend more hours than wives doing outdoor tasks, household repairs, and automobile maintenance. Some tasks, like shopping and paying bills, tend to be gender-neutral, with both husbands and wives spending about the same number of weekly hours on them. It is the typically female tasks that are most time-intensive, however, and thus wives spend more time overall in housework than husbands, even when both spouses are employed (Presser 1994; Robinson and Godbey 1997).

What happens when spouses are both employed, but husbands are home when their wives are not, and vice versa? Do differences in work schedules alter the gender division of household labor? What happens when wives are not available to do the typically female household tasks that need to be done? Drawing on the existing research, there is reason to expect that gender differences in time availability alter family functioning in this regard.

Relevant Literature
Alternative Hypotheses

Time availability is but one of three core perspectives that the literature on household division of labor offers as possible explanations for gender differences. Shelley Coverman (1985, 81, 82, emphasis added) has summarized these leading hypotheses:

(1) The more *resources* (i.e., education, earnings, and occupational position) a husband has, both in absolute terms and relative to his wife, the less domestic labor he does.

(2) The more traditional the husband's *sex role attitudes,* the less domestic labor he performs.

(3) The more domestic task demands on a husband and the greater his capacity to respond to them, especially in terms of *available time,* the greater his participation in domestic labor.

An abundant literature tests these hypotheses (for a thorough review, see Coltrane 2000). The theoretical rationales as well as the findings vary; sometimes they refer to men's share of housework relative to their wives' share, and other times the reference is to the number of hours men devote to housework without relating this to the number of hours their wives put in. This chapter focuses on the "available time" perspective but includes as well the alternative explanations in examining the relationship between nonstandard work schedules and the division of household labor. Thus, we begin with a brief review of the rationales and findings for these perspectives.

Resources   There are two competing explanations for the effect of relative resources between spouses on the division of household labor by gender:

(1) Relative resources tap the relative *power* of spouses to implement their preferences regarding household work (Blood and Wolfe 1960), which are usually to minimize such work.

(2) Relative resources measure the extent to which it is economically *efficient* for households to allocate (more) paid labor to the spouse who can draw greater earnings and (more) unpaid labor to the other spouse (Becker 1973).[2]

Coverman (1985) found only a minimal effect of resources, whereas other studies (for example, Ross 1987) support their relevance, both in absolute terms and relative to the other spouse.

Gender Role Ideology   Coverman's (1985) "sex role attitudes" are commonly referred to as gender role ideology. Such an ideology results from early and intensive socialization by parents, teachers, and society about appropriate "male" and "female" behavior. Research on the effects of gender role ideology on the division of household labor by gender has had mixed results. For example, Coverman found that egalitarian views have an unexpected negative effect on the husband's participation in housework, while other studies have found the predicted positive effect, particularly when the husband holds egalitarian views (Bird, Bird, and Scruggs 1984; Kamo 1988; Ross 1987).

Time Available for Housework   Some researchers view the availability of time as the most important of the three variables, and they
usually define it as (1) whether a spouse is employed or (2) as the cumulative number of hours of employment. Sometimes the definition of
available time takes account of the presence and ages of children.[3] Coverman (1985) found that variables relating to available time were the
most powerful predictors of husbands' hours of housework. Available
time was measured as the husband's cumulative hours of employment
and whether his wife was employed. Frances Goldscheider and Linda
Waite (1991), however, showed that husbands share more of the housework in response to the number of hours their wife is employed, not to
their wife's employment status per se. Moreover, among dual-earner
couples, they found that the wife's hours of employment have a stronger
effect on the husband's share of household tasks than do the husband's
hours of employment. April Brayfield (1992) reported similar findings for
dual-earner couples in Canada.

Nonstandard Work Schedules and Housework

Research using national samples to study the relationship between specific work schedules and family life is minimal. The few studies that
have examined work schedules in relation to household tasks have methodological problems that restrict generalization and interpretation.

Graham Staines and Joseph Pleck's (1983) analysis of the 1977 Quality of Employment Survey (QES) addressed the effect of nonstandard
work schedules on many aspects of family life, but their definition of
such schedules is problematic as noted in chapter 4. They defined part-
time afternoon workers, but not part-time morning workers, as nonday
workers. Because women are more likely than men to have part-time
jobs, the classification of afternoon workers as nonday workers contributed to the finding that wives among dual-earner couples are more
likely to work nondays than comparable husbands, the reverse of what
is found when more precise national estimates of nonday schedules are
used (Mellor 1986; Presser and Cain 1983). Thus, Staines and Pleck's
findings that husbands with nondaytime work schedules spend significantly more time in housework than do husbands with daytime work
schedules, and that the wife's work schedule does not affect housework
time, must be treated as tentative.

Sampson Lee Blair and Daniel Lichter's (1991) analysis of the household division of labor based on data from the National Survey of Families and Households examined shift work for males but not for females;
moreover, they did not define shift work. With fewer variables in their

model than the present analysis, they found that shift work for males does not significantly affect men's share of hours spent on female tasks, but that it does negatively affect men's share of hours spent on *all* household tasks. The study did not consider the number of hours women and men spend on female tasks or the number of hours women spend on all tasks.

Another study based on the 1977 QES studied the "family workday" in relation to housework (Kingston and Nock 1985). The family workday was defined in two ways: the total hours of paid work of both spouses, and the number of hours only one spouse was at paid work. The family is treated as a single unit, without distinguishing between the husband's and the wife's hours of employment, thus precluding a gender perspective. The authors found that neither measure was significantly related to time spent on household chores.

Steven Nock and Paul Kingston's (1988) analysis of the 1981 Study of Time Use (STU) examined the effect of employment schedules on the time parents spent doing housework *with children,* defined as housework done "in the company of a child" (up to age twenty). Significantly less time was spent doing housework with children if husbands (but not wives) were employed during the night or late afternoons.[4] Conversely, fathers who were more available because of their employment schedule were more likely to participate with their children in housework. This study did not, however, address the effect of work schedules on time spent on housework without children present.

The limited literature on work schedules and child care also suggests that, for men, increased time available for family labor leads to greater participation. For example, when dual-earner parents have different work schedules, most fathers are the principal providers of child care when the mother is employed (see chapter 6). Here we examine whether such availability substantially increases the time men spend in housework apart from child care.

General Hypotheses

Despite the considerable literature on the three hypotheses, they are rarely examined simultaneously. I regard them as complementary rather than competing influences and therefore assess the influence of time availability after controlling for the alternative explanations. Also, I define time availability in terms of the specific employment schedules of both spouses as well as the number of hours employed. Moreover, I add the presence of children and other measures of the life course as relevant controls.

Two basic hypotheses are considered in this chapter:

(1) Nonstandard work schedules increase the number of hours husbands participate in female-type household tasks and decrease wives' number of hours, thereby increasing husbands' share of female-type household tasks.

(2) This relationship is most evident among couples who have children.

These hypotheses are tested in relation to dual-earner couples, and the work schedules of both spouses are considered. Work schedules include both nonstandard hours and weekend employment. Regressions are done for all dual-earner couples and for those with children.

The rationale for these hypotheses is based primarily on the fact that when the employment schedules of dual-earner spouses do not overlap—thereby reducing their time at home together—the wife is less available to do certain tasks simultaneously for herself and her husband, particularly tasks traditionally done by females (such as preparing dinner and cleaning up after meals). Moreover, a husband who has time for housework while his wife is employed may feel an obligation to increase his share in these tasks. This may be especially the case for couples who have children.

An alternative possibility is that husbands perform *less* household labor when the spouses have different employment schedules. Being at home while his wife is at paid work may reduce the pressure on a husband to do housework, because his wife is not there to request his labor. Moreover, the particular shift of each spouse—the other aspect of employment schedules—may be relevant. For example, a husband employed on a nonday shift may expect his wife with a daytime shift to do extra work for him because of his late schedule (for example, prepare meals ahead of time to be reheated when he comes home). His wife may also feel that she should do this extra work.

The extent of the husband's participation in household labor among dual-earner couples may also depend on which spouse's job has nonstandard hours. I expect that husbands whose jobs are in the evening or at night may spend more time than other husbands in housework because daytime traditionally is associated with work—both unpaid or paid—rather than leisure. Although this may be more true of tasks traditionally done by males, like yard work and automobile maintenance (which are best done during daytime), it may also apply to tasks traditionally done by females. This expectation holds only for husbands who are not sleeping during most of the day.

Sample and Variables

The sample for this analysis is over 1,600 married dual-earner couples in the first wave of the NSFH (1,617 for model 1 and 1,625 for model 2). For these couples we have complete data for both spouses on household work, the specific hours of employment, and all of the other variables used in the regression models.[5]

Dependent Variables:
Time Spent on Household Tasks

The major dependent variable is the *relative* division of household labor between husbands and wives, in particular the husband's share of the total time spent on household tasks traditionally done by females. The *absolute* number of hours each spouse spent on these tasks is also analyzed to help interpret the results for husbands' share of housework. As Goldscheider and Waite (1991) argued, analyzing the relative allocation of household labor between husbands and wives has the advantage of using a single indicator based on the total amount of time spent on housework by both spouses. This total amount of time may vary among couples because of differences in standards of household maintenance, in the efficiency of the spouses, and in the extent to which others (paid or unpaid) provide domestic help to the household—all sources of variation that the NSF did not measure. However, examining the determinants of the husband's share of household labor without regard to the total amount of couple time essentially standardizes for such differences *among couples.*

The data on household work are self-reports by the main respondents and their spouses on the number of hours they and their spouses spend performing household tasks. Consistent with other survey data (Berk and Shih 1980), husbands and wives tended to report spending more hours on household tasks than their spouses reported for them. This analysis uses the self-reports of each spouse.

I focus on the husband's share of the four most time-intensive tasks: preparing meals, washing dishes and cleaning up after meals, cleaning house, and washing, ironing, and mending clothes. These tasks are disproportionately performed by women and thus are denoted here as "female tasks." Thus, a substantial change toward greater equality *between spouses* in their shares of household labor requires a significant increase in the husband's participation in these tasks or a substantial decline in the wife's participation. A decline in the wife's participation without an increase in the husband's would mean that more services are being purchased outside the home (for example, the family is eating out

TABLE 5.1   *Mean Hours per Week Spent on Household Tasks by Dual-Earner Married Couples, by Type of Household Task*

Household Task	Husband	Wife
Female tasks	6.8	25.0
Preparing meals	2.4	8.6
Washing dishes and cleaning up after meals	2.0	5.2
Cleaning house	1.7	6.9
Washing, ironing, and mending clothes	0.7	4.2
Male tasks	7.4	1.6
Working outdoors and doing other housework maintenance (yard work, household repair, painting, etc.)	5.4	1.4
Maintaining and repairing automobiles	2.0	0.2
Neutral tasks	3.7	5.8
Shopping for groceries and other household goods	1.3	2.7
Paying bills and keeping financial records	1.3	1.6
Driving household members to work, school, or other activities	1.1	1.5
Total	17.8	32.4
Number of respondents	1,617	1,617

Source: NSFH, wave 1.
Notes: Means are weighted; numbers of respondents are unweighted. Sample consists of respondents with complete data for regression analyses.

often), domestic help is being hired, or the standard of household maintenance has been reduced.

Nine household tasks were surveyed in the NSFH, including two traditionally "male tasks" (outdoor and other household maintenance tasks and automobile maintenance and repair) and three "neutral tasks" (shopping, paying bills and keeping financial records, and driving others around) in addition to the four "female tasks." Table 5.1 shows the mean hours per week that husbands and wives spent on each of the nine household tasks.[6] These measures are presented only for couples for whom we have complete data on household tasks and on all the variables in the regression analysis. The means are similar to those for all dual-earner couples (Presser 1994).

As expected, wives in dual-earner marriages spent substantially more time than did husbands on the four tasks traditionally done by females, 18.2 more hours per week, and husbands spent more time than did wives on tasks traditionally done by males, 5.8 more hours per week. Also, wives spent 2.1 more hours per week on neutral tasks than do husbands. Overall, wives spent almost twice as many hours on the nine household tasks as husbands spent: 32.4 hours versus 17.8 hours.

Because these are dual-earner couples, the hours spent in household labor were in addition to hours spent in paid labor and thus are not trivial. For couples in this sample, the total number of hours per week usually worked for pay was 36.3 for women and 46.8 for men.[7] Accordingly, the total workload (paid employment plus unpaid housework on the nine tasks) is somewhat greater for women than for men (68.7 and 64.6, respectively). These figures exclude child care and thus understate the excess of women's total workload relative to men's.

Independent Variables:
Factors Affecting Housework Time

The particular times that spouses are employed affects their availability for domestic labor. I use three sets of variables characterizing *work schedules*. The first two sets relate to the *hours* in which spouses work; the third set relates to the *days* of work.

With regard to work hours, one set of measures relates to *the overlap in spouses' work schedules* in the previous week. (If the respondent was employed but not at work in the previous week, I used usual hours worked. For all those employed, respondents were instructed not to include hours worked at home for their job.) I calculated the cumulative number of hours in the previous week that each spouse was employed while the other spouse was not, and the number of hours in the previous week that both spouses were at work at the same time. The hypothesis is that the fewer the hours of overlap in time employed—particularly hours when the wife is employed and the husband is not—the greater the husband's share of the four female tasks.

The second set of measures on hours considers *each spouse's employment shift*, that is, whether he or she worked a fixed daytime schedule, a fixed nonday schedule, or a rotating schedule. Because of the small sample size when examining only dual-earners, fixed evenings and fixed night shifts are combined in the analyses as "fixed nonday" shifts. The majority of those working fixed nonday shifts worked evenings rather than nights. My expectation is that husbands do a greater share of the female tasks if neither spouse works a fixed day shift, particularly if the husband is home during the day and the wife works a fixed nonday shift or a rotating shift.

With regard to workdays, the measures are *whether or not each spouse worked weekends*. This is a simple dichotomy for each spouse on whether he or she worked Saturday and/or Sunday. I hypothesize that husbands participate more in female tasks when their wives work weekends; however, I do not expect that wives participate more in such tasks when their husbands work weekends.

With regard to *resources,* consistent with Coverman's (1985) analysis, I consider education, earnings, and occupation as resources and add the age difference between spouses. Although I focus on the relative resources of spouses, I also include a control for the husband's earnings (which is highly correlated with the wife's earnings).[8]

The survey questions on *education* differed for the interviewed respondent and the spouse. Thus, I measure relative education by determining whether one spouse had more than two years of schooling than the other, one or two years more, or the same years of schooling. As a control, I code the husband's education as "less than high school graduate," "high school graduate only," or "more than a high school education."

Relative earnings are measured as the log of the ratio of the husband's earnings to the wife's earning. As a control measure, I include the log of the husband's earnings. For cases with missing data on earnings, I use the mean earnings of husbands and wives for the respective spouse and included a dummy variable indicating whether earnings data were imputed. This procedure allows for an adjustment on selectivity as to who neglected to report earnings.

Occupation is a dichotomous measure denoting whether a spouse has a professional or managerial occupation. The absolute and relative influences are inferred from comparing couples in which both spouses, the husband only, or the wife only worked in a professional or managerial occupation with couples in which neither spouse worked in a professional or managerial occupation.

The husband's age minus the wife's age (in months) is a proxy measure of the power he has to implement resources. I assume that age stratification operates within a couple such that the older spouse has greater authority (Presser 1971). A competing view holds that youth is a "premium" in our society, particularly for women, and thus younger wives have more bargaining power. Although this power of youth may be used to obtain paid help in place of female domestic labor, I expect it does not increase male domestic labor.

Generally, I hypothesize that the greater a wife's resources relative to her husband's, the greater the husband's share in traditionally female household tasks, primarily because the wife's greater resources lower the number of hours she spends on such tasks.

The *gender role ideology scale* in this chapter is limited to four of the five items used in chapter 4. The excluded item is: "If a husband and a wife both work full-time, they should share household tasks equally." Because the sample is of dual-earner couples, such a question could produce measurement error toward consistency with the dependent variable and inflate the correlations, as occurred in Blair and Lichter's (1991) analysis.

The responses to each of the four statements were coded from 1 to 5, ranging from "strongly agree" to "strongly disagree," using reverse coding as appropriate. Cronbach's alpha for the four items is .45 for husbands and .50 for wives. Coded responses were then summed to obtain an overall score for each spouse. The scale ranges from 4 to 20, with higher numbers indicating more egalitarian attitudes. Each spouse's score on the gender role ideology scale is included in the models.[9]

Although there are mixed findings from other research on the effects of gender ideology, I tentatively hypothesize a positive relationship for both husbands and wives between their scores on the gender role ideology scale and the husband's share of traditionally female household tasks, possibly as a result of a positive effect on the husband's participation *and* a negative effect on the wife's participation.

To examine the changing social context for gender-related behavior, I include the *wife's age cohort,* coded as younger than age thirty, age thirty to forty-four, and age forty-five and over. As Goldscheider and Waite (1991) noted, young cohorts have more egalitarian attitudes than older cohorts. Age cohort may also be a proxy measure for different stages of the women's movement—women age forty-five and over in the mid-1980s were not exposed to this movement during their childhood (even though many were politicized in their middle years). Thus, I hypothesize that the younger the age cohort, the greater the husband's share of traditionally female household tasks.

Finally, with regard to *stage in the life course,* I include four measures as controls. Two variables indicating whether the husband or the wife was previously married are included. A previously married spouse may be more likely to negotiate the division of household chores before marriage, to the wife's benefit. In particular, previously married husbands may make a greater effort in a subsequent marriage to share more equitably in traditionally female household tasks. Masako Ishii-Kuntz and Scott Coltrane's (1992) finding that remarriage is associated with husbands' greater participation in household tasks (among couples with children) lends support to this expectation.

The *duration of current marriage* (in months) is highly correlated with age (which is why age is not included in the models) and also taps the changing nature of the marital relationship over the life course. Goldscheider and Waite (1991) reported that the husband's share of household tasks is greatest early in marriage, that is, prior to childbearing, and does not return to this level until the "empty nest" stage of the life course. However, with controls for the presence of children, as well as women's age cohort, the duration of current marriage may not have a significant effect.

The *number of children under age five* is both a life course variable and an indication of competing demands on time. Biological children, stepchildren, adopted children, and foster children are included. Caring for young children while at home clearly limits the time available for household tasks, yet children can also provide household labor. The evidence concerning the relationship between the presence of children and the husband's share of household tasks is mixed (Bergen 1990). This relationship may depend on the extent to which fathers trade off time spent with children and time spent on household tasks. Among dual-earner couples, most fathers of preschool-aged children are the primary caregivers of their children during the hours they are not employed but their wives are (Presser 1988; see also chapter 7). If there is a trade-off for such caregiving time, then I expect that the more children there are under age five, the less likely husbands will be to share in household tasks. However, Elizabeth Bergen's (1990) analysis showed that the presence of young children significantly *increases* the number of hours, and the relative share of hours, that husbands spend on some household tasks. Perhaps the presence of children engages husbands more both in child care and in housework.

Older children can both create more household labor and share in such work. Thus, the expected relationship between the *number of children age five to eighteen* and housework is more ambiguous. Bergen (1990) found no effect of the presence of school-aged children for any of the nine household tasks considered, and I hypothesize accordingly.

It may be that having children, regardless of age, interacts with all of the variables being considered; that is, the effects of available time, spouses' resources, gender role ideology, and stage in the life course may be conditional on whether children are present. Accordingly, the analysis looks separately at couples with and without children.

Table 5.2 provides summary measures for the variables included in the analysis. Special note should be taken of the work schedule measures for these dual-earner couples. Considerable lack of overlap is seen in the employment schedules of spouses among dual-earner couples. The mean number of overlapping hours of employment in the previous week is 27.6. However, wives were employed an average of 10.8 hours per week when their husbands were not employed, and husbands were employed an average of 21.2 hours when their wives were not employed. There is no overlap in any employment hours for 7.8 percent of these dual-earner couples (not shown in table 5.2).

For 74.8 percent of the couples, both spouses worked fixed daytime shifts. For 12.0 percent of these couples, the wife worked a nonday or

TABLE 5.2   *Summary Measures for Variables in the Analysis of Dual-Earner Married Parents*

Variables	Measures
Overlap in work schedules	
Mean hours husband and wife are both employed	27.6
Mean hours husband is not employed while wife is employed	10.8
Mean hours wife is not employed while husband is employed	21.2
Work shift	
Wife nondaytime or rotating shift, husband day shift	12.0%
Husband nondaytime or rotating shift, wife day shift	10.8
Both spouses employed day shifts	74.8
Both spouses nondaytime or rotating shifts	2.4
Weekend employment	
Husband works on weekends	35.0
Wife works on weekends	27.7
Spouse's resources	
Husband less than high school graduate	8.9
Husband high school graduate only	31.6
Husband more than high school graduate	59.5
Wife's schooling more than two years more than husband's	8.5
Wife's schooling one or two years more than husband's	16.4
Wife's schooling same as husband's	40.4
Husband's schooling one or two years more than wife's	23.4
Wife professional/managerial, husband in other occupation	17.4
Both spouses professional/managerial	17.7
Husband professional/managerial, wife in other occupation	21.2
Neither spouse professional/managerial	43.7
Mean earnings ratio, husband/wife (log)	0.9
Mean husband's earnings	$34,320
Mean wife's earnings	$15,694
Mean husband's earnings minus wife's earnings	$18,670
Earnings data missing	14.7%
Mean husband's age minus wife's age (in months)	27.3
Gender role ideology	
Mean husband's scale score	13.4
Mean wife's scale score	14.3
Mean age of wife	38.0
Cohort: wife's age younger than thirty	24.0%
Cohort: wife's age thirty to forty-four	49.6
Stage in life course	
Wife married more than once	18.1
Husband married more than once	19.7
Mean duration of current marriage (in months)	171.3
Mean number of children under age five	0.3
Mean number of children age five to eighteen	0.9
Number of cases	1,617

Source: NSFH, wave 1.

rotating shift while the husband worked a fixed day shift; for 10.8 percent, the husband worked a nonday shift or a rotating shift while the wife worked a fixed day shift; and for 2.4 percent of couples, both spouses worked a nonday shift or a rotating shift.[10] That over one-fourth of dual-earner couples had at least one spouse working a nonday shift or rotating shift reinforces the need to acknowledge diversity in employment schedules when studying the time available for household labor.

Findings
All Dual-Earner Couples

Table 5.3 shows the ordinary least squares (OLS) regressions for three dependent variables in the sample of all dual-earner couples: the *husband's share* of total hours spent on the four traditionally female household tasks; the *number of hours the husband* spent on female tasks; and the *number of hours the wife* spent on female tasks. Two models were calculated for each dependent variable: model 1 includes measures of the degree of overlap in spouses' hours of employment in the previous week; model 2 includes measures of both spouses' employment shifts. (The two models are considered separately because measures of overlap are highly correlated with measures of type of shift.) Both models include weekend employment.

Measures of overlap in spouses' hours of employment generally show the predicted relationships. The number of same hours that husbands and wives were both employed is not related to the husband's share in female household tasks or to the husband's number of hours spent on these tasks. However, it is significantly related to the wife's number of hours on these tasks: the more the overlap in spouses' work hours, the fewer hours wives spent doing female household tasks. This finding suggests that couples with high degrees of overlap may be more likely to eat out and buy household services traditionally performed by wives, since husbands are not at home to take over these tasks.

We see in table 5.3 that the more hours the husband was *not* employed while the wife *was* employed, the more the husband's share of household tasks increased. This greater share results from both a significant increase in the husband's hours spent on housework and a significant reduction in the wife's hours. There is no such significant effect on the housework hours of either spouse, however, the more hours the wife was not employed while the husband was employed.

A couple's employment shifts also affect the husband's participation in housework. Relative to couples in which both spouses worked day shifts, husbands were significantly more likely to do female tasks on both a relative and absolute basis if they worked a nonday or rotating shift and their wives a day shift. Employment shifts in which both spouses or wives only worked a nonday or rotating shift significantly increased the number of hours wives spent on female household tasks. Thus, being home alone—particularly during the day—appears to be an important factor increasing a spouse's share of traditionally female household tasks, for both husbands and wives.

The relative educational levels of husbands and wives are not significant determinants of the husband's share of housework hours for either model. However, the control variable—the husband's education—is highly relevant. For both sets of employment schedule measures (models 1 and 2), husbands with more than a high school education (relative to those without a high school degree) did a significantly larger share of female household tasks, and this is a result of both a reduction in the number of hours wives spent on housework and an increase in husbands' hours. Compared with husbands who were not high school graduates, husbands who were high school graduates did not significantly differ on their share of housework, but their wives' housework hours were significantly reduced.[11] Moreover, wives' housework hours were significantly reduced when they had the same or more education than their husband.

For both models, the husband's share of household work was significantly greater if both spouses were in professional or managerial occupations relative to couples in which neither spouse was in a professional or managerial occupation. This increase in the husband's share was a result of a significant reduction in the wife's hours spent on housework rather than an increase in the husband's hours. The same pattern obtains when wives were in professional occupations and husbands were not, but it is not significant. These findings suggest that it is the wife's professional or managerial occupation that is particularly important in reducing gender differences in hours spent on housework rather than the relative difference between spouses. Wives with high-status occupations may be more likely to regard housework as tedious than wives in other occupations (in contrast to the satisfactions derived from their jobs), and thus they may be more willing to hire domestic help or accept reduced standards of order and cleanliness. This result is net of the earnings variables, which tap the affordability of help. Myra Marx Ferree (1984) found that full-time housewives who previously held high-status occupations were less satisfied with housework than were housewives who previously held low-status jobs, providing tangential support for this interpretation.

The wife's earnings relative to her husband's (and net of his earn-

TABLE 5.3 OLS Coefficients for Regressions of Hours Spent in the Previous Week on Female Household Tasks on Selected Independent Variables for Dual-Earner Married Couples

| | Husband's Share of Female Tasks | | Hours Spent on Female Tasks | | | |
| | | | Husband | | Wife | |
	Model 1	Model 2	Model 1	Model 2	Model 1	Model 2
Overlap in work schedules						
Hours husband and wife both employed	0.001	—	0.017	—	−0.085*	—
Hours husband is not employed while wife is employed	0.003***	—	0.094***	—	−0.115***	—
Hours wife is not employed while husband is employed	−0.0001	—	0.011	—	0.026	—
Work shift						
Both spouses nondaytime or rotating shifts	—	0.026	—	1.753	—	3.170
Wife nondaytime or rotating shift, husband day shift	—	−0.011	—	0.585	—	4.568***
Husband nondaytime or rotating shift, wife day shift	—	0.034*	—	1.942***	—	0.599
Weekend employment						
Husband works weekends	−0.016	−0.020*	−0.699+	−0.690+	1.737*	2.039**
Wife works weekends	−0.010	0.024*	−0.282	0.661	1.351+	−0.648

Spouse's resources						
Husband high school graduate only	0.026	0.017	0.309	−0.110	−3.562**	−3.543**
Husband less than high school graduate	0.102***	0.090***	1.916*	1.409+	−7.505***	−7.449***
Wife's schooling more than two years more than husband's	0.034	0.029	0.917	0.667	−4.926**	−4.836**
Wife's schooling one or two years more than husband's	0.027	0.022	0.384	0.221	−3.773**	−3.575**
Wife's schooling same as husband's	0.020	0.015	0.468	0.306	−2.611*	−2.475*
Husband's schooling one or two years more than wife's	0.011	0.008	0.580	0.486	−1.861	−1.743
Wife professional/managerial, husband in other occupation	0.019	0.018	0.284	0.281	−0.409	−0.464
Both spouses professional/managerial	0.051***	0.048***	0.501	0.484	−2.904**	−2.601*
Husband professional/managerial, wife in other occupation	−0.001	−0.005	−0.123	−0.203	−0.442	−0.235
Earnings ratio, husband/wife (log)	−0.018***	−0.023***	−0.326	−0.451*	1.587***	1.903***
Husband's earnings (log)	−0.002	−0.005	−0.572+	−0.653*	−1.628**	−1.658**
Earnings data missing	−0.021+	−0.021+	−1.013*	−1.049*	−0.567	−0.482
Husband's age minus wife's age (in months)	−0.0001	−0.0001	−0.008*	−0.007*	0.0001	−0.002
Gender role ideology						
Husband's scale score	0.005**	0.006***	0.098	0.114	−0.500***	−0.529***
Wife's scale score	0.007***	0.008***	0.192**	0.233**	−0.327*	−0.375***

TABLE 5.3   Continued

| | Husband's Share of Female Tasks | | Hours Spent on Female Tasks | | | |
| | | | Husband | | Wife | |
	Model 1	Model 2	Model 1	Model 2	Model 1	Model 2
Cohort: wife's age younger than 30	0.025	0.027	1.136	1.175	−2.579	−2.647
Cohort: wife's age thirty to forty-four	0.011	0.012	−0.094	−0.060	−3.600**	−3.563**
Stage in life course						
Wife married more than once	0.021	0.020	0.701	0.636	−2.241*	−2.331*
Husband married more than once	0.018	0.021	0.786	0.878	−0.037	−0.180
Duration of current marriage (in months)	−0.0001	−0.0001	−0.001	−0.001	−0.006	−0.005
Number of children under age five	−0.017*	−0.020*	0.729*	0.626*	4.592***	4.599***
Number of children age five to eighteen	−0.010+	−0.010*	0.278	0.302	1.983***	2.106***
Intercept	−0.033	0.019	5.130	6.966	63.121***	60.568***
Adjusted r-square	0.179***	0.153***	0.085***	0.068***	0.183***	0.178***
Number of cases	1,617	1,625	1,617	1,625	1,617	1,625

Source: NSFH, wave 1.
Note: Omitted categories of dummy variables: both spouses day shifts, husband less than high school graduate, wife's education over two years less than husband's, neither spouse professional/managerial, wife's age forty-five or over.
$^{+}$p = < 0.10; *p = < 0.05; **p = < 0.01; ***p = < 0.001.

ings) is an especially important variable. Table 5.3 shows that the greater the logged ratio of the husband's earnings to the wife's earnings, the lower the husband's share of housework. However, this decrease in the husband's share is attributable primarily to a significant increase in the wife's hours of housework, although the husband's hours of housework decline significantly in model 2. The husband's earnings (logged and net of the earnings ratio) had no significant effect on his share of household work.[12] The husband's earnings are highly correlated with the wife's earnings, and thus this variable also controls for family income. High earnings by husbands reduce the hours of household work for both spouses—again, probably as a result of increased spending on domestic cleaning services and restaurant meals.

The dummy variable denoting missing data on earnings is significant for husbands' hours of housework (and near-significant for their share), indicating that husbands who are allocated earnings values do less of the housework than husbands in other couples. This finding affirms the importance of including couples with missing data on earnings in the analysis so that the other variables are adjusted for the effect of these missing data.

The age difference between husband and wife shows the predicted negative association with the husband's hours of housework (but not his share). The older the husband relative to the wife, the fewer the husband's hours of housework. This finding supports the age-stratification perspective, which links the older age of husbands to a greater ability to exercise their preferences.

In sum, this analysis provides limited support for the relative resource hypothesis. Husbands' share is influenced only by the relative earnings of spouses, not by the other relative measures. The older the husband relative to the wife, the less likely he is to do housework, in absolute hours, but his share of housework is not significantly greater. Absolute measures of education are significant determinants of housework, but the relationships are not as predicted by the resource thesis. A husband's high education increases his hours of housework and reduces his wife's hours of housework. Education may be tapping an egalitarian gender role ideology for both spouses, beyond the ideology measures used in the analysis. If husbands and wives both have a professional or managerial occupation, wives do less housework.

Husbands' and wives' gender role ideology scores are significantly related to the husband's share of housework: the more egalitarian their ideologies, the greater the husband's share of housework. This occurs because, for each spouse, a more egalitarian gender role ideology is associated with significantly fewer hours of housework for the wife. Only the wife's gender role ideology score increases the husband's hours of housework. Men appear to be more responsive to their wife's gender role expectations than to their own when it comes to doing tasks traditionally done by females.

Gender ideology, when tapped indirectly with the age cohort measures, is not significantly related to the husband's share of housework. This result is net of gender role ideology scores and thus measures the influence of cohort support. Table 5.3 shows a significant relationship between age cohort and the wife's hours of housework only for wives age thirty to forty-four, compared with wives age forty-five and over.

Whether husbands were previously married has no significant effect on any of the dependent variables. If the wife was married previously, her hours of housework are significantly reduced in both models, but this reduction does not significantly affect the husband's share of housework. Moreover, the duration of the current marriage is not significant in any of the regressions, which was expected given the controls for gender role ideology and number of children.

The number of children under age five shows a significant relationship to housework for all six models. The greater the number of children under age five, the smaller the husband's share of household tasks. However, this is not because husbands contribute fewer hours; rather, husbands and wives both do significantly more, but wives' hours increase more than do husbands' hours. The number of children age five to eighteen significantly increases women's, but not men's, absolute hours of housework, producing a decrease in men's share.

Among couples with children, are the husbands who do more traditionally female housework also those who do more child care? In other words, does parenthood lead those husbands who are most willing to do housework to participate more directly in child rearing than do other fathers, or is their greater involvement in female housework a substitute for greater participation in child care tasks? The answer seems to be the first alternative: doing more of one type of traditionally female family work is correlated with doing more of another type. A question on parents' time spent caring for children's physical needs was asked of randomly selected children under age five.[13] The zero-order correlation between the hours fathers spent on such care for this child and husbands' share of typically female housework is positive and significant, although not very high ($r = .13$, $p = .015$).[14] Of course, some of this child care may occur simultaneously with the performance of household tasks (as it may also for wives), particularly if fathers are home caring for children while mothers are employed. This sequential parenting occurs when spouses work different shifts. The questions about child care included the option of reporting on fathers' care while mothers are employed.

Husbands who reported such care did a significantly greater share of the housework (24.7 percent) than did fathers who did not provide care in this situation (20.2 percent, t-test, p = .043).

The adjusted r-squares in table 5.3 show that 17.9 percent and 15.3 percent of the total variation in husbands' share of household tasks traditionally done by females is explained by these models. The difference between the two models indicates that knowing the number of non-overlapping hours of spouse employment is a somewhat better predictor of the husband's share of housework than is knowing the couple's work shifts.

In terms of hours spent on housework, the models explain more of the wife's hours than the husband's hours—about 18 percent versus 7 to 8 percent, respectively. This finding is consistent with prior discussion of the individual variables: to understand the determinants of the husband's share of these tasks it is important to understand how these determinants affect the wife's hours spent on such tasks—more so than the husband's.[15] Moreover, when both spouses' hours spent on housework are significantly affected by these determinants, the relationship differs for husbands and wives. For example, the number of hours husbands are not employed while wives are employed significantly increases husbands' share in these tasks as a result of significantly reducing wives' hours of housework and significantly increasing husbands' hours.

Dual-Earner Couples with Children

As previously noted, it is relevant to consider whether the effects of work schedules on the time spent on female household tasks for husbands and wives obtains when looking separately at those who have children. As we have seen with regard to marital disruption, the effects could be specific to those with children, in that their presence changes family dynamics.

Table 5.4 presents the same set of regressions as shown in table 5.3, for parents only. The sample sizes are reduced from 1,617 to 1,625 couples to 1,058 to 1,065 couples, and thus significance levels are harder to reach. Nevertheless, we see that with regard to overlapping hours and shifts, the relationships between nonstandard schedules and hours spent on female household tasks that were significant in table 5.3 also obtain in table 5.4. With regard to weekend employment, we see some new significant relationships indicating notable decreases in husbands' absolute and relative hours of participation in household tasks, despite the smaller sample (model 1 for overlapping hours and model 2 for employ-

TABLE 5.4 OLS Coefficients for Regressions of Hours Spent in the Previous Week on Female Household Tasks on Selected Independent Variables for Dual-Earner Married Parents

| | Husband's Share of Female Tasks | | Hours Spent on Female Tasks | | | |
| | | | Husband | | Wife | |
	Model 1	Model 2	Model 1	Model 2	Model 1	Model 2
Overlap in work schedules						
Hours husband and wife are both employed	0.001	—	0.013	—	-0.118**	—
Hours husband is not employed while wife is employed	0.003***	—	0.100***	-	-0.152***	—
Hours wife is not employed while husband is employed	0.0002	—	0.012	—	0.023	—
Work shift						
Both spouses nondaytime or rotating shifts	—	0.039	—	1.681	—	-0.578
Wife nondaytime or rotating shift, husband day shift	—	-0.016	—	0.164	—	3.346*
Husband nondaytime or rotating shift, wife day shift	—	0.044*	—	2.428***	—	0.789
Weekend employment						
Husband works weekends	-0.030*	-0.032**	-1.054+	-1.116*	2.487*	2.798**
Wife works weekends	-0.005	-0.031*	-0.044	1.197*	1.634+	0.069

	(1)	(2)	(3)	(4)	(5)	(6)
Spouse's resources						
Husband high school graduate only	0.025	0.015	−0.005	−0.458	−2.997+	−2.682
Husband less than high school graduate	0.099***	0.085***	2.073*	1.404	−6.863***	−6.458***
Wife's schooling more than two years more than husband's	0.056*	0.046	2.114+	1.584	−5.308*	−5.322*
Wife's schooling one or two years more than husband's	0.034	0.030	1.060	0.947	−3.955*	−3.821*
Wife's schooling same as husband's	0.039*	0.032+	1.324+	1.096	−2.937+	−2.760+
Husband's schooling one or two years more than wife's	0.021	0.017	1.119	0.975	−2.522+	−2.388
Wife professional/managerial, husband in other occupation	0.027+	0.028+	0.515	0.572	−0.085	−0.092
Both spouses professional/managerial	0.050**	0.045**	0.780	0.725	−3.704**	−3.127*
Husband professional/managerial, wife in other occupation	−0.002	−0.006	0.367	0.275	−0.503	−0.169
Earnings ratio, husband/wife (log)	−0.021***	−0.025***	−0.466+	−0.550*	1.542***	2.012***
Husband's earnings (log)	0.009	0.005	−0.362	−0.503	−2.108**	−2.052+
Earnings data missing	−0.023	−0.023	−1.120+	−1.075+	−0.514	−0.260
Husband's age minus wife's age (in months)	−0.00003	0.00001	−0.004	−0.003	0.001	−0.002
Gender role ideology						
Husband's scale score	0.004+	0.005+	0.083	0.091	−0.330+	−0.390*
Wife's scale score	0.008***	0.009***	0.225*	0.279**	−0.428*	−0.514***

TABLE 5.4   Continued

| | Husband's Share of Female Tasks | | Hours Spent on Female Tasks | | | |
| | | | Husband | | Wife | |
	Model 1	Model 2	Model 1	Model 2	Model 1	Model 2
Cohort: wife's age younger than thirty	0.042	0.039	2.450*	2.282+	-3.726+	-3.569
Cohort: wife's age thirty to forty-four	0.028	0.027	0.998	0.911	-4.444**	-4.293**
Stage in life course						
Wife married more than once	0.017	0.016	0.813	0.779	-2.098	-2.092
Husband married more than once	0.001	0.005	0.306	0.390	0.238	-0.051
Duration of current marriage (in months)	-0.0001	-0.0001	-0.001	-0.001	-0.010	-0.010
Number of children under age five	-0.023*	-0.024*	0.293	0.246	4.559***	4.574***
Number of children age five to eighteen	-0.011	-0.011	0.119	0.126	2.153***	2.183***
Intercept	-0.164	-0.086	1.547	4.077	69.178***	65.188***
Adjusted r-square	0.180***	0.154***	0.088***	0.071***	0.185***	0.167***
Number of cases	1,058	1,065	1,058	1,065	1,058	1,065

Source: NSFH, wave 1.
Note: Omitted categories of dummy variables: both spouses day shifts, husband less than high school graduate, wife's education over two years less than husband's, neither spouse professional/managerial, wife's age forty-five or over.
+p = < 0.10; *p = < 0.05; **p = < 0.01; ***p = < 0.001.

ment shifts). With regard to wives' hours of housework, this now shows a significant increase for husbands' absolute hours (model 2) that was not evident in table 5.3.[16]

Overall, then, the regressions show that nonstandard work schedules affected the division of household labor by gender for those with children as it did for the total, and that among those couples with a spouse employed on weekends, it was especially likely when children were present that the husband's hours in such tasks would decrease and the wife's hours would increase. There are some differences in significant relationships between the control variables and the hours spent in the previous week on female household tasks for parents as compared with the total sample. Generally, these differences are that parents showed some nonsignificant relationships that were significant for the total. In almost all cases the direction of the relationship remains the same, and the lack of significance may be largely due to the different sample sizes. The r-squares are about the same for parents as for the total sample, indicating that the variables in the models explain about the same amount of variation in the housework of husbands and wives.

Discussion

We have seen that a major form of family functioning—the performance of household tasks traditionally done by wives—is affected by nonstandard work schedules. Both husbands and wives do more housework when they are home and their spouse is not. Given the substantial lack of overlap in the employment schedules of husbands and wives and the great number of spouses working nonday shifts, this structural aspect of "available time" is relevant to a large portion of dual-earner American couples.

Interestingly, husbands and wives differ in their domestic responses to nonstandard employment patterns, net of their resources, gender role ideology, and stage in the life course: the more hours husbands are not employed while wives are employed, the more likely husbands are to do housework that is traditionally done by females, breaking traditional gender expectations. In contrast, the hours wives spend not employed while husbands are employed seem to encourage wives to spend more hours on traditionally female tasks, reinforcing traditional gender expectations.

These findings demonstrate the relevance of external factors for the division of labor within the family. The growth of the service sector may increase the demand for employment during nonstandard hours, thereby influencing the temporal patterns of family life. This indirect influence on the family narrows the gender gap in housework—albeit to a small extent—when husbands are in a situational bind: their wives are unavailable for housework while they are available. Although some spouses may select particular employment schedules to accommodate family needs, reversing the causal direction, we have seen that most spouses, particularly husbands, work nontraditional hours mainly because it is a job requirement (chapter 2). Nonetheless, one consequence may be a modest alteration of gender-specific behavior within the family.[17]

Some aspects of the relative resources of spouses—namely, earnings and age—also reduce the gender gap in housework. Further, if both spouses are professionals or managers, the gender gap is smaller. These findings suggest that the less the resource gap favors husbands, the greater is the power of wives to narrow the housework gap, although such power may decrease the wife's participation instead of, or in addition to, increasing the husband's participation. Future surveys should obtain data on standards of household maintenance and the purchase of domestic services in order to assess their effects on husbands' and wives' participation in housework.

The need to consider the determinants of hours of housework separately for husbands and wives before considering the determinants of the husband's share of housework is also evident when considering the role of gender ideology. The husband's share of housework increases, as expected, the more egalitarian the gender role ideologies of the husband and the wife are. But the husband's gender role ideology has no significant effect on his hours of housework, only a significant negative effect on his wife's hours, whereas the wife's gender role ideology significantly increases the husband's hours *and* significantly decreases her own hours. Husbands may be more responsive to their wives' gender ideologies than their own when the work is not pleasurable, but why this may be so merits further study.

The effect of the number of children also illustrates the importance of considering the absolute number of hours as well as relative shares of hours of housework for each spouse. The significant negative effects of these variables on husbands' share of housework suggest, at first glance, that husbands do less housework the more children they have. In fact, they do significantly more hours of housework, but wives' hours increase even more (especially as they have more children under age five), leading to a reduced share of housework for husbands. The relevant question, then, is why having children generates a greater domestic burden for women than it does for men.

When the analysis is limited to couples with children, the results are similar. Nonstandard work schedules affect the gender division of household labor, net of the relative resources of the spouses, their gender role ideologies, and their stage in the life course.

Overall, the implications of these findings are sobering for advocates of egalitarian marriages. The narrowing of the gender gap in housework may continue to be slow, judging from the small amount of variation explained by these theoretically important variables.[18] Moreover, nonstandard work schedules may increase the domestic workload for both spouses.

On the other hand, wives are likely to continue doing less housework, regardless of their husband's participation, as long as their representation in professional and managerial occupations increases, the gender gap in earnings narrows, gender ideologies become more egalitarian, and more domestic services are purchased. Whether wives will have fewer children—a factor strongly linked to a reduction in women's domestic workload—is more speculative.

We turn now from the issue of how nonstandard work schedules affect the sharing of household tasks to the impact of such schedules on parent-child interactions, another important aspect of family functioning.

6

Parent-Child Interaction

IN THE past two chapters, the focus has been on married couples, both parents and nonparents. The aim was to assess the effect of nonstandard work schedules on the quality and stability of marriages, as well as on the division of household labor, and to determine whether the presence of children was relevant. We turn now to a consideration of parents only, both married and nonmarried. The objective in this chapter is to examine the extent to which parent-child interaction is affected by the nonstandard work schedules of parents and whether marital status is relevant.

Parent-child interaction is considered to be of central importance to children's cognitive, social, and emotional development (Amato 1998; Brown et al. 2001; Hoffman et al. 1999). Although there are different types of parental involvement with children, such as setting rules and expectations and distilling values, we are specifically interested in the direct engagement of parents with their children in specific activities on a regular basis.[1]

The potential for such direct engagement is clearly constrained by the employment status of parents, including the number of hours and days they are employed. But what about *which* hours they are employed? Does working nonstandard hours enhance or reduce parent-child interaction? It might seem that working nondaytime hours would provide parents with more opportunities for parent-child interaction, especially if they work nights and are home during their children's waking (and nonschool) hours. But this scenario assumes both that parents working nights are not sleeping when children are home and that the opportunity for parent-child interaction that their work schedule allows is in fact realized in that way. And what about weekend employment—does this limit parent-child interaction? School-aged children are usually more available for family outings and other types of parental interaction on nonschool days, but parents may not be able to take advantage of these opportunities if they work on weekends.

Relevant Literature

Prior research on this topic at the national level that considers both work schedules and parental time with children is limited to two studies, and these are limited to the examination of work hours, not weekend employment. The study based on the 1999 National Survey of America's Families (NSAF) (Phillips 2002) looked specifically at low-income families and found a positive as well as a negative relationship between nonstandard work hours and parental involvement with children age six to eleven. Among married-couple households with such children, working late hours was linked to greater parental involvement in their children's school, but the children of such parents were less likely to be engaged in extracurricular activities. This study does not distinguish the type of shift and defines "night hours" as employment mostly between 6:00 P.M. and 6:00 A.M. The other study, also of married couples only, is based on the 1981 Study of Time Use (STU). This study found little relationship between work schedules—the number of minutes the husband and the wife were employed within certain ranges of hours around the clock—and the amount of parental time spent with children, but children in this study included all those under age twenty (Nock and Kingston 1988).

A few other studies do not look specifically at parental involvement but do consider child outcomes in relation to nonstandard work schedules. Preliminary findings based on an analysis of one thousand children in the Study of Early Child Care sponsored by the National Institute of Child Health and Human Development (NICHD) (Han 2002) show that children of mothers who had ever worked some nonstandard hours—evenings, nights, or variable schedules—had lower cognitive scores at ages up to thirty-six months than children whose mothers worked only standard hours. Moreover, it is the night hours that seem to matter most, with children of mothers who worked those hours showing the lowest scores. Another large study, based on the National Longitudinal Survey of Youth (NLSY) (Heyman 2000), shows that school-aged children with poor educational outcomes in 1996 were more likely than other children to have parents (presumably of either gender) who worked evenings some or all of their employed years between 1990 and 1996. (Evening shifts were self-defined without specification of which hours this encompassed.) A three-city study (Boston, Chicago, and San Antonio) of low-income families in 1999 found more problem behaviors and fewer positive behaviors among children whose parents worked nonstandard hours or weekends (grouped together) compared with those who worked fixed-daytime weekday-only schedules (Bogen and Joshi 2001).

Small-scale studies in other countries also suggest some negative effects of nonstandard schedules. J. Barton, Jan M. Aldridge, and Peter A. Smith's (1998) study of 190 eight- to eleven-year-olds (from an unspecified European country) found that daughters—but not sons—of fathers who worked shifts were more likely to have poorer perceptions of their academic competence, their competencies overall, and their perceptions of self-worth than daughters of fathers who worked day schedules. A Belgian study of elementary school children found lower academic achievement when their fathers worked nonday shifts, but this was attributed to differences in the children's intelligence (Maasen 1978). A study of male rotating-shift workers in two factories in Bangladesh explored different rotation systems and reported that fathers on weekly, as distinct from fortnightly, rotation had significantly fewer "opportunities" for contact with their children than other fathers (actual engagement was not measured), as well as greater family problems (Rahman and Pal 1993–94).

Qualitative studies with very small samples suggest some positive as well as negative aspects of parental nonstandard work schedules for children—and for parents too, especially mothers. Anita Ilta Garey's (1999) interviews with seven nurses working the night shift full-time indicated that these mothers liked the fact that this late work schedule allowed them to maximize family time and do traditional maternal tasks at home, as though they were full-time "at-home moms." Such tasks included helping with homework and being able to participate in or facilitate their children's school and extracurricular activities. Moreover, they preferred the night shift to the evening shift because they were able to supervise dinner and bedtime and married respondents had more time with their spouses. The cost to these mothers, which they were all willing to assume, was considerable sleep deprivation—most got four to five hours of sleep a night. Sleep deprivation problems among shift workers and the desire to be a "good mother" by working late hours were also relayed in interviews with women in the Midwest (Hattery 2001; sample size not provided). But sleep deprivation can hinder mothering, as exemplified by a mother in Jody Heyman's (2000, 17) in-depth study of one hundred parents who referred to her three years on the night shift as a "nightmare":

> I always wanted to try to catch some sleep so I could get there the next day. I just couldn't even think. It just clogged my memory and everything. It really did a job on me, and I haven't been right since. . . . It is just not good if you have kids at their age [preschoolers]. I just couldn't spend any valuable time with them. I was always sleepy or cranky. "Hurry up because I gotta get some sleep and I gotta go to work."

Fathers who work late hours have also been found to have problems with scheduling sleep, work, and home activities. A qualitative study of ninety male security guards on rotating shifts found that many who were fathers deprived themselves of sleep in order to participate in family life—for instance, eating meals with their family even though doing so put them "out of sync with their biological rhythm" (Hertz and Charlton 1989, 502). Among thirty couples in a New England study (Deutsch 1999), fathers on late shifts displayed some resistance to assuming greater responsibility for parental tasks such as cooking and bathing children ("women's work"), but they also expressed satisfaction with learning how to listen to their children.

The connection between the frequency of parent-child interaction and child outcomes cannot be addressed in the present study, since cell sizes are too small for an analysis that distinguishes different shifts (which is important) as well as the gender of parents. Indeed, an important limitation of the empirical studies on child outcomes by Han (2002) and by Bogen and Joshi (2001) is that they group all nonstandard schedules together, whereas different parental shifts (in these studies maternal shifts) may have different effects on children.

Ideally, one would want to view the frequency of parent-child interaction as an intermediary factor, one that is affected by nonstandard work schedules and in turn has an impact on child outcomes. But we are able to consider here only the first part of this process—the relationship between nonstandard work schedules and the extent of parent-child interaction. Although more frequent parent-child interaction does not necessarily lead to higher-quality parenting (especially among the sleep-deprived), we can expect there to be a strong correlation.

There have been some analyses of the frequency of parent-child activity based on the NSFH data (Acock and Demo 1994), but that research examined how parent-child activities vary by family structure, not by work schedules. The authors found that family structure did not matter much.

General Hypotheses

The basic hypothesis of this chapter is that nonstandard work schedules affect the extent of parental interaction with children *within* family types. Moreover, this effect varies depending on which nondaytime shift the parent works and which type of parent-child interaction is at issue. Since we know that mothers and fathers engage in different types of activities with children (Brown et al. 2001; Hoffman et al. 1999), the gender of the parent is expected to be another source of variation.

The specific types of engagement between parents and children to be considered here are eating meals together (breakfast and dinner separately) and one-on-one types of parent-child interaction: time spent together in leisure activities away from home, time spent together at home working on a project or playing together, the extent to which the parent and child have private talks, and parental help with reading or homework. (In the next chapter, we consider how nonstandard work schedules relate to fathers' participation in child care.) Specific hypotheses about how these interactions are affected by nonstandard work schedules are discussed along with the analyses.

Sample and Variables

The data for this analysis are based on the subsample of parents in wave 1 of the NSFH with children age five to eighteen. The questions of interest were not asked of parents with regard to younger children in the household. For our purposes, this restriction to older children is appropriate. For example, infants and toddlers can be disruptive at dinner, but older children are especially likely to benefit from dining with parents and possibly other family members (older siblings, for example) on a regular basis. It should be noted, however, that for couples with more than one child for the age range considered, we do not know whether it was one or more of the children the parents were referring to when they indicated the extent of their interaction. Accordingly, the responses should be interpreted as the time parents spent with children, and not the time children spent with parents.

There were several questions asked of parents that are of specific interest in this chapter:

(1) "How many days last week did you eat breakfast or dinner with at least one of the children?" (Responses for each meal ranged from 1 to 7.)

(2) "How often do you spend time with the children:
   a. in leisure activities away from home (picnics, movies, sports, etc.);
   b. at home working on a project or playing together;
   c. having private talks;
   d. helping with reading or homework?" (Responses for each activity were: "never or rarely," "once a month or less," "several times a month," "about once a week," "several times a week," and "almost everyday." The values assigned to their categorical frequencies ranged from 1 ("never or rarely") to 6 ("almost everyday").

The responses to these questions are presented for all married couples with children and for single mothers. For married couples, the sample is limited to those couples with data for both the main respondent and the spouse and with at least one spouse employed. For single mothers, the sample is drawn from main respondents only. Because the question about how often parents ate breakfast and dinner with their children related to the previous week, the analysis is restricted to those who were at work in the previous week (not on leave or vacation). For the other questions, the analysis includes all those employed, including the relatively few who were not at work during the previous week. Since eating meals is a daily activity for all families, we focus on which hours but not which days parents were employed; when considering one-on-one parent-child interaction, the relevance of weekend employment as well as work shifts is considered.

Findings: Parents and Children Eating Meals Together

Of special interest is the effect of nonstandard work schedules on the "family dinner," since this activity may be the most significant day-to-day organizing feature of family life. Typically, it is the only daily event that allows for meaningful family interaction.[2] As Marjorie DeVault (1991, 35, 39) has stated, eating is "profoundly social," and its day-to-day nature creates a family's "reality."[3] Thus, it is significant that this form of family connectedness has been on the decline in recent decades. According to Robert Putnam (2000), the proportion of American families who definitely agreed to the statement "Our whole family usually eats dinner together" declined from about 50 percent to 35 percent between 1977 and 1999. Putnam did not report the percentages for those with and without children but did indicate that while they differed, the trend over time was identical. Most of the decline occurred between 1980 and 1990.[4]

Since dinner is time-bound and usually occurs in the evening—at least on weekdays—it is important to consider what happens to the family dinner when parents work evenings or rotating schedules.[5] Breakfast is also time-bound but typically considered a less important—and less frequent—context for social interaction among family members. Because it may be more important than dinner for families who do not have dinner together, however, it is of potential significance.

The only empirical study I am aware of that relates work schedules to family meals is based on a sample of parents in England and Wales (La Valle et al. 2002). The family evening meal is defined in this study as one that includes the mother, her partner (if applicable), and at least one of their children. While it was found that "atypical" schedules (early mornings, late afternoons, evenings, nights, and weekends, grouped) were associated with less frequent family dining, for both dual-earner and single-mother families, the particular work schedules were not de-lineated. Clearly the evening shift would have had the most impact.

Although this analysis delineates the shifts, a limitation is that we cannot determine which days of the week parents were eating meals with their children. For married couples, we know the total number of days during the previous week each parent ate with the children. Unless it was seven days for both parents, however, we cannot determine how many days both parents were eating together with their children—that is, on the same days. It should be noted that eating meals with one's children is not place-specific and thus includes dining out as well as at home together.

Before considering the relevance of work schedules, it is of interest to examine the extent to which mothers and fathers dined with their children in general, since such information is limited. Figure 6.1 presents the frequency distributions on the number of days mothers and fathers ate dinner with their children age five to eighteen, separately for those married and for those single-defined here as separated or not married. Among the married, figures are presented for parents in households with at least one earner and for the subset of dual-earner households only.

We see sharp gender differences in the frequency with which parents dined with their children. Among all married couples with children, 64.1 percent of mothers and 47.4 percent of fathers had dinner with at least one of their children all seven days of the previous week. Only 36.7 percent of these couples reported that both parents ate dinner with their children all seven days. Also striking are the substantial proportions of parents who ate dinner with their children less than five days a week: 14.9 percent of mothers and 27.9 percent of fathers; 8.2 percent reported that both parents ate breakfast less than five days a week with their children.

These figures may result in part because of the absence of children at dinner, particularly very young and teenage children, rather than because of the absence of parents. When we look at couples who had only children age five to thirteen, the percentages are somewhat higher: 70.5 percent of mothers and 52.8 percent of fathers ate dinner with their children all seven days of the previous week, and 41.4 percent reported that both parents did so.

As would be expected, restricting the analysis to dual-earner couples reveals even lower frequencies of parents eating dinner with at least one of their children seven days a week: 58.9 percent of mothers and

FIGURE 6.1   *Frequency Distribution of the Number of Days Employed Mothers and Fathers Ate Dinner with Their Children Age Five to Eighteen in the Previous Week, by Family Type*

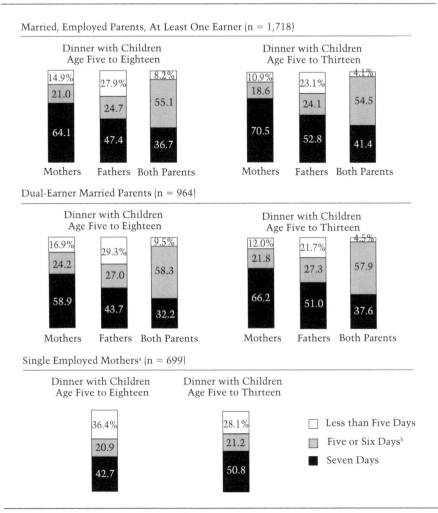

Married, Employed Parents, At Least One Earner (n = 1,718)

Dual-Earner Married Parents (n = 964)

Single Employed Mothers[a] (n = 699)

Source: NSFH, wave 1.

Notes: Percentages are weighted; numbers of cases are not weighted. Sample is limited to those couples with data for both main respondent and spouse. Earners are those who were employed and worked in the previous week.

[a]Main respondents only; includes married with spouse absent and single with a partner present.

[b]For both parents, this category includes all combinations other than both "fewer than five days" and "seven days."

43.7 percent of fathers in these families did so, as did both parents in 32.2 percent of these families. When further limiting the sample to dual-earner couples with children age five to thirteen only, the frequencies are 66.2 percent, 51.0 percent, and 37.6 percent, respectively.

Separated and nonmarried employed mothers are less likely to have dinner with their children than married mothers, even those in dual-earner households. We see at the bottom of figure 6.1 that only 42.7 percent of these single mothers ate dinner with their children seven days in the previous week, and 36.4 percent less than five days. The frequencies are somewhat higher when looking at single mothers with children age five to thirteen only, but they are still remarkably low: 50.8 percent ate dinner with their children all seven days in the previous week and 28.1 percent less than five days. It cannot be determined with the NSFH data whether these children were eating dinner with others when their mothers were absent or alone.[6]

As expected, the frequencies at which parents ate breakfast with their children are substantially lower than they are for dinner (figure 6.2). This may be because some parents do not themselves eat breakfast and also because it is easier for children to make their own breakfast than their own dinner. For all married couples with at least one earner, only 35.4 percent of mothers ate breakfast all seven days of the previous week with their children, and only 16.5 percent of fathers; 10.0 percent reported that both parents did so. The majority of mothers (54.6 percent) and fathers (75.0 percent) reported that they ate breakfast less than five days a week with their children, and close to half (46.0 percent) of these families reported that both parents ate breakfast this infrequently with the children. These percentages are somewhat higher when looking at couples with children age five to thirteen only.

Dual-earner parents are less likely than married couples more generally to have breakfast with their children. Only 26.9 percent of mothers and 15.0 percent of fathers in dual-earner families (both on the job during the previous week) ate breakfast all seven days of that week with their children, and just 8.4 percent of these families reported that both parents did this. Over three-fourths (62.5 percent) of such mothers and three-fourths (75.7 percent) of such fathers ate breakfast less than five days of the week with their children, and in over half (52.8 percent) of these families both parents ate with the children this infrequently. Again, couples with children age five to thirteen only ate breakfast with their children more frequently.

Single employed mothers were less likely than married mothers to have breakfast with their children (although more likely than married fathers). Only 18.8 percent ate breakfast with their children seven days a week; 70.5 percent did so less than five days a week. Among those with

FIGURE 6.2   *Frequency Distribution of the Number of Days*
Employed Mothers and Fathers Ate Breakfast with
Their Children Age Five to Eighteen in the Previous
Week, by Family Type

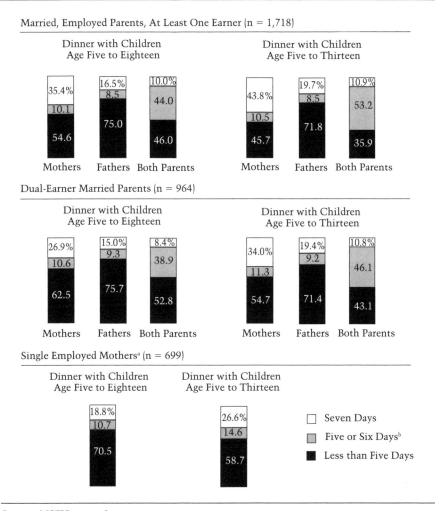

Source: NSFH, wave 1.
Notes: Percentages are weighted; numbers of cases are not weighted. Sample is limited to those couples with data for both main respondent and spouse. Earners are those who were employed and worked in the previous week.
[a]Main respondents only; includes married with spouse absent and single with a partner present.
[b]For both parents, this category includes all combinations other than both "fewer than five days" and "seven days."

children age five to thirteen only, the figures are 26.6 percent and 58.7 percent, respectively.

We see, then, that parents did not eat with their children as frequently at breakfast as at dinner, but that patterns by gender of parents and family type were the same for both meals. Moreover, for both meals parental presence was higher in families with children age five to thirteen only than in families that included preschoolers and teenagers age fourteen to eighteen.

It is possible that parents who do not eat dinner with their children are more likely to eat breakfast with them than parents who do eat dinner with their children; that is, parents may compensate for their absence from dinner this way. However, for all married couples with at least one earner, the correlation between eating breakfast and dinner is positive, both for mothers ($r = .25$; $p = <.001$) and for fathers ($r = .28$; $p = <.001$), refuting this hypothesis. (The correlations are positive and significant as well for the subgroup of dual-earner couples and for non-married mothers.)

Shift Work and Dinner

The work schedules of parents would seem highly relevant to their presence at dinner. We would expect evening and rotating shifts to reduce parental availability, and thus presence, at dinnertime. Night and day shifts, on the other hand, may maximize parental availability.

The data in table 6.1 support this expectation for both married and single employed mothers. (It should be kept in mind that since this table refers to employed mothers only, the category of "married and at least one earner" eliminates the traditional family of employed fathers and full-time housewives and is thus not much larger than the subsample of dual-earner couples.) Over two-fifths (42.9 percent) of employed married mothers who worked fixed evenings and one-third (33.4 percent) of those who were rotators ate dinner with their children less than five days a week, in contrast to 16.3 percent of those working fixed days and 10.3 percent of those working fixed nights. Accordingly, the mean number of dinner days for those working fixed evening (4.8) and rotating shifts (5.1) is significantly smaller than it is for those working fixed days (5.9). The difference in dinner frequency between mothers working fixed nights and fixed days is small and not significant.

The adjusted mean controls for the number of hours and days worked by mothers, as well as education, since these factors may contribute to parental unavailability and attitudes about the importance of eating dinner with school-aged children. We see that these controls change the values of the means only minimally and that the significant differences by shift status remain.

TABLE 6.1   *Frequency Distribution and Unadjusted and Adjusted Means of the Number of Days Employed Mothers Ate Dinner with Their Children Age Five to Eighteen in the Previous Week, by Shift Status*

Marital and Employment Status of Mother	Number of Days Ate Dinner with Children in the Previous Week	Shift During the Previous Week			
		Fixed Day	Fixed Evening	Fixed Night	Rotating
Married mothers, at least one earner					
Children age five to eighteen (n = 1,151)	Fewer than five days	16.3	42.9	10.3	33.4
	Five or six days	25.0	18.8	26.6	25.0
	Seven days	58.7	38.3	63.1	41.6
	Mean number of days	5.9	4.8***	6.1	5.1***
	Adjusted mean number of days	5.9	4.6***	6.1	5.0***
	Number of cases	958	73	36	84
Children age five to thirteen (n = 993)	Fewer than five days	9.5	39.8	10.8	31.5
	Five or six days	22.9	16.3	21.0	27.3
	Seven days	67.6	43.9	68.2	41.2
	Mean number of days	6.2	5.1**	6.1	5.3***
	Adjusted mean number of days	6.2	5.0***	6.2	5.1***
	Number of cases	504	42	24	51
Married mothers, dual-earner					
Children age five to eighteen (n = 997)	Fewer than five days	16.1	47.2	9.0	31.1
	Five or six days	26.0	20.4	26.1	23.1
	Seven days	58.0	32.5	65.0	45.8
	Mean number of days	5.9	4.6***	6.3	5.3**
	Adjusted mean number of days	5.9	4.4***	6.3	5.2***
	Number of cases	833	62	30	72
Children age five to thirteen (n = 536)	Fewer than five days	9.5	45.2	7.4	30.3
	Five or six days	23.4	19.6	19.2	25.5
	Seven days	67.1	35.2	73.4	44.2
	Mean number of days	6.2	4.9***	6.3	5.3**
	Adjusted mean number of days	6.2	4.8***	6.5	5.2***
	Number of cases	434	35	21	46
Single mothers[a]					
Children age five to eighteen	Fewer than five days	32.2	62.7	40.3	44.6
	Five or six days	22.3	11.8	20.9	17.4

TABLE 6.1   *Continued*

Marital and Employment Status of Mother	Number of Days Ate Dinner with Children in the Previous Week	Shift During the Previous Week			
		Fixed Day	Fixed Evening	Fixed Night	Rotating
(n = 685)	Seven days	45.5	25.6	38.8	38.0
	Mean number of days	5.2	4.1***	4.9	4.6*
	Adjusted mean number of days	5.2	4.0***	4.8	4.7*
	Number of cases	535	49	27	74
Children age five to thirteen (n = 344)	Fewer than five days	22.7	63.8	41.5	38.9
	Five or six days	22.1	12.5	18.9	19.6
	Seven days	55.2	23.7	39.6	41.5
	Mean number of days	5.6	4.5*	4.9	4.6*
	Adjusted mean number of days	5.6	4.4**	4.9	4.7**
	Number of cases	270	18	14	42

Source: NSFH, wave 1.

Notes: Percentages and all means are weighted; numbers of cases are not weighted. Sample is limited to those mothers employed in the previous week with data on all relevant variables, including employment status of spouses. However, fathers may have missing values on these relevant variables, and thus the numbers of cases may differ between tables on mothers and fathers. Adjusted means are calculated by using coefficients from OLS regressions that control for education and number of hours worked in the previous week. Numbers of cases for adjusted means may lose a few cases owing to missing cases for these control variables.

Differences from day shift are significant at: *p = <0.05; **p = <0.01; ***p = <0.001

ᵃMain respondents only; includes married with spouse absent and nonmarried with a partner present.

As previously noted, teens age fourteen to eighteen may be choosing not to eat dinner with their parents rather than vice versa. When focusing on married mothers with children age five to thirteen only, we see that the negative relationship between evening and rotating work and the frequency of dinnertime spent with children obtains. This is true for the adjusted means as well.

Similar patterns are evident when we look specifically at mothers in dual-earner households and at single mothers. For each shift status, single mothers ate dinner with their children less frequently than married mothers, but the relationship between shift status and frequency of dining with children was the same for both groups. Moreover, this is true even after adjusting the means for differences in education and the number of hours and days worked and also when looking specifically at mothers with children age five to thirteen only.

As can be seen in table 6.2, employed fathers' presence at dinner

TABLE 6.2   *Frequency Distribution and Unadjusted and Adjusted Means of Number of Days Employed Fathers Ate Dinner with Their Children Age Five to Eighteen in the Previous Week, by Shift Status*

Marital and Employment Status of Father	Number of Days Ate Dinner with Children in the Previous Week	Shift During the Previous Week			
		Fixed Day	Fixed Evening	Fixed Night	Rotating
Married fathers, at least one earner					
Children age five	Fewer than five days	25.4	60.4	31.5	35.3
to eighteen	Five or six days	25.4	15.1	20.2	31.1
(n = 1,642)	Seven days	49.2	24.5	48.3	33.6
	Mean number of days	5.5	3.6***	5.2	5.0*
	Adjusted mean number of days	5.5	3.6***	5.2	5.1+
	Number of cases	1,352	90	68	132
Children age five	Fewer than five days	19.9	59.0	24.0	28.0
to thirteen	Five or six days	25.5	11.4	13.4	28.2
(n = 929)	Seven days	54.7	29.6	62.6	43.8
	Mean number of days	5.7	4.0***	5.6	5.3*
	Adjusted mean number of days	5.7	4.0***	5.5	5.3+
	Number of cases	757	55	40	77
Married fathers, dual-earner					
Children age five	Fewer than five days	26.1	61.9	33.1	32.5
to eighteen	Five or six days	27.1	11.4	27.6	38.4
(n = 993)	Seven days	46.8	26.8	39.3	29.1
	Mean number of days	5.4	3.7***	5.1+	5.0+
	Adjusted mean number of days	5.4	3.6***	5.0	5.1
	Number of cases	825	54	37	77
Children age five	Fewer than five days	17.7	59.4	32.2	25.5
to thirteen	Five or six days	27.6	4.9	17.4	33.2
(n = 531)	Seven days	54.7	35.7	50.4	41.2
	Mean number of days	5.8	4.2***	5.1	5.1+
	Adjusted mean number of days	5.8	4.1***	5.1+	5.2*
	Number of cases	435	32	22	42

Source: NSFH, wave 1.

Notes: Percentages and all means are weighted; numbers of cases are not weighted. Sample is limited to those fathers employed in the previous week with data on all relevant variables, including employment status of spouse. However, mothers may have missing values on these relevant variables, and thus the numbers of cases may differ between tables on mothers and fathers. Adjusted means are calculated by using coefficients from OLS regressions that control for education and number of hours worked in the previous week. Numbers of cases for adjusted means may lose a few cases owing to missing cases for these control variables.

Differences from day shift are significant at: +$p = <0.10$; *$p = <0.05$; **$p = <0.01$; ***$p = <0.001$

with their children is also related to shift status. Like mothers, fathers who worked evening and rotating shifts were significantly less likely than those who worked fixed days to dine with their children. About three-fifths (60.4 percent) of fathers who worked evenings ate dinner less than five days a week with their children, as compared with one-fourth (25.4 percent) of fathers with fixed day schedules. The mean difference is almost two days less per week, even when adjusting for education and the number of hours and days worked. The effect of evening work appears to be stronger for fathers than for mothers, with a mean difference of a little more than one day (see table 6.3). Like mothers, fathers were somewhat more likely to be present at the dinner table with their children when their children were age five to thirteen years of age only than were fathers whose children were in the broader age range of five to eighteen.

Specific Evening Work Hours and Dinner

It is clear that evening and rotating shifts still permit some parents to have dinner with their children regularly because of the specific hours of these shifts. Another way of viewing parental presence at dinner in terms of work schedules is to consider the extent to which they are working during standard dinner hours, regardless of their shift. I define work at dinner hours here as employment during the entire range of 4:30 P.M. to 7:29 P.M., rounded to 5:00 to 7:00 P.M. in the data presented.[7] This is an especially broad range (four hours) when one considers that commuting time would extend it further.

There is, of course, a strong correlation between shift status and employment during the hours of 5:00 to 7:00 P.M. Among mothers in our married sample with at least one earner, 87.5 percent of those working evening shifts worked at least one day during the hours of 5:00 to 7:00 P.M. (rounded), in contrast to 51.3 percent of rotators, 22.1 percent of night workers, and 11.3 percent of day workers (figures not shown). For fathers, the figures are 89.6 percent, 52.0 percent, 11.7 percent, and 14.6 percent, respectively.

The data for the analysis of employment between 5:00 and 7:00 P.M., as for the shift analysis, refer only to parents who did paid work outside the home. But unlike the shift analysis, we are describing here the frequency of days during the previous week when the respondent was engaged in evening employment at specific dinnertime hours, rather than whether he or she worked the most hours in the evenings (4:00 P.M. to midnight) for most of the days in the previous week.

Table 6.3 shows that 65.6 percent of mothers who were not em-

ployed during typical dinner hours for any of the seven days in the previous week ate dinner with at least one of their school-aged children all
seven days. As expected, the frequency with which mothers had dinner
with their children declines with the unavailability of mothers during
dinnertime. Yet 30.2 percent of mothers did report eating dinner all
seven days with their children, even though they worked three or more
days during the 5:00 to 7:00 P.M. range. It may be that many of these
mothers had a dinner break from their employment covering this time
range and were able to eat with children during this break; others may
have eaten dinner at very early or late times with their children. Over
twice as many employed mothers (65.6 percent) who did not work at all
in the previous week between 5:00 and 7:00 P.M. ate dinner with their
children all seven days, leaving about one-third who did not. When we
contrast employed mothers who were not at work during dinnertime
any of the preceding seven days with those who were at work at least
three of those days, we find a mean difference in days dining with children of 1.8. This greater average difference for the former group obtains
when controlling for education and number of hours employed. When
focusing specifically on mothers with children age five to thirteen only,
the frequency with which mothers had dinner with their children increases somewhat for all categories of mothers' days of dinnertime employment, but the contrasts between these categories are similar.

Focusing on dual-earner couples—or more specifically, dual-earner
couples with children age five to thirteen only—the frequency with
which mothers had dinner with their children decreases for all categories of mothers' days of dinnertime employment, just as it does when
looking at evening shifts. And also as in the shift analysis, single
mothers dined with their children less frequently than married mothers,
even when they seemed to be available. It is notable that 31.6 percent of
single mothers who were not working during traditional dinnertime
hours any of the seven days of the previous week ate dinner with their
children less than five days of that week; 22.1 percent if their children
were aged five to thirteen only. Again, we cannot determine with whom
these children were eating dinner, if anyone, in the absence of their
mothers. Also, although single mothers ate dinner less often with their
children than married mothers, we do not know whether this was because single mothers were more likely than married mothers to dine out
without their children.

Table 6.4 shows the expected relationship for married fathers of
lower frequencies of dining with their children the more days they were
employed between 5:00 and 7:00 P.M. And as we saw with regard to shift
work and parental presence at dinner, married fathers consistently show
lower percentages dining with their children for all of the subgroups.

TABLE 6.3 *Frequency Distribution and Unadjusted and Adjusted Means of the Number of Days Mothers Employed Between 5:00 and 7:00 P.M. Ate Dinner with Their Children Age Five to Eighteen in the Previous Week*

Marital and Employment Status of Mother	Number of Days Ate Dinner with Children in the Previous Week	Number of Days Employed Between 5:00 and 7:00 P.M.[a] in the Previous Week		
		Zero Days	One or Two Days	Three or More Days
Married mothers, at least one earner				
Children age five to eighteen (n = 1,825)	Fewer than five days	13.2	24.8	52.3
	Five or six days	21.2	29.0	17.5
	Seven days	65.6	46.2	30.2
	Mean number of days	6.1	5.6***	4.3***
	Adjusted mean number of days	6.0	5.6**	4.2***
	Number of cases	1,606	121	98
Children age five to thirteen (n = 1,040)	Fewer than five days	8.6	21.7	49.2
	Five or six days	18.1	27.4	16.2
	Seven days	73.3	51.0	34.5
	Mean number of days	6.3	5.7***	4.6***
	Adjusted mean number of days	6.3	5.7***	4.5***
	Number of cases	917	65	58
Married mothers, dual-earner				
Children age five to eighteen (n = 1,010)	Fewer than five days	14.1	24.4	56.6
	Five or six days	25.0	30.6	19.8
	Seven days	60.9	44.9	23.6
	Mean number of days	6.0	5.7**	4.0***
	Adjusted mean number of days	6.0	5.5**	4.1***
	Number of cases	818	109	83
Children age five to thirteen (n = 548)	Fewer than five days	7.8	21.0	57.3
	Five or six days	22.1	29.2	19.5
	Seven days	70.1	49.8	23.2
	Mean number of days	6.3	5.7**	4.2***
	Adjusted mean number of days	6.3	5.7***	4.2***
	Number of cases	439	61	48
Single mothers[b]				
Children age five to eighteen (n = 679)	Fewer than five days	31.6	37.8	62.9
	Five or six days	21.9	34.3	9.7
	Seven days	46.5	28.0	27.4
	Mean number of days	5.2	4.7+	4.1***

152

TABLE 6.3 *Continued*

Marital and Employment Status of Mother	Number of Days Ate Dinner with Children in the Previous Week	Number of Days Employed Between 5:00 and 7:00 P.M.[a] in the Previous Week		
		Zero Days	One or Two Days	Three or More Days
	Adjusted mean number of days	5.2	4.8	4.1***
	Number of cases	544	54	81
Children age five to thirteen (n = 341)	Fewer than five days	22.1	22.3	64.8
	Five or six days	21.7	40.0	9.6
	Seven days	56.2	37.7	25.6
	Mean number of days	5.7	5.4	4.1***
	Adjusted mean number of days	5.6	5.4	4.1***
	Number of cases	273	29	39

Source: NSFH, wave 1.
Notes: Percentages and all means are weighted; numbers of cases are not weighted. Sample is limited to those mothers employed in the previous week with data on all relevant variables, including employment status of spouse. However, fathers may have missing values on these relevant variables, and thus the numbers of cases may differ between tables on mothers and fathers. Adjusted means are calculated by using coefficients from OLS regressions that control for education and number of hours worked in the previous week. Numbers of cases for adjusted means may lose a few cases owing to missing cases for these control variables.
Differences from day shift are significant at: $^+$p = <0.10; *p = <0.05; **p = <0.01; ***p = <0.001
[a]Rounded for the actual range of 4:30 to 7:29 P.M.
[b]Main respondents only; includes married with spouse absent and single with a partner present.

Over one-fourth of fathers (26.7 percent) reported that they dined with their children all seven days in the previous week even though they worked three or more days during the 5:00 to 7:00 P.M. interval. The percentages are only slightly less if they had children age five to thirteen only or were in dual-earner households. In contrast, only 51.2 percent of fathers in households with at least one earner and children age five to eighteen who were theoretically available for dinner with their children all seven days of the week in fact did so. The figures are slightly higher for those with children age five to thirteen only, and somewhat lower for those in dual-earner households.

Shift Work and Breakfast

In contrast to their effect on dinnertime, night shifts would seem to conflict with breakfast more than evening shifts, since many parents on night (and rotating) shifts come home in the early hours to sleep, not eat. Evening shifts, on the other hand, might be most conducive to eat-

TABLE 6.4   *Frequency Distribution and Unadjusted and Adjusted Means of the Number of Days Fathers Employed Between 5:00 and 7:00 P.M. Ate Dinner with Their Children Age Five to Eighteen in the Previous Week*

Marital and Employment Status of Mother	Number of Days Ate Dinner with Children in the Previous Week	Number of Days Employed Between 5:00 and 7:00 P.M.[a] in the Previous Week		
		Zero Days	One or Two Days	Three or More Days
Married fathers, at least one earner				
Children age five	Fewer than five days	23.3	28.3	55.6
to eighteen	Five or six days	25.5	27.9	17.7
(n = 1,754)	Seven days	51.2	43.8	26.7
	Mean number of days	5.6	5.4	4.1***
	Adjusted mean number of days	5.5	5.5	4.1***
	Number of cases	1,397	136	221
Children age five	Fewer than five days	17.1	18.5	57.3
to thirteen	Five or six days	24.6	31.2	16.2
(n = 993)	Seven days	58.3	50.2	26.5
	Mean number of days	5.9	5.8	4.1***
	Adjusted mean number of days	5.8	5.9	4.1***
	Number of cases	785	81	127
Married fathers, dual-earner				
Children age five	Fewer than five days	23.9	28.8	59.6
to eighteen	Five or six days	28.6	30.6	17.2
(n = 997)	Seven days	47.5	40.5	23.3
	Mean number of days	5.5	5.3	3.9***
	Adjusted mean number of days	5.5	5.3	4.0***
	Number of cases	803	75	119
Children age five	Fewer than five days	16.5	12.8	59.0
to thirteen	Five or six days	27.3	33.5	15.6
(n = 533)	Seven days	56.1	53.7	25.4
	Mean number of days	5.9	6.0	3.9***
	Adjusted mean number of days	5.9	6.0	3.9***
	Number of cases	431	41	61

Source: NSFH, wave 1.
Notes: Percentages and all means are weighted; numbers of cases are not weighted. Sample is limited to those fathers employed in the previous week with data on all relevant variables, including employment status of spouse. However, mothers may have missing values on these relevant variables, and thus the numbers of cases may differ between tables on mothers and fathers. Adjusted means are calculated by using coefficients from OLS regressions that control for education and number of hours worked in the previous week. Numbers of cases for adjusted means may lose a few cases owing to missing cases for these control variables.
Differences from day shift are significant at: [+]p = <0.10; *p = < 0.05; **p = <0.01; ***p = <0.001
[a]Rounded for the actual range of 4:30 to 7:29 P.M.

ing breakfast with children, since unlike most parents on a day shift, parents working an evening shift do not have to leave early to go to work.

The data in table 6.5 support this expectation. Among all married couples with at least one earner and children age five to eighteen, the mean number of days employed mothers ate breakfast with their children was significantly higher only for those working fixed evenings compared with those working fixed days—3.9 and 3.1, respectively. This significance does not obtain when we adjust for differences between shift groups in education and number of hours and days employed. The means then become 3.4 and 3.1, respectively. When looking specifically at couples with children age five to thirteen only, not only were mothers more likely to eat breakfast with their children, but the mean difference in breakfast days by shift status is larger. Again, the difference in means between fixed evenings (4.6) and fixed days (3.5) is significant and becomes smaller and nonsignificant after adjusting for education and number of hours and days employed—4.2 and 3.6, respectively. Mothers in dual-earner households show the same patterns, and the differences in means between fixed evenings and fixed days in the frequency with which they ate breakfast with their children are significant only when unadjusted.

Single mothers, in contrast to married mothers, show a different pattern. Among single mothers, it is the rotators who show a relatively high prevalence of eating breakfast with their children. The difference in mean frequency for single mothers who worked rotating shifts rather than fixed days is significant (3.6 and 2.6, respectively), and the significance obtains for the adjusted means (3.7 and 2.6, respectively). When looking specifically at single mothers with children age five to thirteen only, the means are high for both fixed evening and rotating shifts, 4.3 and 4.1, but near-significant for the latter only when contrasting with fixed days (3.3, p = <.10), because rotators were a larger group than evening workers. When adjusting for education and the number of hours and days worked, the mean for fixed days remains the same (3.3) but increases to 4.3 for rotating shifts, and the difference between the two becomes significant (p = <.05).

Married fathers show higher means in the frequency with which they ate breakfast with their children age five to eighteen for those working all nonday shifts relative to those working fixed days (table 6.6). But like single mothers, it is only those on rotating shifts who show significantly more frequent breakfasts with children relative to fixed days. This pattern of statistical significance holds for fathers in all households with at least one earner and for fathers in dual-earner households, with regard to both the unadjusted and adjusted means. Fathers employed fixed nights also show a higher mean number of breakfasts

TABLE 6.5   *Frequency Distribution and Unadjusted and Adjusted Means of the Number of Days Employed Mothers Ate Breakfast with Their Children Age Five to Eighteen in the Previous Week, by Shift Status*

Marital and Employment Status of Mother	Number of Days Ate Breakfast with Children in the Previous Week	Shift During the Previous Week			
		Fixed Day	Fixed Evening	Fixed Night	Rotating
Married mothers, at least one earner					
Children age five to eighteen (n = 1,146)	Fewer than five days	65.3	55.1	62.5	63.7
	Five or six days	10.3	7.5	1.2	12.1
	Seven days	24.4	37.4	36.3	24.2
	Mean number of days	3.1	3.9*	3.6	3.2
	Adjusted mean number of days	3.1	3.4	3.5	3.1
	Number of cases	949	72	38	87
Children age five to thirteen (n = 619)	Fewer than five days	58.0	39.2	62.4	58.5
	Five or six days	11.6	10.1	0.0	9.3
	Seven days	30.4	50.6	37.6	32.2
	Mean number of days	3.5	4.6*	3.4	3.7
	Adjusted mean number of days	3.6	4.2	3.7	3.4
	Number of cases	501	42	24	52
Married mothers, dual-earner					
Children age five to eighteen (n = 992)	Fewer than five days	65.1	56.1	61.1	59.7
	Five or six days	10.8	8.0	1.4	13.9
	Seven days	24.2	36.0	37.5	26.4
	Mean number of days	3.1	3.8*	3.7	3.4
	Adjusted mean number of days	3.1	3.5	3.6	3.3
	Number of cases	823	62	32	75
Children age five to thirteen (n = 533)	Fewer than five days	57.4	40.0	65.5	54.4
	Five or six days	12.2	12.1	0.0	10.2
	Seven days	30.4	47.9	34.5	35.4
	Mean number of days	3.6	4.5*	3.2	3.8
	Adjusted mean number of days	3.6	4.3	3.6	3.5
	Number of cases	430	35	21	47
Single mothers[a]					
Children age five	Fewer than five days	73.1	67.5	84.5	54.0

TABLE 6.5   *Continued*

Marital and Employment Status of Mother	Number of Days Ate Breakfast with Children in the Previous Week	Shift During the Previous Week			
		Fixed Day	Fixed Evening	Fixed Night	Rotating
to eighteen	Five or six days	8.7	15.7	5.8	20.3
(n = 689)	Seven days	18.2	16.9	9.8	25.6
	Mean Number of days	2.6	2.9	2.5	3.6**
	Adjusted mean number of days	2.6	2.8	2.6	3.7***
	Number of cases	533	51	29	76
Children age five	Fewer than five days	62.5	48.5	90.5	40.6
to thirteen	Five or six days	12.6	16.4	4.2	26.3
(n = 347)	Seven days	24.9	35.1	5.3	33.1
	Mean number of days	3.3	4.3	2.6	4.1+
	Adjusted mean number of days	3.3	4.2	2.8	4.3*
	Number of cases	269	19	15	44

Source: NSFH, wave 1.
Notes: Percentages and all means are weighted; numbers of cases are not weighted. Sample is limited to those mothers employed in the previous week with data on all relevant variables, including employment status of spouse. However, fathers may have missing values on these relevant variables, and thus the numbers of cases may differ between tables on mothers and fathers. Adjusted means are calculated by using coefficients from OLS regressions that control for education and number of hours worked in the previous week. Numbers of cases for adjusted means may lose a few cases owing to missing cases for these control variables.
Differences from day shift are significant at: $^+$p = <0.10; *p = <0.05; **p = <0.01; *** p = <0.001
[a]Main respondents only; includes married with spouse absent and nonmarried with a partner present.

with their children, relative to those who worked fixed days, that is near-significant (p = <.10), for the adjusted means only.

Fathers in families with children age five to thirteen only, like mothers in such families, were more likely to have breakfast with their children than when they had older teenagers in the household as well. Again, the mean differences in frequency are significantly higher specifically when fathers worked fixed night and rotating shifts relative to fixed days, and they become near significant (p = <.10) when adjusting for the control variables.

In sum, we have seen that nonstandard work schedules alter the extent to which parents eat breakfast and dinner with their school-aged children, and that they do so for all family types and for fathers as well as mothers. Moreover, these schedules can increase as well as decrease

TABLE 6.6 *Frequency Distribution and Unadjusted and Adjusted Means of the Number of Days Employed Fathers Ate Breakfast with Their Children Age Five to Eighteen in the Previous Week, by Shift Status*

Marital and Employment Status of Father	Number of Days Ate Breakfast with Children in the Previous Week	Shift During the Previous Week			
		Fixed Day	Fixed Evening	Fixed Night	Rotating
Married fathers, at least one earner					
Children age five to eighteen (n = 1,649)	Fewer than five days	76.8	73.7	71.8	75.5
	Five or six days	7.6	9.6	9.0	9.1
	Seven days	15.6	16.7	19.2	15.4
	Mean number of days	2.5	2.7	2.9	3.0*
	Adjusted mean number of days	2.5	2.8	3.0+	3.1**
	Number of cases	1,361	91	66	131
Children age five to thirteen (n = 931)	Fewer than five days	73.3	64.7	64.6	74.8
	Five or six days	8.3	12.3	9.5	4.1
	Seven days	18.4	23.1	25.9	21.0
	Mean number of days	2.8	3.2	3.4	3.1
	Adjusted mean number of days	2.7	3.3	3.5+	3.3+
	Number of cases	763	53	39	76
Married fathers, dual-earner					
Children age five to eighteen (n = 997)	Fewer than five days	76.9	74.0	66.2	71.9
	Five or six days	8.2	8.2	13.5	14.9
	Seven days	14.9	17.7	20.3	13.2
	Mean number of days	2.4	2.7	3.2	3.1*
	Adjusted mean number of days	2.4	2.8	3.3+	3.2*
	Number of cases	832	54	35	76
Children age five to thirteen (n = 529)	Fewer than five days	72.4	60.4	60.2	71.7
	Five or six days	9.3	9.9	11.8	7.5
	Seven days	18.3	29.7	28.1	20.8
	Mean number of days	2.8	3.4	3.7	3.4
	Adjusted mean number of days	2.8	3.5	3.9+	3.5+
	Number of cases	437	30	21	41

Source: NSFH, wave 1.

Notes: Percentages and all means are weighted; numbers of cases are not weighted. Sample is limited to those fathers employed in the previous week with data on all relevant variables, including employment status of spouse. However, mothers may have missing values on these relevant variables, and thus the numbers of cases may differ between tables on mothers and fathers. Adjusted means are calculated by using coefficients from OLS regressions that control for education and number of hours worked in the previous week. Numbers of cases for adjusted means may lose a few cases owing to missing cases for these control variables.

Differences from day shift are significant at: $^{+}p = <0.10$; $^{*}p = <0.05$; $^{**}p = <0.01$

FIGURE 6.3   Unadjusted and Adjusted Means of the Number of Days Employed Parents Ate Dinner or Breakfast with Their Children Age Five to Eighteen in the Previous Week, for Nonday Shifts Compared with Fixed Days

| | Dinner | | | | | | Breakfast | | | | | |
| | Mother | | | Father | | | Mother | | | Father | | |
	Fixed Evening	Fixed Night	Rotating	Fixed Evening	Fixed Night	Rotating	Fixed Evening	Fixed Night	Rotating	Fixed Evening	Fixed Night	Rotating
Married parents, at least one earner												
Children age five to eighteen												
Unadjusted means	−		−	−		−	+					+
Adjusted means	−		−	−		=					#	+
Children age five to thirteen only												
Unadjusted means	−		−	−		−	+					+
Adjusted means	−		−	−		=					#	#
Married, dual-earner parents												
Children age five to eighteen												
Unadjusted means	−		−	−	=	=	+				#	+
Adjusted means	−		−	−		−						+
Children age five to thirteen only												
Unadjusted means	−		−	−	=	=	+				#	+
Adjusted means	−		−	−		−						+
Single mothers												
Children age five to eighteen												
Unadjusted means	−		−	▨	▨	▨			+	▨	▨	▨
Adjusted means	−		−	▨	▨	▨			+	▨	▨	▨
Children age five to thirteen only												
Unadjusted means	−		−	▨	▨	▨			#	▨	▨	▨
Adjusted means	−		−	▨	▨	▨			+	▨	▨	▨

Source: NSFH, wave 1.
Note: All shift comparisons are relative to fixed days. Plus (+) and minus (−) signs denote significant relationships (p = <.05); other signs (#, =) denote near-significance (p = <.10), positively and negatively, respectively.

the extent to which parents eat meals with their children, depending on the type of shift they work and whether it is breakfast or dinner. Figure 6.3 shows the significant and near-significant relationships for both the unadjusted and adjusted means. The general pattern is as follows: certain nonstandard schedules—namely, evening and rotating shifts—generally decrease the frequency with which parents have dinner with their children, both for married mothers and fathers and for single mothers. In contrast, certain nonstandard schedules increase breakfast time with children: evening schedules for married mothers, night and rotating schedules for married fathers, and rotating shifts for single mothers.

I turn next to a consideration of the relationship between nonstandard work schedules and other types of parent-child interactions.

Findings: One-on-One Parent-Child Interactions

Again, the only study I am aware of that empirically examines the relationship between work schedules and family activities is for England and Wales (La Valle et al. 2002). This study shows that "atypical" work (early mornings, late afternoons, evenings, nights, or weekends, grouped as well as Sunday separately) limits various aspects of family activities.

As noted earlier, I am particularly interested in one-on-one parent-child interactions, namely: working on a project or playing together, private talks between parent and child, and parental help with reading or homework.[8] Leisure activity away from home is also considered, although this interaction is less likely than the others to be one-on-one. As previously noted, the responses are categorical, ranging from "never or rarely" to "almost every day," and are assigned values of 1 to 6.

Shift Work

Table 6.7 shows that mothers on average interacted with their children more frequently than fathers for all these activities, regardless of family type. The mean values are consistently lower for fathers even when adjusting for education and the number of hours and days worked.

For all married households with at least one earner and children age five to eighteen, mothers who worked the night shift were significantly less likely to engage in leisure activity away from the home with their children compared with mothers who worked fixed days. This significance holds for the adjusted means. Among fathers, it was working a rotating shift that significantly decreased such leisure activity with their children, but this difference does not obtain for the adjusted means. For neither mothers nor fathers was the frequency of work on projects with their children significantly affected by their work schedule.

The frequency of talks with children and help with homework was not related to the mothers' work schedule, but it is with the fathers'. Here nonstandard work schedules *increased* fathers' engagement. Fathers who worked rotating shifts had significantly more frequent private talks with their children than fathers who worked fixed days, after adjusting for the relevant controls. And fathers who worked night shifts were significantly more likely to help with homework, again, after adjusting for the control variables.

When looking at dual-earner households, the general patterns obtain, although they are less likely to show statistical significance, particularly for fathers. This can be attributed to the fact that the number of cases is reduced more substantially for fathers than mothers when looking at dual-earners, since far more employed mothers than fathers in households with at least one earner are in dual-earner households.

Like married mothers, single mothers engaged in less leisure activity away from home with their children when they worked fixed nights relative to those who worked fixed days, but the difference is only near significance for both the unadjusted and adjusted means (<.10). Unlike married mothers, however, single mothers were significantly more likely to have private talks with their children if they worked fixed evenings rather than fixed days.

Parent-child interaction is greater overall when focusing on households with children age five to thirteen only and removing teens age fourteen to eighteen (compare total means in tables 6.7 and 6.8).[9] This finding is true for all family types. However, the exclusion of teens (and the smaller sample size) reduces the number of significant relationships between shift status and the extent of parent-child interaction. These relationships are in the same direction as when significant, but they are not as strong.

On the other hand, there are some new significant relationships for these households with children age five to thirteen only that were not evident for the larger sample. There are two for married couples: married fathers working fixed evenings are now significantly less likely to have private talks with their children than fathers working fixed days, although the difference is not significant when adjusting for the control variables. And married mothers who are rotators are now significantly less likely to help with homework than mothers working fixed days, but only after adjusting for the control variables.

Among single mothers, all four parent-child interaction variables now show significant relationships rather than only parent talks. Working fixed nights and rotating shifts now significantly reduces the extent

TABLE 6.7   Unadjusted and Adjusted Means of Employed Parents' Interaction with Children Age Five to Eighteen, by Family Type and Shift Status

Parent-Child Interaction Items		Mothers					Fathers				
		Total	Fixed Day	Fixed Evening	Fixed Night	Rotating	Total	Fixed Day	Fixed Evening	Fixed Night	Rotating
Married parents, at least one earner[a]											
Leisure activity away from home (1) "never" to (6) "daily"	Unadjusted means	3.52	3.54	3.46	2.95*	3.53	3.37	3.39	3.32	3.37	3.17
	Adjusted means	3.51	3.53	3.36	2.95*	3.50	3.37	3.38	3.31	3.39	3.23
	Number of cases	1,220	1,022	78	33	87	1,742	1,440	100	62	140
Work on project with child (1) "never" to (6) "daily"	Unadjusted means	4.12	4.12	4.08	3.93	4.28	4.03	4.04	3.95	3.99	3.99
	Adjusted means	4.11	4.12	3.92	3.88	4.24	4.02	4.03	3.92	4.05	3.97
	Number of cases	1,216	1,018	78	33	87	1,742	1,438	101	62	141
Private talks (1) "never" to (6) "daily"	Unadjusted means	4.27	4.26	4.35	4.36	4.37	3.46	3.45	3.26	3.56	3.65
	Adjusted means	4.27	4.25	4.36	4.36	4.39	3.45	3.43	3.31	3.64	3.71
	Number of cases	1,210	1,015	77	32	86	1,717	1,420	100	59	138
Help with homework (1) "never" to (6) "daily"	Unadjusted means	4.20	4.19	4.16	4.12	4.39	3.45	3.45	3.21	3.84+	3.43
	Adjusted means	4.19	4.19	4.03	4.09	4.38	3.45	3.43	3.24	4.03**	3.57
	Number of cases	1,215	1,018	77	33	87	1,738	1,436	100	62	140
Married dual-earner parents[a]											
Leisure activity away from home (1) "never" to (6) "daily"	Unadjusted means	3.54	3.55	3.45	3.03*	3.68	3.39	3.42	3.28	3.23	3.19
	Adjusted means	3.53	3.55	3.34	3.02+	3.65	3.38	3.41	3.23	3.25	3.28
	Number of cases	1,090	914	70	29	77	1,118	937	59	34	88

Work on project with child (1) "never" to (6) "daily"	Unadjusted means	4.15	4.12	4.16	4.04	4.51*	3.94	3.94	4.07	3.68	3.90
	Adjusted means	4.15	4.14	3.98	3.96	4.44+	3.93	3.93	4.02	3.76	3.93
	Number of cases	1,087	911	70	29	77	1,120	938	60	34	88
Private talks (1) "never" to (6) "daily"	Unadjusted means	4.29	4.27	4.35	4.41	4.48	3.41	3.38	3.43	3.37	3.63
	Adjusted means	4.28	4.26	4.36	4.39	4.51	3.40	3.37	3.46	3.51	3.71
	Number of cases	1,081	908	69	28	76	1,108	929	59	32	88
Help with homework (1) "never" to (6) "daily"	Unadjusted means	4.23	4.22	4.17	4.02	4.55	3.45	3.42	3.56	3.90	3.49
	Adjusted means	4.22	4.23	4.00	3.94	4.52	3.45	3.41	3.53	4.01+	3.58
	Number of cases	1,086	911	69	29	77	1,115	934	60	34	87
Single Mothers[b]											
Leisure activity away from home (1) "never" to (6) "daily"	Unadjusted means	3.54	3.56	3.46	3.09+	3.60	—	—	—	—	—
	Adjusted means	3.53	3.56	3.53	3.01+	3.50	—	—	—	—	—
	Number of cases	767	590	62	26	89	—	—	—	—	—
Work on project with child (1) "never" to (6) "daily"	Unadjusted means	4.23	4.22	4.38	3.87	4.30	—	—	—	—	—
	Adjusted means	4.25	4.23	4.40	3.99	4.32	—	—	—	—	—
	Number of cases	770	594	61	27	88	—	—	—	—	—
Private talks (1) "never" to (6) "daily"	Unadjusted means	4.48	4.45	4.86*	4.28	4.41	—	—	—	—	—
	Adjusted means	4.49	4.46	4.96**	4.26	4.45	—	—	—	—	—
	Number of cases	746	575	58	26	87	—	—	—	—	—
Help with homework (1) "never" to (6) "daily"	Unadjusted means	4.29	4.30	4.25	4.30	4.23	—	—	—	—	—
	Adjusted means	4.30	4.34	4.15	4.14	4.17	—	—	—	—	—
	Number of cases	769	592	62	26	89	—	—	—	—	—

Source: NSFH, wave 1.

Notes: Shift status in usual week. Current employment status includes with a job but not at work. Adjusted means are calculated by using coefficients from OLS regressions that control for education, hours of work, and days of work in the previous week. Numbers for adjusted means may lose a few cases owing to missing cases for these control variables.

[a] Married sample includes main respondents' spouses (that is using couples data), and includes those whose spouse's shift information is missing.

[b] Main respondents only; includes married with spouse absent and single with a partner present.

Differences from day shift are significant at: +p < 0.10; *p < 0.05, **p < 0.01.

TABLE 6.8   Unadjusted and Adjusted Means of Employed Parents' Interaction with Children Age Five to Thirteen Only, by Family Type and Shift Status

Parent-Child Interactions	Means/Number of Cases	Mothers					Fathers				
		Total	Fixed Day	Fixed Evening	Fixed Night	Rotating	Total	Fixed Day	Fixed Evening	Fixed Night	Rotating
Married parents, at least one earner[a]											
Leisure activity away from home (1) "never" to (6) "daily"	Unadjusted means	3.77	3.80	3.66	3.45	3.70	3.56	3.58	3.60	3.75	3.30+
	Adjusted means	3.75	3.79	3.52	3.56	3.60	3.55	3.56	3.59	3.80	3.32
	Number of cases	653	536	45	20	52	989	809	62	36	82
Work on project with child (1) "never" to (6) "daily"	Unadjusted means	4.59	4.61	4.60	4.23	4.56	4.43	4.44	4.26	4.48	4.41
	Adjusted means	4.56	4.60	4.48	4.35	4.37	4.42	4.43	4.22	4.54	4.39
	Number of cases	655	538	45	20	52	986	805	62	36	83
Private talks with child (1) "never" to (6) "daily"	Unadjusted means	4.42	4.41	4.47	4.65	4.39	3.72	3.73	3.33*	3.90	3.90
	Adjusted means	4.40	4.39	4.46	4.73	4.25	3.72	3.71	3.40	4.12	3.95
	Number of cases	650	534	45	20	51	970	793	61	34	82
Help with home-work (1) "never" to (6) "daily"	Unadjusted means	4.91	4.96	4.69	4.85	4.65	3.92	3.94	3.64	4.32	3.82
	Adjusted means	4.89	4.94	4.65	4.97	4.55*	3.94	3.93	3.69	4.48*	3.94
	Number of cases	654	537	45	20	52	993	812	62	36	83
Married, dual-earner parents[a]											
Leisure activity away from home (1) "never" to (6) "daily"	Unadjusted means	3.78	3.79	3.72	3.46	3.85	3.57	3.57	3.73	3.53	3.44
	Adjusted means	3.76	3.79	3.58	3.58	3.73	3.55	3.56	3.68	3.55	3.44
	Number of cases	583	477	40	18	48	601	500	34	19	48

		C1	C2	C3	C4	C5	C6	C7	C8	C9	C10
Work on project with child (1) "never" to (6) "daily"	Unadjusted means	4.61	4.60	4.73	4.26	4.74	4.40	4.41	4.51	3.87[+]	4.42
	Adjusted means	4.58	4.59	4.63	4.38	4.56	4.39	4.39	4.44	3.97	4.42
	Number of cases	586	480	40	18	48	600	499	34	19	48
Private talks (1) "never" to (6) "daily"	Unadjusted means	4.43	4.40	4.56	4.60	4.50	3.73	3.73	3.45	3.52	3.98
	Adjusted means	4.40	4.39	4.56	4.68	4.36	3.73	3.71	3.52	3.79	4.01
	Number of cases	580	475	40	18	47	594	495	33	18	48
Help with homework (1) "never" to (6) "daily"	Unadjusted means	4.92	4.97	4.68	4.81	4.69	4.02	4.02	4.19	3.79	4.01
	Adjusted means	4.91	4.96	4.65	4.93	4.60[+]	4.01	4.01	4.14	3.97	3.94
	Number of cases	585	479	40	18	48	604	503	34	19	48
Single mothers[b]											
Leisure activity away from home (1) "never" to (6) "daily"	Unadjusted means	3.76	3.83	4.14	3.08*	3.38*	—	—	—	—	—
	Adjusted means	3.76	3.83	4.17	2.93*	3.35*	—	—	—	—	—
	Number of cases	386	295	25	13	53	—	—	—	—	—
Work on project with child (1) "never" to (6) "daily"	Unadjusted means	4.58	4.60	5.06*	4.17	4.32	—	—	—	—	—
	Adjusted means	4.61	4.62	5.05[+]	4.27	4.42	—	—	—	—	—
	Number of cases	389	298	24	14	53	—	—	—	—	—
Private talks with child (1) "never" to (6) "daily"	Unadjusted means	4.66	4.71	5.07	4.43	4.26*	—	—	—	—	—
	Adjusted means	4.70	4.72	5.16[+]	4.35	4.45	—	—	—	—	—
	Number of cases	372	286	22	13	51	—	—	—	—	—
Help with homework (1) "never" to (6) "daily"	Unadjusted means	4.99	5.05	5.32	4.75	4.62[+]	—	—	—	—	—
	Adjusted means	4.99	5.04	5.37	4.68	4.52**	—	—	—	—	—
	Number of cases	389	298	25	13	53	—	—	—	—	—

Source: NSFH, wave 1.

Notes: Shift status in usual week. Current employment status includes with a job but not at work. Adjusted means are calculated by using coefficients from OLS regressions that control for education, hours of work, and days of work in the previous week. Numbers for adjusted means may lose a few cases owing to missing cases for these control variables.

[a] Married sample includes main respondents' spouses (i.e., using couples data), and includes those whose spouse's shift information is missing.

[b] Main respondents only; includes married with spouse absent and single with a partner present.

Differences from day shift are significant at: [+] $p < 0.10$; * $p < 0.05$, ** $p < 0.01$

TABLE 6.9 Unadjusted and Adjusted Means of Employed Parents' Interaction with Children Age Five to Eighteen, by Family Type and Weekend Employment Status

Parent-Child Interactions	Children Age Five to Eighteen						Children Age Five to Thirteen Only					
	Mothers			Fathers			Mothers			Fathers		
	Total	Weekday Only	Weekend[a]	Total	Weekday Only	Weekend[a]	Total	Weekday Only	Weekend[a]	Total	Weekday Only	Weekend[a]
Married parents, at least one earner[b]												
Leisure activity away from home (1) "never" to (6) "daily"												
Unadjusted means	3.51	3.57	3.36*	3.37	3.41	3.30+	3.74	3.82	3.58+	3.55	3.62	3.45*
Adjusted means	3.51	3.56	3.39+	3.37	3.37	3.36	3.74	3.79	3.61	3.55	3.63	3.43+
Number of cases	1,176	789	377	1,686	1,038	648	631	432	199	952	567	385
Work on project with child (1) "never" to (6) "daily"												
Unadjusted means	4.11	4.18	3.96*	4.02	4.04	3.97	4.56	4.63	4.41+	4.42	4.47	4.35
Adjusted means	4.11	4.15	4.15	4.02	4.02	4.01	4.56	4.58	4.52	4.42	4.52	4.27*
Number of cases	1,172	794	378	1,685	1,040	645	633	433	200	948	566	382
Private talks with child (1) "never" to (6) "daily"												
Unadjusted means	4.26	4.30	4.19	3.45	3.44	3.47	4.39	4.41	4.36	3.72	3.75	3.67
Adjusted means	4.26	4.26	4.27	3.45	3.38	3.57+	4.39	4.35	4.48	3.72	3.71	3.73
Number of cases	1,167	792	375	1,660	1,025	635	629	431	198	932	555	377
Help with homework (1) "never" to (6) "daily"												
Unadjusted means	4.19	4.26	4.06+	3.45	3.44	3.47	4.89	4.97	4.73*	3.94	3.96	3.92
Adjusted means	4.19	4.23	4.13	3.46	3.41	3.54	4.89	4.93	4.82	3.94	3.91	3.98
Number of cases	1,171	794	377	1,682	1,037	645	632	432	200	955	569	386

Married, dual-earner parents												
Leisure activity away from home (1) "never" to (6) "daily"												
Unadjusted means	3.53	3.59	3.40*	3.38	3.43	3.30	3.76	3.84	3.58*	3.56	3.61	3.47
Adjusted means	3.53	3.58	3.43	3.39	3.40	3.36	3.76	3.82	3.62+	3.56	3.62	3.45
Number of cases	1,052	717	335	1,092	676	416	564	386	178	584	355	229
Work on project with child (1) "never" to (6) "daily"												
Unadjusted means	4.14	4.20	4.03+	3.93	3.94	3.90	4.58	4.65	4.42*	4.39	4.43	4.33
Adjusted means	4.14	4.18	4.07	3.93	3.90	3.99	4.58	4.60	4.53	4.39	4.45	4.29
Number of cases	1,049	713	336	1,094	679	415	567	388	179	583	355	228
Private talks with child (1) "never" to (6) "daily"												
Unadjusted means	4.28	4.31	4.22	3.40	3.38	3.44	4.40	4.43	4.34	3.73	3.75	3.70
Adjusted means	4.28	4.28	4.29	3.40	3.31	3.57*	4.40	4.37	4.47	3.73	3.68	3.82
Number of cases	1,044	714	333	1,082	672	410	562	385	177	577	352	225
Help with homework (1) "never" to (6) "daily"												
Unadjusted means	4.23	4.28	4.11	3.45	3.42	3.50	4.91	4.99	4.74*	4.02	3.99	4.06
Adjusted means	4.22	4.26	4.15	3.45	3.09	3.29	4.91	4.98	4.85	4.02	3.96	4.11
Number of cases	1,048	713	335	1,089	675	414	566	387	179	587	357	230
Single mothers[c]												
Leisure activity away from home (1) "never" to (6) "daily"												
Unadjusted means	3.52	3.52	3.53	—	—	—	3.75	3.83	3.64	—	—	—
Adjusted means	3.53	3.53	3.52	—	—	—	3.75	3.84	3.62	—	—	—
Number of cases	722	449	273	—	—	—	365	226	139	—	—	—

TABLE 6.9   Continued

| | Children Age Five to Eighteen | | | | | | Children Age Five to Thirteen Only | | | | | |
| | Mothers | | | Fathers | | | Mothers | | | Fathers | | |
Parent-Child Interactions	Total	Weekday Only	Weekend[a]	Total	Weekday Only	Weekend[a]	Total	Weekday Only	Weekend[a]	Total	Weekday Only	Weekend[a]
Work on project with child (1) "never" to (6) "daily"												
Unadjusted means	4.25	4.21	4.30	—	—	—	4.62	4.60	4.64	—	—	—
Adjusted means	4.25	4.16	4.39+	—	—	—	4.62	4.58	4.67	—	—	—
Number of cases	725	452	273	—	—	—	368	228	140	—	—	—
Private talks with child (1) "never" to (6) "daily"												
Unadjusted means	4.49	4.42	4.60	—	—	—	4.71	4.70	4.74	—	—	—
Adjusted means	4.50	4.41	4.63+	—	—	—	4.71	4.68	4.74	—	—	—
Number of cases	701	438	263	—	—	—	351	218	133	—	—	—
Help with home- work (1) "never" to (6) "daily"												
Unadjusted means	4.29	4.28	4.31	—	—	—	4.98	4.99	4.95	—	—	—
Adjusted means	4.30	4.30	4.28	—	—	—	4.98	5.00	4.94	—	—	—
Number of cases	724	452	272	—	—	—	368	228	140	—	—	—

Source: NSFH, wave 1.

Notes: Current employment status includes with a job but not at work. Adjusted means are calculated by using coefficients from OLS regressions that control for education, hours of work, and days of work in the previous week. Numbers for adjusted means may lose a few cases owing to missing cases in education and hours and days of work last week.

[a] Working on weekdays and weekend or on weekend only.

[b] Married sample includes main respondents' spouses (i.e., using couples data), and includes those whose spouse's shift information is missing.

[c] Main respondents only, including those married with spouse absent, and those nonmarried with a partner present.

Differences from weekday-only employment are significant at: [+]p < 0.10, [*]p < 0.05, [**]p < 0.01

to which single mothers spend leisure time away from home with their children (both with and without controls). Further, working rotating shifts significantly reduces private talks (without controls only) and help with housework (controls only, near-significance without controls); the positive relationship of evening employment and private talks is still there, but it is no longer significant. Finally, working fixed evenings increases the frequency of parental work with children on projects (significant without controls, near-significant with controls).

Weekend Employment

What about weekend employment? We would expect that particularly with regard to leisure activity away from home and work on projects, the greater availability of parents on weekends would be linked with greater frequency of parent-child interaction.

The data presented in table 6.9 do not show consistently strong relationships. Among all couples with at least one earner and children age five to eighteen, the weekend employment of mothers significantly reduced leisure activity away from home with children; fathers' weekend employment was also associated with lower leisure activity, but it was only near-significant. When considering the subset of those with children age five to thirteen only, the relationship is significant for both mothers and fathers. However, in all cases the relationship becomes weaker (and not significant) after adjusting for the controls.

Similarly, among couples with at least one earner and children age five to eighteen, weekend employment significantly reduced the frequency with which mothers worked on projects with children; the relationship is near-significant for mothers with children age five to thirteen only. For fathers in both child-age groups, there is no relationship. Moreover, when adjusting for controls, the relationships for mothers weakens, but it becomes significant for fathers with children age five to thirteen only.

As for private talks with their children for this sample of couples, there is no significant relationship between the frequency of such talks and the weekend employment of either parent (only one near-significant positive relationship for fathers after adjusting for the controls). The help these parents gave with homework shows but one significant relationship: less when mothers worked weekends and had children age five to thirteen only; this relationship is near-significant for mothers with children age five to eighteen. Neither relationship is significant when comparing adjusted means.

Thus, for all married couples with at least one earner, and for all four types of parent-child interaction, there is only one significant rela-

FIGURE 6.4   *Unadjusted and Adjusted Means of Employed Parents' Interactions with Their Children Age Five to Eighteen for Nonday Shifts Compared with Fixed Days, and for Weekend Compared with Weekday Employment*

	Leisure Away								Project							
	Mother				Father				Mother				Father			
	Eve	Ngt	Rtg	Wknd	Eve	Ngt	Rtg	Wknd	Eve	Ngt	Rtg	Wknd	Eve	Ngt	Rtg	Wknd
Married parents, at least one earner																
Children age five to eighteen																
Unadjusted means		—					—	=				—				
Adjusted means		—						=								—
Children age five to thirteen only																
Unadjusted means				—			=	—				=				
Adjusted means				=			=	=							=	
Married, dual-earner parents																
Children age five to eighteen																
Unadjusted means		—									+	=				
Adjusted means		=									#				=	
Children age five to thirteen only																
Unadjusted means				—								—				
Adjusted means				=												
Single mothers																
Children age five to eighteen																
Unadjusted means	=	=							+			#				
Adjusted means	=	=							#							
Children age five to thirteen only																
Unadjusted means	—	—														
Adjusted means	—	—														

Private Talks   Homework Help

	Private Talks — Mother				Private Talks — Father				Homework Help — Mother				Homework Help — Father			
	Eve	Ngt	Rtg	Wknd	Eve	Ngt	Rtg	Wknd	Eve	Ngt	Rtg	Wknd	Eve	Ngt	Rtg	Wknd
Married parents, at least one earner																
Children age five to eighteen																
Unadjusted means							+							#		
Adjusted means								#				=			+	
Children age five to thirteen only																
Unadjusted means					−											
Adjusted means											−	−			+	
Married, dual-earner parents																
Children age five to eighteen																
Unadjusted means							+									
Adjusted means								+								
Children age five to thirteen only																
Unadjusted means														#		
Adjusted means											=					
Single mothers																
Children age five to eighteen																
Unadjusted means	+															
Adjusted means	+			+												
Children age five to thirteen only																
Unadjusted means			−								=	−				
Adjusted means	#															

Source: NSFH, wave 1.

Note: All shift comparisons are relative to fixed days, and weekend comparisons are relative to weekday employment status. Plus (+) and minus (−) signs denote significant relationships (p = <.05); other signs (#, =) denote near-significance (p = <.10), positively and negatively, respectively.

Eve = fixed evening; Ngt = fixed night; Rtg = rotating; Wknd = weekend tionship after adjusting for the control variables: fathers had a lower frequency of work on projects with their children when they worked weekends and their children were age five to thirteen only. Confining the analysis to dual-earner couples, there is also but one significant relationship after adjustment: fathers had a higher frequency of private talks with their children when those children were age five to thirteen only and when the fathers worked weekends. The adjusted means are not significant in any instance for married mothers.

Single mothers show no significant relationships between weekend employment and parent-child interaction for either the unadjusted or adjusted means. There are only two near-significant relationships for adjusted means among those with children age five to eighteen. With regard to work on projects and private talks, weekend employment increased the frequency of parent-child interaction for these mothers. This was not the case when they had children age five to thirteen only.

In sum, as shown in figure 6.4, we see a mixed picture of the relationship between parents' shift status and the extent of one-on-one parent-child interaction. We can describe a general pattern. With regard to the work shifts and the frequency of leisure activities outside the home, working nights may have minimized such activities for mothers, both married and single; rotating shifts seem to have done this for married fathers and single mothers. As for the frequency with which parents worked on projects with their children, this may have increased when dual-earner mothers worked rotating shifts and single mothers worked evenings; shift status is not associated with this activity for fathers, with the exception of one near-significant relationship. As for the frequency of private talks, single, but not married, mothers show a relationship to shift status (positive when they worked evenings and nights, negative when they rotated); married fathers show a reverse pattern from single mothers (a negative relationship with evening work and a positive relationship with rotating shifts). As for help with homework, the significant relationships for mothers of both marital statuses are negative when they were on rotating shifts, and positive for fathers when they worked night shifts. The few significant or near-significant relationships with regard to weekend employment also show a mixed picture, with only some activities seemingly related and with differences in direction by gender of parent.

Discussion

Overall, the data suggest that working nonstandard hours has an effect on parent-child interaction, particularly with regard to parental presence at meals, but also with regard to one-on-one interaction. This effect seems to be generally negative with regard to dinnertime spent together, positive with regard to breakfast time spent together, and quite mixed with regard to one-on-one parent-child interaction. There are contingencies relating to which parent, which shift, marital status, whether both spouses are employed (among the married), and whether the family has children age five to thirteen only. Most significant relationships are maintained after adjusting for the control variables.

Accordingly, we can conclude from this first look at these relationships that nonstandard work hours affect the frequency of parent-child interaction. We clearly need to undertake larger and more focused studies to better understand why there are these various contingencies. For example, a single mother is generally more likely to have private talks with her children than a married mother, which may be due in part to the fact that the children are not competing with a spouse for private time with her. But, among single mothers, why are night and evening work schedules associated with more frequent private talks than daytime schedules?

We need to also address the question of the impact on child outcomes of the frequency of parental interaction with children. What difference does it make, for instance, when parents eat meals together with their children and spouses (if married) more frequently? As noted earlier, there is a small body of literature on the effects of shift work on child outcomes suggesting some negative effects, but the frequency of parent-child interaction is not considered as a mediating factor. It is important that we explore this issue.

A form of parent-child interaction that we have not yet considered is fathers' participation in child care as a consequence of available time for such an activity because of employment during nonstandard times, either on their part or on the part of mothers. In the next chapter, we consider this issue, along with the more general topic of the greater complexity of child care when parents work nonstandard schedules.

7

The Complexity of Child Care

T HE LIMITED availability of affordable, quality child care is a serious problem in the United States. The abundance of research on
various dimensions of this problem is a response to the dramatic
growth in paid employment among mothers with young children in recent decades and the corresponding need to expand and improve child
care options (see, for example, Hayes, Palmer, and Zaslow 1990; Blau
2001; Helburn and Bergmann 2002). This discourse on the child care
needs of preschool-aged children focuses implicitly, if not explicitly, on
day care. We know that a minuscule proportion of all child care centers
are open evenings and that only somewhat higher proportions are open
on weekends.[1] With such limited availability of formal options for the
care of young children, how do parents manage when they work nonstandard schedules?

Obviously, they have to rely for the most part on informal care, and
this can mean considerable juggling with multiple caregivers. Among
dual-earner couples, this includes the sharing of child care by mothers
and fathers when the other is at work. Single mothers, who have no
spouse with whom to share child care and who usually work more
hours than married mothers, may find the juggle especially difficult.
From this perspective, it is important to look at the child care arrangements of those married and single mothers with young children who
work nonstandard schedules and compare them with the types of child
care used by mothers who work at standard times.

In this chapter, we address this issue utilizing the NSFH data. The
analysis is basically descriptive and provides the most detailed examination to date of the relationships between nonstandard work schedules
and child care use.[2] This examination includes a specification of care by
relatives and care by nonrelatives, according to family type. The extent
of multiple child care use, both including and excluding father care, is
also shown by family type. Further, among dual-earner couples, the extent of spouse overlap in employment (regardless of shift) is related to
the type of child care used.

These various dimensions of child care tap the highly complex situation that parents often face when mothers are employed. At issue in this chapter is whether this is particularly the case when mothers work nonstandard schedules and whether family type matters. Ideally, to better assess the situation we would have measures of the perceived or actual availability of alternative child care providers along with child care preferences, but the NSFH does not ask these questions. Moreover, the extent to which child care issues influenced parents' work schedule decisions cannot be determined, since NSFH respondents were not asked why they worked at nonstandard times. However, relying on the May 1997 CPS data, we are able to consider in the next chapter the extent to which "better child care arrangements" is a reason given by low-educated mothers for working nonstandard hours. (The type of child care they use is not asked in this CPS, so its relation to their reason for working nonstandard hours cannot be examined.)

What about child care arrangements for school-aged children? The NSFH did not collect such data, but we are able to consider from this survey an important aspect of parental supervision: whether they are home when children age five to eleven leave and return from school. Here is where working nonstandard schedules may be of benefit to children's well-being, as such schedules may enable a parent to be at home at such times. But as noted in the previous chapter, parental presence at home is potentially positive only if the parent is not sleeping and leaving young children alone unsupervised. Putting this issue aside, however (for lack of data), are parents more likely to be home before and after school at such times when they work nonstandard hours? And to what extent is this more the case among married dual-earner parents than among single mothers? These questions will be addressed in this chapter as well. First, let us consider what the existing literature tells us about the issues raised.

Relevant Literature

The limited literature on the relationship between parents' employment schedules and the care of children shows a heavy reliance on relative care; among dual-earner couples, many fathers provide child care when mothers are employed late and rotating hours.

National studies published in the early 1980s first began to point to these relationships with indirect evidence. James Morgan (1981), using the Panel Survey of Income Dynamics (PSID), found that among employed parents in 1979 with children under age twelve, over one-fourth reported working different shifts from their spouses as their mode of child care, although data on the specific work schedules of these parents were not reported. In an earlier work on women and child care (Presser 1982), I analyzed the June 1977 CPS and found a high prevalence of father care for preschool-aged children when mothers were employed in occupations that had high proportions working nonday shifts, but work shifts were not specifically asked in this CPS.

I directly assessed the relationship between relative care, including father care, and work shifts using data from the June 1982 CPS (Presser 1986) in a paper that included for the first time data on both child care and work shifts, but with regard to women's employment only.[3] This study showed much greater reliance on relatives when mothers worked nonday rather than day schedules. For married mothers working nondays, the primary relative providing child care was the child's father; for nonmarried mothers, the primary relative was the grandparent. Employed mothers were also asked whether the lack of satisfactory child care at reasonable cost was constraining the number of hours they worked. A significantly larger proportion of mothers who worked nondays rather than days described such constraints. Moreover, when the principal caregiver was the father, mothers were more likely to report constraint than for any other mode of child care used. I concluded that although father care may facilitate the employment of mothers with young children, it may also constrain the number of hours they work. This raises the issue of the extent to which mothers and fathers who do split-shift parenting have non-overlapping hours of employment, an issue addressed later in this chapter.[4]

Data from the 1984 wave of the National Longitudinal Survey of Labor Market Experience—Youth Cohort (NLSY) also demonstrated heavy reliance on relatives when parents worked nonday shifts (Presser 1988). Among married couples with at least one spouse age nineteen to twenty-six years and with children under age five in this sample, about half were couples with at least one spouse working a nonday shift—consistent with the finding in chapter 2 that nonday employment is higher the younger the worker.

More recent studies based on the Survey of Income and Program Participation (SIPP) for various years confirm the positive relationship between relative care and nonday shifts (O'Connell 1993; Casper 1997; Casper and O'Connell 1998). April Brayfield's (1995) analysis of the 1990 National Child Care Survey (NCCS) also considered women's weekend employment and showed significantly more father care at such times. There appears to be no research on whether multiple caregiving is more prevalent when parents work nonstandard schedules.

The literature is even more limited on the issue of parental presence when young children leave for and return from school and the relevance of parental work schedules. At best, there are occasional references in qualitative studies to certain problems of nonstandard schedules, such as keeping awake at such times or surreptitiously having children along on the job before and after school. For example, a study (Hoffman et al. 1999, 63) describes one family's situation:

> When [eight-year-old] Alexis arrived home from school on the afternoon she described, her [twelve-year-old] sister was home, and her father was home but sleeping. Soon, Alexis's mother came home, and by suppertime, the whole family was awake and ate at the same time, although the parents ate in front of the television while the children ate in the kitchen. During the meal, the babysitter arrived, and first Alexis's mother and then her father left for work. The babysitter helped get the children into bed and stayed as the children slept. In the morning, Alexis washed and dressed as her mother, who had returned home at some point during the early morning, slept. Her father came home from work in time to make breakfast for the children, and to see them off to school. The typical pattern in this family is that the father is sleeping in the afternoon when the children come home from school, and the mother is sleeping in the morning as the children wake up and get ready for school.

In another study, a night nurse who hired a woman to pick up her son from kindergarten says: "I still have to wake up to get him in [the house] and that breaks my sleep already and I try to go back to sleep but then you cannot really go to sleep because leaving a five-year-old alone [laughs]—you don't know what he's getting into" (Garey 1999, 135).

Taking children to work surreptitiously before and after school was reported in a qualitative study of bus drivers working shifts, even though it was explicitly against city transit policy (Grosswald 1999). The children would ride the bus while their parent drove. However, most shift workers are in occupations (for example, waitressing, nursing, sales) that would make it exceedingly difficult to disregard company policy in this way.

This study is not qualitative in nature. In this chapter, the objective is to add to the literature by descriptively portraying in some detail how nonstandard work schedules affect child care patterns for preschool-aged children and parental presence at home for school-aged children.[5]

General Hypotheses

The general hypothesis is that child care varies substantially by work schedule status and by family status. It is expected that parents working rotating shifts and weekends with preschool-aged children rely on the most complex forms of child care, as compared with parents on fixed day and weekday only schedules. Moreover, single parents rely on more complex forms of child care than married couples. It is also expected that parents will be present at home when school-aged children leave and return from school more frequently when they work other than fixed days.

Sample Considerations

Mothers who were main respondents in the NSFH were asked for all the types of child care used for their children under age five while they were employed.[6] The reference period was the previous week. Of the 753 employed mothers with such young children who answered the child care questions, 698 also answered the work schedule questions. Although mothers were asked how many hours each provider cared for their child, when there were two or more young children, one cannot determine whether these hours referred to caring for these children simultaneously or separately. Because of this lack of specificity for mothers with more than one child under age five and the small number of such mothers, some of the analyses were done separately for those with only one child and compared with all mothers with young children, whether one or more.

As previously noted, mothers with school-aged children were not asked detailed questions in the NSFH about after-school child care arrangements. However, they were asked whether a parent is at home when children leave and return from school and, if not, who cares for the child at these times (if anyone). The number of main respondent mothers with school-aged children who answered questions about before- and after-school care as well as work schedule questions is 1,018 and 984, respectively.

Findings: Work Schedules and Child Care for Children Under Age Five

Figure 7.1 shows the distribution of child care arrangements made while mothers were employed, for the total and for dual-earners and single mothers separately. The latter group is further refined to consider only single mothers who did not have a partner in the household, since some of these partners may have been the child's father, although the number reporting a partner present was only thirty-six.[7] Mothers indicated all of their arrangements for their children under age five while they were working. Those who worked fully at home are excluded from this analysis (and all other tables), since they were not asked the work schedule questions.[8]

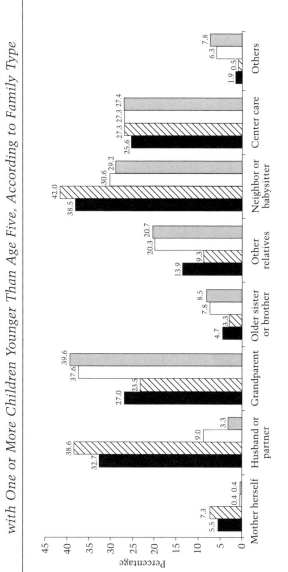

FIGURE 7.1   Distribution of Child Care Arrangements in the Previous Week of Employed Mothers with One or More Children Younger Than Age Five, According to Family Type

- ■ All employed mothers (n = 751–753)[a]
- ▨ Dual-earner married mothers (n = 352–354)[a]
- ☐ All employed single mothers (n = 276)
- ▨ Employed single mothers without partner present (n = 240)

Source: NSFH, wave 1.
Note: Respondents may report more than one arrangement; thus sums may exceed 100 percent. All employed mothers include separated and nonmarried mothers. Some fathers in single-mother households who do not live in the same household may be included as care provider. Center care includes daycare center, nursery school, preschool, and kindergarten.
[a]Numbers vary owing to missing values.

For all employed mothers, the most common arrangement (38.5 percent) was a neighbor or baby-sitter (often referred to as "family day care"), followed closely by the husband or partner (32.7 percent), then a grandparent (27.0 percent) and center care (25.6 percent). The basic difference between dual-earner married mothers and single mothers was the higher use by the former of care by husbands or partners and neighbors or baby-sitters; single mothers (with and without a partner present) relied more heavily than those married on grandparent care and other relatives. The same rankings and differences obtain when considering the subset of mothers with only one child under five (595 of the 753 mothers).

To what extent does the mother's work schedule affect the type of arrangements made? As noted earlier, we would expect that those working at nonstandard times would rely more on relatives for child care than those on standard schedules. It is not only that formal arrangements such as child care centers and family dare care are typically restricted to standard daytime hours and weekdays, but that parents may prefer not using formal care outside the home at late hours. Among dual-earner couples, spouses may accommodate to these restraints by working different shifts and splitting child care. However, their shifts are often not completely different, leaving some hours during which both spouses are at their jobs and other caregivers may be needed. Similarly, when employed mothers working nonstandard hours rely on grandmothers or other relatives employed during the daytime to provide evening or night care, other caregivers also may be needed because of some overlap in their work hours. The extent of non-overlap in work hours is addressed here but limited to dual-earner spouses, since the work schedules of other relatives were not obtained in the NSFH.

Work Shifts and Types of Child Care

Table 7.1 shows the distribution of child care arrangements for children under age five while mothers were employed, according to work shift and family type. Considering first the work shift of all employed mothers, we see that late and rotating shifts enhanced the likelihood of husbands or partners caring for children while the mothers were at work (64.4 percent and 50.2 percent, respectively). Grandparent care was relatively high when mothers were on rotating shifts (42.7 percent) as compared with fixed shifts, whether they were fixed days, evenings, or nights. Center care and care by neighbors or baby-sitters was highest for those working fixed days relative to other shifts. Mothers cared for children while they were at work infrequently; this was almost exclusively

TABLE 7.1 Distribution of Child Care Arrangements in the Previous Week of Employed Mothers with One or More Children Younger Than Age Five, by Mother's Shift Status, According to Family Type

Care Provider	All Employed Mothers			Dual-Earner Married Mothers			All Employed Single Mothers[a]			Employed Single Mothers Without Partner Present		
	Day	Evening and Night	Rotating	Day	Evening and Night	Rotating	Day	Evening and Night	Rotating	Day	Evening and Night	Rotating
Mother herself	6.0%	2.6%+	2.8%	8.1%	4.9%	5.0%	0.3%	0.0%	0.9%	0.4%	0.0%	1.1%
Husband or partner[b]	24.9	64.4***	50.2***	29.2	80.9***	61.5***	5.0	17.9*	15.9+	1.6	5.0	9.2
Grandparent	24.0	22.2	42.7***	22.7	7.6**	40.8*	30.9	36.5	57.5**	32.4	40.1	57.3**
Older sister or brother	3.3	7.7	6.8	2.3	1.4	7.4	5.5	15.5+	9.9	6.9	18.5+	5.6
Other relatives	14.3	15.8	18.6	9.8	13.8	8.8	19.3	22.3	26.6	21.0	26.7	18.9
Neighbor or baby-sitter	41.9	22.7***	35.1	47.5	18.2***	35.9	29.9	28.3	27.7	27.3	27.1	27.4
Center care[c]	32.3	12.9***	10.3***	33.8	12.7***	9.7***	37.3	7.1***	17.4**	38.5	8.5***	14.5**
Others	2.2	0.7	2.9	0.8	0.0	0.0	6.7	2.7	9.3	8.4	3.2	11.6
Number of cases	504–6[d]	103	89	241–43[d]	43	37	178	41	41	153	36	36

Source: NSFH, wave 1.

Note: Respondents may report more than one arrangement; thus, sums may exceed 100 percent.

[a] Includes separated and nonmarried mothers.

[b] Some fathers who do not live in the same household may be included.

[c] Includes day care center, nursery school, preschool, and kindergarten.

[d] Numbers vary owing to missing values.

T-tests for significance compare the weighted mean for the standard work schedule category with that of each of the other nonstandard work schedule categories: $^+p = <.10$; $^*p = <.05$; $^{**}p = <.01$; $^{***}p = <.001$

the practice of dual-earner married mothers. Over half (54.9 percent) of all the mothers who reported that they cared for their own children while employed were child care workers (not shown), a fact that would explain the higher prevalence of mother care during day shifts relative to other shifts. (Again, mothers who worked fully at home are excluded from this analysis; accordingly, so are mothers who provided family day care in their own home.)

Family type makes a difference in caregiving arrangements. The prevalence of father care is most striking among dual-earner married couples, particularly when mothers were employed nondays (and virtually all fathers were employed during the daytime). Among such couples with children under age five, when mothers worked fixed evenings or nights, 80.9 percent of fathers (husbands and/or partners) cared for these children; when mothers worked a rotating shift, the figure was 61.5 percent. Whereas grandparent care for children of dual-earner parents was not very prevalent when mothers worked evenings or nights (only 7.6 percent), it was quite high (40.8 percent) when these mothers were on rotating schedules. This suggests that grandparents are often needed to complement father care, because even when spouses work different shifts, some of the hours they work may be the same—an issue to be addressed shortly.

Single employed mothers (separated or not married) do not have the benefit of husbands in the household to provide child care, although a notable minority appeared to have a partner living with them who did so, as well as a partner not residing in the household providing such care. Single employed mothers compensated for the general absence of fathers to share child care with much greater reliance on grandparents as providers (36.5 percent when mothers worked evenings or nights, and 57.5 percent when they were rotators) relative to married employed mothers. The minimal use of center care when single mothers worked evenings and nights (7.1 percent) is in line with the limited availability of center care at such late hours. Center care was higher when single mothers were rotators (17.4 percent); the extent to which this was day care utilized when rotators were on the day shift or center care available around the clock is undeterminable.[9]

The unavailability of formal child care arrangements when mothers worked weekends also put heavier demands on child care by relatives. In cases when there was more than one caregiver, and more than one type of nonstandard work schedule (nonday shifts and weekend employment), we cannot differentiate which caregiver was providing child care at which time. Considering both shift work and workdays simultaneously, we can assess the extent to which the mother's working one or both types of nonstandard schedules affected the type of child care used.

We see in table 7.2 the high reliance on relatives when mothers worked nondays and/or weekends, with about two-thirds of fathers (64.3 percent) caring for their children in dual-earner households under such conditions and over two-fifths (40.8 percent) of grandparents providing such care in single-parent households.

Work Shifts and Relative Care: Sole and Combination

The heavy reliance on fathers, grandparents, and other relatives for child care during nonstandard hours raises the important issue of the extent to which those working nonstandard schedules are relying on relatives exclusively for child care when mothers are employed, given the scarcity of formal child care arrangements at such times, or are depending on nonrelative care as well (both formal and informal). This issue also relates to whether the number of care arrangements made when mothers work nonstandard schedules is greater than when they work at more standard times.[10]

As may be seen in table 7.3, reliance on relative care *only* was significantly greater when women worked nonstandard rather than standard schedules: for all employed mothers, the percentages are 49.6 percent and 29.3 percent, respectively. The combination of relative and nonrelative care was also significantly greater for those working nonstandard than standard schedules: 31.5 percent and 23.2 percent, respectively. Sole reliance on nonrelatives for child care was the predominant mode when mothers were working standard hours—close to one-half, as compared with only one-fifth when mothers worked nonstandard schedules.

Sole reliance on relative care was about as frequent for all family types presented (almost half). However, consistent with the previous analysis, the role of fathers differed by family type. Among dual-earner couples, it is notable that over one-fifth of husbands (20.8 percent) provided the sole care of children when mothers were employed on a nonstandard schedule. An additional 13.9 percent did so in conjunction with other relatives. Among single mothers, it was other relatives who constituted almost all of the sole relative care. Combinations of relative and nonrelative care were somewhat higher among those who worked nonstandard than standard schedules for all family types. Correspondingly, reliance on nonrelatives only was substantially higher for mothers who worked standard rather than nonstandard schedules—about one half for all family types.

TABLE 7.2 Distribution of Child Care Arrangements in the Previous Week of Employed Mothers with One or More Children Younger Than Age Five, by Mother's Shift and Weekday and/or Weekend Working Status, According to Family Type

Care Provider	All Employed Mothers		Dual-Earner Married Mothers		All Employed Single Mothers[a]		Employed Single Mothers Without Partner Present	
	Day Shift and Weekday Employment Only	Nonday Shift or Weekend Employment	Day Shift and Weekday Employment Only	Nonday Shift or Weekend Employment	Day Shift and Weekday Employment Only	Nonday Shift or Weekend Employment	Day Shift and Weekday Employment Only	Nonday Shift or Weekend Employment
Mother herself	7.0%	2.4%**	9.2%	3.9%+	0.0%	0.7%	0.0%	0.9%
Husband or partner[b]	21.5	51.3***	23.2	64.3***	4.1	13.7*	2.4	4.7
Grandparent	22.2	31.4**	21.1	25.5	29.2	40.8	31.2	41.5
Older sister or brother	2.5	7.1**	1.6	4.6	6.4	9.6	8.1	9.7
Other relatives	12.0	18.4*	8.6	12.6	13.9	26.9*	14.2	27.3*
Neighbor or baby-sitter	41.8	34.2*	45.5	37.8	32.2	27.9	29.3	27.1
Day care center[c]	32.2	19.6***	32.7	21.6*	39.6	19.9**	41.7	19.1**
Others	1.9	2.3	1.0	0.0	6.5	6.8	8.2	8.5
Number of cases	380–81[d]	310–11[d]	189–90[d]	131–32[d]	122	135	104	118

Source: NSFH, wave 1.

Note: Respondents may report more than one arrangement; thus, sums may exceed 100 percent.

[a] Includes separated and nonmarried mothers.

[b] Some fathers who do not live in the same household may be included.

[c] Includes daycare center, nursery school, preschool, and kindergarten.

[d] Numbers vary owing to missing values.

T-tests for significance compare the weighted mean for the standard work schedule category with that of the nonstandard work schedule category: + p = <.10; * p = <.05; ** p = <.01; *** p = <.001

TABLE 7.3 Distribution of Combinations of Child Care Arrangements in the Previous Week of Employed Mothers with One or More Children Younger Than Age Five, by Mother's Shift and Weekday and/or Weekend Working Status, According to Family Type

Care Provider	All Employed Mothers		Dual-Earner Married Mothers		All Employed Single Mothers[a]		Employed Single Mothers Without Partner Present	
	Day Shift and Weekday Employment Only	Nonday Shift or Weekend Employment	Day Shift and Weekday Employment Only	Nonday Shift or Weekend Employment	Day Shift and Weekday Employment Only	Nonday Shift or Weekend Employment	Day Shift and Weekday Employment Only	Nonday Shift or Weekend Employment
Relatives only	29.3%	49.6%***	26.2%	47.7%***	28.9%	47.9%***	30.0%	48.5%*
Husband or partner only[b]	2.8	14.5***	2.0	20.8***	1.8	2.5	0.8	0.0
One or more other relatives only[c]	22.2	22.1	20.1	13.2+	27.1	42.4**	29.2	47.6*
Husband and/or partner and other relatives	4.2	13.1***	3.9	13.9**	0.0	2.7+	0.0	0.6
Nonrelatives only[d]	47.4	18.8***	47.5	18.5***	53.8	24.5***	52.1	26.0***
Both relatives and nonrelatives	23.2	31.5*	26.3	33.8	17.3	27.4+	17.9	25.2*
Number of cases	379–81[e]	310–11[e]	188–90[e]	131–32[e]	122	134–35[e]	104	117–18[e]

Source: NSFH, wave 1.
[a]Includes separated and nonmarried mothers.
[b]Some fathers who do not live in the same household may be included.
[c]Includes "mother herself" and/or "grandparent" and/or "older sister or brother" and/or "other relatives" only.
[d]Includes "neighbor or baby-sitter" and/or "center care" and/or "others" only.
[e]Numbers vary owing to missing values.
T-tests for significance compare the weighted mean for the standard work schedule category with that of the nonstandard work schedule category: +p = <.10; *p = <.05; **p = <.01; ***p = <.001

All Multiple Child Care Use

Putting aside the issue of relative versus nonrelative care, to what extent are children cared for by two or more caregivers, and how does this vary by mother's work schedule?

As shown in table 7.4, among all employed mothers with children under age five in this sample, 41.0 percent reported having two or more child care arrangements. This is consistent with the finding from the 1995 SIPP showing that 44 percent of all children under age five were cared for in multiple arrangements (Smith 2000).[11] Family type is relevant, with dual-earner married mothers showing greater reliance on multiple caregiving than single employed mothers. This result, as we will see, is affected by the fact that the child's father is included as a provider for dual-earners.

For each family type, the mother's work schedule was clearly linked to whether she relied on multiple child care arrangements. (The significance tests reported in this table are based on a comparison of weighted means, with the nonstandard schedule compared with the standard schedule.) First, with regard to shift status, we see in table 7.4 that the percentage of all employed mothers using multiple caregivers was significantly higher when mothers worked a rotating (51.0 percent) as compared with a fixed day shift (38.6 percent). The higher percentage for rotators is to be expected, given that shift rotation creates a variable spread of hours—and days—in which child care is needed, making it especially difficult to rely on only one child care source. The especially high prevalence of multiple caregiving among dual-earner couples when mothers rotated points to the difficulties of fathers being available to meet child care needs fully under such conditions. However, because of the smaller number of dual-earner couples as compared with all employed, the contrast in multiple care between such rotating mothers (54.0 percent) and those who worked fixed days (42.8 percent) is not statistically significant. The lack of significance also holds when comparing multiple care for children of single mothers by shift status, even though rotators showed a higher percentage using multiple care (41.9 percent) than those on day shifts (29.6 percent). When single mothers worked fixed evenings or nights, the extent of the multiple care they used was not too different from what they used when they worked fixed days—a finding that is consistent with the results for dual-earner mothers.

It is not only mothers who worked rotating shifts who were most likely to rely on multiple caregivers, but also those who worked weekends. Indeed, the majority of employed mothers who worked weekends (52.9 percent) relied on two or more caregivers, in contrast to one-third

TABLE 7.4   *Employed Mothers of One or More Children Younger Than Age Five with Two or More Child Care Arrangements, by Mother's Work Schedule, According to Family Type*

Mother's Work Schedule	All Employed Mothers	Married Mothers and/or Dual-Earner Couples	All Employed Single Mothers[a]	Employed Single Mothers Without Partner Present
Shift status				
Total	41.0%	43.5%	31.7%	31.6%
	(694)	(320)	(259)	(224)
Day	38.6	42.8	29.6	31.8
	(502)	(240)	(177)	(152)
Evening and night	43.2	38.0	29.3	27.9
	(103)	(43)	(41)	(36)
Rotating	51.0*	54.0	41.9	34.4
	(89)	(37)	(41)	(36)
Weekday/weekend status				
Total	40.3	42.9	30.9	30.6
	(719)	(337)	(264)	(229)
Weekdays only	34.0	36.6	25.3	28.4
	(461)	(235)	(145)	(124)
Weekdays and weekends or weekends only	52.9***	57.8***	38.0*	33.4
	(258)	(102)	(119)	(105)
Shift and weekday and/or weekend status				
Total	41.3	43.6	31.7	31.5
	(688)	(319)	(256)	(221)
Day shift and weekday employment only	33.2	35.9	25.8	28.6
	(379)	(188)	(122)	(104)
Nonday shift or weekend employment	51.7***	54.5***	36.9[+]	34.1
	(309)	(131)	(134)	(117)

Source: NSFH, wave 1.
Note: The number of child care arrangements refers to the previous week and includes mother who takes the child to work; the husband or partner; the child's grandparent; the child's older sister or brother; other relative of child; a neighbor or baby-sitter; a day care center; or another provider. Numbers of cases are in parentheses.
[a]Includes separated and nonmarried mothers.
T-tests for significance compare the weighted mean for the standard work schedule category with that of each of the other nonstandard work schedule categories: [+]p = <.1; *p = <.05; **p = <.01; ***p = <.001

(34.0 percent) of those who worked weekdays. The difference between these two categories was statistically significant not only for all employed mothers but for the subsets of dual-earner married mothers and all single employed mothers.

Since some mothers work both late hours and weekends, it is appropriate to consider their combined schedules in relation to multiple caregiving. We see at the bottom of table 7.4 that mothers who worked a nonday shift and/or weekends were significantly more likely to rely on multiple caregivers for their preschool-aged children (51.7 percent) than those who worked daytime shifts on weekdays only (33.2 percent). A nonstandard schedule was significantly associated with multiple caregiving for the subset of dual-earner married mothers and near-significant for single employed mothers.

In sum, although multiple caregiving was highly prevalent for young children when mothers were employed, regardless of their work schedules, it was especially likely when mothers worked at nonstandard times. This finding holds for both married dual-earner mothers and single employed mothers, although it is not always statistically significant given the smaller numbers when looking at family type subgroups.

Non-overlap in Spouse's Employment and Relative Care

Thus far we have been considering the specific time of day or week that mothers are employed. For dual-earner couples, we can also address the issue of the extent to which there is non-overlap in the wife's and husband's work schedules. Specifically, we can relate the hours or days that a husband is not employed when his wife is employed, and consider the extent to which this enhances father care and other types of relative care. This analysis does not consider the specific shifts of spouses; that is, the extent of non-overlap in spouses' work hours is assessed similarly both for spouses who work the same shift (for example, both working mostly days) and for spouses who work different shifts.

As shown in figure 7.2, among dual-earner married couples, only one-third (32.2 percent) of mothers worked all the previous week's hours within the range of their husband's work hours. Close to one-fifth (19.1 percent) of dual-earner mothers worked twenty or more hours outside this range; that is, their husbands were not employed during at least twenty of the weekly hours they were employed. When we exclude couples in which either the mother or father was not a rotator—that is, both spouses worked a fixed schedule—the extent of non-overlap is somewhat less: 36.8 percent had no hours in which mothers were work-

FIGURE 7.2   *Distribution of the Number of Hours and Days Mothers Worked in the Previous Week When Fathers Were Not Working, for Dual-Earner Married Couples with Children Younger Than Age Five*

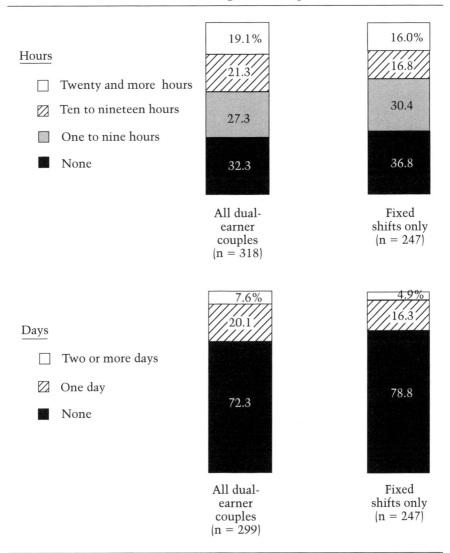

Source: NSFH, wave 1.
Note: The sample selects only from main interview respondents. The category "fixed shifts only" excludes couples in which either the mother or father works a rotating shift.

189

ing when fathers were not, and 16.0 percent had twenty or more hours of such non-overlap.

There is considerable non-overlap in the work days as well as work hours of dual-earner spouses. As may be seen in figure 7.2, over one-fourth (27.7 percent) of mothers were employed at least one day in which their husbands were not employed; the proportion is somewhat less (21.2 percent) when we exclude couples with a rotator. For 7.6 percent of couples, there were at least two days in the week during which mothers were working but fathers were not; this was true for 4.9 percent of fixed shift dual-earners.

Does the increased availability of fathers for child care, as tapped by the extent to which they were not at work when mothers were, generate a greater likelihood that they will participate in such care? As expected, the data indicate this is so.

Figure 7.3 shows the distribution of child care arrangements by the number of hours mothers were employed when fathers were not. Couples with at least one spouse on a rotating schedule are excluded here, since changing hours of employment confound the notion of spouse availability.

We see that the more hours fathers were not at work when mothers were, the more likely fathers were to be the *sole* source of child care, rising to one-fifth (24.6 percent) when the non-overlapping hours were twenty or more. The non-overlap in work hours between spouses is also related to reliance on relative care more generally. Reliance on relative care *only* (including father care) was more likely when spouses had some non-overlap rather than none, and the combination of both relative and nonrelative care was especially likely when there were ten or more hours of non-overlap. Correspondingly, reliance on non-relatives *only* was comparatively high when there were less than ten hours of non-overlap.

As may be seen in figure 7.4, non-overlap in the *days* in which dual-earner spouses worked (excluding rotators) was also associated with greater reliance on father care alone (16.9 percent) than when wives worked all of their days within the same range as their husbands (5.8 percent). So too was the couple's greater reliance on relatives in general, either exclusively or in combination with nonrelatives, when there was some non-overlap in workdays between spouses. Dual-earner spouses were almost four times as like to rely on nonrelative care only when wives worked at least one day in which husbands were not at work (47.2 percent) than when there were no such days (12.8 percent).

FIGURE 7.3   *Distribution of Child Care Arrangements in the*
Previous Week of Dual-Earner Married Mothers with
Children Younger than Age Five, by Mother's Number
of Working Hours Not Overlapped with Father's

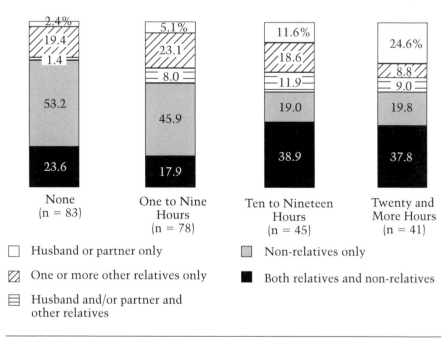

Source: NSFH, wave 1.
Note: Some fathers who do not live in the same household may be included. Relatives
include "mother herself" and/or "grandparent" and/or "older sister or brother" and/or
"other relatives" only. Non-relatives include "neighbor or baby-sitter" and/or "center
care" and/or "others" only. The sample only selects from main interview respondents, and
excludes couples with one or both spouses rotating.

Nonparental Multiple Child Care Use

As we have seen, the availability of fathers among dual-earner couples
to provide child care enhances the use of multiple care among such couples. But one could argue that although father—and mother—care during the hours mothers are employed may add to the stress of juggling
work and family for parents, the child is unlikely to view either type of
parental care as a special child care arrangement but rather as part of the
larger picture of parental care when parents are home. Accordingly, it is
of interest to consider the extent to which parents rely on multiple *non-*

FIGURE 7.4   *Distribution of Child Care Arrangements in the Previous Week of Dual-Earner Married Mothers with Children Younger than Age Five, by Mother's Number of Working Days Not Overlapped with Father's*

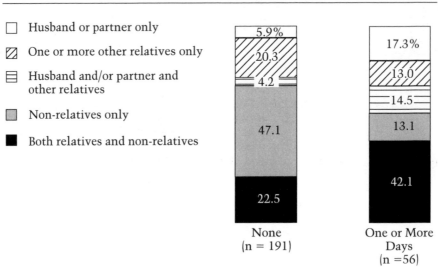

Source: NSFH, wave 1.
Notes: Some fathers who do not live in the same household may be included. Relatives include "mother herself" and/or "grandparent" and/or "older sister or brother" and/or "other relatives" only. Non-relatives include "neighbor or babysitter" and/or "center care" and/or "others" only. The sample only selects from main interview respondents and excludes couples with one or both spouses rotating.

parental caregivers for their children when mothers are employed. We do so by returning to a consideration of specific shifts and weekend employment.

We see in table 7.5 that even when we exclude father and mother care when mothers were employed, the extent of multiple child care arrangements was substantial—over 22 percent. Yet relying on two or more types of nonparental child care was rare among dual-earner couples in which the wife worked evenings or nights (only 1.4 percent). Again, multiple child care was highest among rotators (although the difference relative to day workers was not significantly significant).

Having multiple nonparental caregivers was significantly more common among mothers who worked weekends than weekdays only for all those employed (27.9 percent versus 19.2 percent, respectively). Substantial differences are evident for both married and single mothers, al-

TABLE 7.5　*Employed Mothers of One or More Children Younger Than Age Five with Two or More Nonparental Child Care Arrangements, by Mother's Work Schedule, According to Family Type*

Mother's Work Schedule	All Employed Mothers	Married Mothers and/or Dual-Earner Couples	All Employed Single Mothers[a]	Employed Single Mothers Without Partner Present
Shift status				
Total	22.3%	21.0%	28.6%	30.0%
	(694)	(320)	(259)	(224)
Day	23.3	23.7	28.3	31.8
	(502)	(240)	(177)	(152)
Evening and night	10.9***	1.4***	19.2	22.9
	(103)	(43)	(41)	(36)
Rotating	28.6	26.1	38.4	30.1
	(89)	(37)	(41)	(36)
Weekday/weekend status				
Total	22.1	21.3	27.8	29.0
	(719)	(337)	(264)	(229)
Weekdays only	19.2	19.3	24.2	27.0
	(461)	(235)	(145)	(124)
Weekdays and weekends or weekends only	27.9**	26.0	32.3	31.5
	(258)	(102)	(119)	(105)
Shift and weekday/ weekend status				
Total	22.4	21.0	28.4	29.9
	(688)	(319)	(256)	(221)
Day shift and weekday employment only	19.7	19.7	25.8	28.6
	(379)	(188)	(122)	(104)
Nonday shift or weekend employment	25.7+	22.9	30.8	31.0
	(309)	(131)	(134)	(117)

Source: NSFH, wave 1.

Note: The number of nonparental child care arrangements refers to last week, and includes child's grandparent; child's older sister or brother; other relative of child; neighbor or babysitter; day care center; or other provider.

[a]Includes separated and nonmarried mothers.

T-tests for significance compare the weighted mean for the standard work schedule category with that of each of the other nonstandard work schedule categories: +p = <.1; *p = <.05; **p = <.01; ***p = <.001

193

though when examined separately (and thus having fewer cases), differences are not statistically significant.

When combining shift and weekend status, those working nonstandard schedules were more likely to rely on multiple nonparental child care. However, the difference is only near-significant (<.1) for all employed mothers and not significant when looking at each family type separately.

In sum, use of multiple nonparental child care was widespread, especially when mothers worked nonstandard schedules. Father care when mothers worked fixed evening and night shifts served to deflate substantially the need for nonparental multiple care arrangements for dual-earner couples. For others, and especially for single women who were rotators or working weekends, there was considerable reliance on multiple nonparental care.

Findings: Work Schedules and Parental Presence at Home Before and After School

Although the care of children under age five may be more complex and difficult when parents work other than a regular day shift, the care of school-aged children may benefit when parents work nonstandard hours. In particular, parents who work evenings, nights, or a rotating shift may be more likely to be home when children go off to school and to be there when children return from school than when they work days. This benefit, as noted earlier, may depend on whether parents who work nonstandard hours and are at home during the daytime are in fact awake rather than asleep when their children leave or return from school, a topic generally neglected in studies of employed parents.

The NSFH asked the following question of main respondent mothers with children age five to eleven: "How often are you (or your husband/partner) at home when your child(ren) leave(s) for school in the morning? Would you say it was: always, usually, sometimes, rarely, or never?"[12] Eighty percent of all employed mothers responded "always" or "usually." Mothers were also asked: "How often are you (or your husband/partner) at home when your child(ren) get(s) out of school?," with similar response categories. For these afternoon hours, only 57.4 percent of mothers responded that a parent was home "always" or "usually."[13]

Tables 7.6 and 7.7 show parental presence at home before and after school by mother's shift and according to family type. We see that when mothers worked evenings and nights or on rotating shifts, parents were significantly more likely to be home before their children went to

TABLE 7.6   *Employed Mothers with Children Age Five to Eleven Who Report That a Parent Is Always or Usually Home Before Children Go to School, by Mother's Shift Status, According to Family Type*

Mother's Shift	All Employed Mothers	Dual-Earner Married Mothers[a]	All Employed Single Mothers[b]	Employed Single Mothers Without Partner Present
Day	77.2%	82.3%	61.9%	60.4%
	(807)	(311)	(361)	(329)
Evening and night	94.8***	96.0**	90.2***	88.2***
	(96)	(26)	(55)	(48)
Rotating	87.7**	92.8**	79.1**	74.6*
	(115)	(48)	(53)	(47)
Total	80.0	84.6	67.5	65.4
	(1018)	(385)	(469)	(424)

Source: NSFH, wave 1.
[a]Excludes those married mothers with spouse absent.
[b]Includes separated and nonmarried mothers.
T-tests for significance compare the weighted mean for the standard work schedule with that of each of the other nonstandard work schedule categories: *p = <.05; **p = <.01; ***p = <.001

school, either "always" or "usually." Mothers' evening and night schedules also made it significantly more likely that a parent would be home, "always" or "usually," when children got out of school; rotating shifts also seemed to enhance this likelihood, but the difference relative to fixed days was only near-significant for all employed mothers. Again, although parents who worked late hours were more likely to be at home when the children left for school, many may have been sleeping at such early morning hours. This possibility is most relevant for single mothers, who do not have another parent in the household to supervise at this time.

These relationships for mothers' shift and parental presence were evident both for dual-earner married mothers and single mothers, although the extent of parental presence was always lower for single mothers. This was most evident for those working days. This finding is to be expected, since among married dual-earner couples with a mother working days, the father may be working nondays and thus be present at home when the children leave for or return from school. Most single mothers are not living with their children's father, and thus such parental sharing of care in this way is not typically an option.

TABLE 7.7   *Employed Mothers with Children Age Five to Eleven Who Report That a Parent Is Always or Usually Home When Children Get Out of School, by Mother's Shift Status, According to Family Type*

Mother's Shift	All Employed Mothers	Dual-Earner Married Mothers[a]	All Employed Single Mothers[b]	Employed Single Mothers Without Partner Present
Day	54.7	57.3	35.3	31.5
	(774)	(303)	(339)	(309)
Evening and night	72.3***	77.2*	67.1***	67.7***
	(96)	(26)	(55)	(48)
Rotating	63.9+	71.7+	46.1	39.9
	(114)	(48)	(52)	(46)
Total	57.4	60.6	40.8	37.1
	(984)	(377)	(446)	(403)

Source: NSFH, wave 1.

[a]Excludes those married mothers with spouse absent.

[b]Includes separated and nonmarried mothers.

T-tests for significance compare the weighted mean for the standard work schedule with that of each of the other nonstandard work schedule categories: +p = <.1; *p = <.05; **p = <.01; ***p = <.001

When there was no parent home before or after school, children were generally cared for by others: 84.6 percent before school and 89.3 percent after school. For the remaining families—15.4 percent and 10.7 percent, respectively—children age five to eleven were alone at these times. Children this young rarely had to look after themselves when mothers worked evenings or nights; rather, such self-care was most evident when mothers worked days or on a rotating schedule. Interestingly, even with the small number of cases on which these percentages of children in self-care are based by shift, they did not differ much by family type (data not shown). The total percentages were consistent with the findings of other national studies—for example, the 1999 National Survey of America's Families, which reported that 10 percent of children age six to twelve take care of themselves when parents are employed (Sonenstein et al. 2002). However, all survey estimates are probably an underestimate of the number of "latchkey" children, since parents may be very reluctant—for security reasons as well as to avoid embarrassment—to report to an interviewer that their child is at home alone.

The shift pattern of married dual-earner couples determines the availability of parents to be home before children leave for school and

TABLE 7.8   *Employed Mothers with Children Age Five to Eleven*
              Who Report That a Parent Is Always or Usually Home
              When Children Leave for and Return from School, by
              Couple's Shift Status, According to Family Type

Couple's Shift	Before School	After School
Both day	81.1%	52.9%
	(241)	(233)
One or both nonday	90.4*	72.4***
	(109)	(109)

Source: NSFH, wave 1.
Notes: Only mothers/main respondents were asked the question. The sample excludes those married mothers with spouse absent.
T-tests for significance compare the weighted mean for the couple's day shifts with one or both nonday shifts:*p = <.05; **p = <.01; ***p = <.001

when they return. As may be seen in table 7.8, when one or both spouses worked a nonday schedule (including rotating), it was significantly more likely that a parent would be home both when the child left for school and when he or she returned, relative to the traditional pattern of both spouses working days.

Discussion

Public discourse on the complexity of child care when mothers work nonstandard hours is minimal. The limited care options outside the family at such times are, as the Women's Bureau (U.S. Department of Labor 1995, 25) aptly puts it, "a sleeper issue relative to other work/family issues." The bureau further states that it would take "a 'champion'—either from management, labor, or the community—to make the issue a priority." To date, there has been no such champion. Most people, including the press, missed the statement that First Lady Hillary Rodham Clinton made at the Democratic National Convention in Chicago in 1996: "Right now there are mothers and fathers just finishing a long day's work, and there are mothers and fathers just going to work. Some to their second and third jobs of the day." Although it is remarkable that she explicitly acknowledged in this political speech the late hours that parents work, she did not mention the child care constraints of such late-hour employment, even though she has had a long-term interest in the care and well-being of America's children. Perhaps in her current role as a U.S. senator she has discussed the child care dilemma in other talks, or will in the future; it may require a person with her stature and commitment to child care issues to bring this issue to the fore politically.

Some people might argue that the heavy reliance on relatives for child care at nonstandard times negates the problem, and that we therefore need not be concerned. For example, Ron Haskins (1988, 13), in his article "What Day Care Crisis?," notes the high level of relative care for preschool-aged children and concludes: "Thus, millions of parents can vote with their feet in the child care market." This conclusion does not acknowledge the possibility that in this "vote," the "list of candidates" may consist of few, if any, alternatives—especially for parents of young children who work nonstandard schedules. Nor does this it allow for the possibility that although care by relatives facilitates women's employment—because it is generally free or of low cost (Casper 1995)—it also constrains the number of hours women work and thus their total earnings (Presser and Baldwin 1980; Presser 1988; Mason and Kuhlthau 1992).

Also, many of the relatives who provide child care when mothers are employed—most of whom are fathers and grandmothers—are often themselves otherwise employed, but at different hours than the mother. Among dual-earner couples, this is so for fathers by definition. But as noted in chapter 3, mothers and grandmothers also split shifts and share care. The only national data on the employment status of grandmothers who care for young children indicate that one-third of these grandmothers are otherwise employed; moreover, those who care for the children of their nonmarried daughters are more likely to be employed than those who care for the children of their married sons and daughters (Presser 1989b).

This complex situation leads one to ask whether child care by relatives generates considerable stress for the caregivers, perhaps more so than with nonrelative care, and whether it may be less stable over time. As I stated in an earlier study on grandmother care (Presser 1989b, 588): "The underlying assumption is that a relative is more emotionally committed to the child and will provide more loving care than a nonrelative. This may be true in most cases—although never empirically tested— but it is only one factor of many that should be considered when assessing care provided by a relative."

The need to assess many factors when looking at relative care also applies to father care among dual-earner couples. There may be special benefits to both father and child in the greater day-to-day interaction of such a caregiving arrangement. For example, as we have seen in chapter 6, fathers who work nights may have more one-on-one interaction with their children with regard to such activities as helping with homework. But we have also seen in chapter 4 that among married couples, when parents work night shifts (facilitating their involvement in daytime child care), the marriage is less stable. These findings point to the need to weigh the short-term family benefits among dual-earner couples of split-shift caregiving against possible long-term family costs.

We have seen that, in addition to greater reliance on relative care, nonstandard work schedules are associated with greater use of multiple child care providers. Multiple caregiving is especially vulnerable to disruption, because there are multiple possibilities of these arrangements breaking down. And there is a general sense (in the absence of data) that instability in child care arrangements is not good for children as well as stressful for parents. The NSFH data suggest that it is single mothers who are working weekends or a rotating schedule who are especially at risk of such problems. And as we have seen from the CPS data presented in chapter 3, single mothers working nonstandard schedules are especially likely to have low earnings, further limiting their child care options.

Child care for school-aged children may be less complex when parents work nonstandard rather than standard schedules than it is for children under age five. We have seen that when mothers work evenings, nights, or a rotating shift, or when either partner of a dual-earner couple does so, children are more likely to go off to school and come home with a parent present—in contrast to when parents work days. As cautioned earlier, parental presence is beneficial at these times if we assume that parents working late or rotating hours are in fact awake rather than asleep when their children leave or return from school and thus are providing supervision. Otherwise, unless there are other caregivers around, these children must be added to the ranks of "latchkey" children, the notable minority of children age five to eleven who are home alone when they leave for and return from school. The parents of these latter children are more likely to work days or on a rotating schedule than evenings or nights.

The small sample size for parents with children in the NSFH precludes detailed analysis of the low-income population. Moreover, the NSFH does not provide data on the extent to which child care is the main reason for working nonstandard schedules. In the next chapter, we address this issue for low-educated mothers using data from the May 1997 CPS. Although this data source is large enough to analyze the work schedules of these mothers in detail, it does not include data on their child care arrangements. Nevertheless, we get a good picture of the misfit between their work schedules and the availability of formal types of child care.

8

Implications for Low-Educated Mothers

THE PROVISION of child care subsidies for poor women has been a special concern of public policy, particularly in the context of moving those on welfare into paid jobs (Blau, Ferber, and Winkler 2001; Helburn and Bergmann 2002). Researchers and policy analysts focus most commonly on the limited range of hours that child care is available relative to parents' daytime work—and commuting—hours; rarely do they examine the lack of fit between evening and night employment and child care availability. In the previous chapter, we saw that the arrangements made by parents who work nonstandard hours and weekends are highly complex and that they rely heavily on informal caregivers, particularly relatives. The potential stress and instability of such arrangements and the declining availability of relatives as caregivers (Presser 1989a) are issues that raise the question of whether there should be more subsidization of child care not only during the daytime for poor employed mothers who need such care, the current policy focus, but at nonstandard times as well. Our ability to address both needs has a direct bearing on the extent to which women with young children are able to move from welfare to paid employment and remain employed, as well as on the effectiveness of employment and child care policies in general.

The few studies that address the unmet need for child care at nonstandard hours include one conducted by the Women's Bureau, which highlighted the experiences of some companies and communities around the nation that have served as a resource for helping to manage the problem (U.S. Department of Labor 1995). Similarly, focusing on New York City, the United Neighborhood Houses prepared a policy brief on the need for around-the-clock child care, indicating that as of November 1998, among 1,478 licensed, center-based, child care providers included in the city's central resource and referral database, only one offered care on a twenty-four-hour-a-day schedule, only twenty offered care during some evening and night hours, and only three offered weekend child care hours (Marks, Edelstein, and Turetsky 1998). A study of twelve companies from major industries in the greater Boston area that employed nonstandard workers showed that most were aware of the need for child care at nonstandard hours, especially during the "shoulder hours"—early morning and evening during the week and weekend hours. But few of these companies subsidized child care at such times, and only one company, the MBTA (Massachusetts Bay Transportation Authority), conducted research to assess the need among its employees. Indeed, companies that offered on-site care were reluctant to offer care during nonstandard hours, citing the higher cost, logistical barriers, or philosophical concerns (Fried and Clifton 1998; WEIU and PUCC 1998). A recent study of child care for low-income families in the United States indicated that the most frequently reported child care shortage was during nonstandard work hours (Collins et al. 2000).

Neither the NSFH nor the CPS data permit a direct assessment of the need for subsidized child care at nonstandard times. However, the May 1997 CPS data do allow us to view the labor force context that produces the demand for late-hour care by examining the work schedules of low-educated employed mothers—the labor force group closest to mothers on welfare.[1] (Education rather than income is the socioeconomic measure, since we have data on income only for a subset of this sample.)

A first consideration is the extent to which such mothers work nonstandard schedules relative to higher-educated mothers. In other words, are the needs for child care at nonstandard times greater for the lower-educated? The second consideration is the specific jobs that low-educated mothers hold. Are their occupations a source of variation in their work schedule behavior? Third, we consider the main reasons that low-educated mothers give for working nonstandard schedules, with a special interest in assessing the extent to which they report personal-familial reasons as distinct from job constraining reasons. Are most low-educated women with young children who work nonstandard schedules choosing to do so primarily for child care purposes—they can share child care with relatives or others who work during the daytime—or do most of these mothers have to find child care at nonstandard times because they have the kinds of jobs that demand such schedules? This question is further addressed in a multivariate analysis that assesses the relative influence of personal and job characteristics.

Sample Considerations

This chapter relies on the same data source described in chapter 2, the May 1997 CPS. From this sample of about fifty thousand households, I selected for this chapter women age eighteen to thirty-four who had a

TABLE 8.1   Distribution of Work Schedules of Employed Women Age Eighteen to Thirty-Four, by Education, Parental Status, and Marital Status, and Comparisons with Employed Women Age Eighteen and Over

| Work Schedules | Employed Women Age Eighteen to Thirty-four with Children Under Age Fourteen | | | | | All Employed Women Age Eighteen and Over with Children Under Age Fourteen | All Employed Women Age Eighteen and Over |
| | With High School Education or Less | | | With More Than a High School Education | | | |
	Single	Married	Total	Total	Total		
Hours							
Fixed day	74.6%	81.7%	78.8%	81.4%	80.1%	82.6%	81.8%
Fixed evening	11.1	8.5	9.6	9.3	9.4	7.6	8.0
Fixed night	7.2	3.7	5.2	3.7	4.4	4.2	3.7
Hours vary	3.8	3.3	3.5	3.0	3.3	3.2	3.7
Rotating	3.3	2.7	2.9	2.6	2.8	2.4	2.7
Days							
Weekday only, five days	55.1	61.4	58.8	61.4	60.1	61.4	61.4
Weekday only, fewer than five days	5.9	11.8	9.3	12.1	10.7	12.2	10.7
Seven days	7.2	4.7	5.7	6.1	5.9	6.0	6.9
Weekday and weekend, fewer than seven days	30.9	21.4	25.4	19.7	22.5	19.7	20.2
Weekend only, one or two days	1.0	0.7	0.8	0.8	0.8	0.7	0.8
Combination							
Fixed day, weekdays only	51.4	64.8	59.3	65.3	62.3	62.6	64.8
Other than fixed day, weekdays only	9.5	8.4	8.9	8.1	8.5	8.5	7.3
Fixed day with at least some weekend	23.2	16.9	19.5	16.1	17.8	17.9	17.1
Other than fixed day, plus weekend	15.9	10.0	12.4	10.5	11.4	11.1	10.8
Number of cases	659	1,002	1,661	1,762	3,423	7,412	23,203

Source: May 1997 CPS.

Notes: Percentages are weighted; numbers of cases are not weighted. Sample includes only those who have data on both work hours and work days in previous week.

high school education or less, at least one child under age fourteen, and at least one job for pay the previous week, and whose primary occupation (the one in which they worked the most hours) was in non-agricultural. The number of respondents who had these characteristics as well as complete data on the work schedule variables is 1,661, and they represented about 4.1 million persons. For comparison purposes, I also present data on the broader sample of employed women. (The numbers are shown at the bottom of table 8.1.) All percentages reported are weighted for national representativeness.

The work schedules are defined exactly as in chapter 2. The specific work hour shifts and workday patterns are shown separately and in combination.

Work Schedule Behavior

We see in table 8.1 that about three-fourths (78.8 percent) of low-educated employed women age eighteen to thirty-four with children under age fourteen worked fixed daytime hours, and about two-thirds (68.1 percent) worked weekdays only, five days or less. When measures on hours and days are combined, we see that about three-fifths (59.3 percent) of these mothers worked a standard, fixed daytime schedule during weekdays only—and two-fifths (40.7 percent) did not. Moreover, one-eighth (12.4 percent) of these mothers worked both nonstandard hours *and* weekends.

Single mothers comprise two-fifths (39.7 percent) of those who are low-educated in this age range. Almost half of them (48.6 percent), as compared with one-third of married mothers (35.2 percent), did not work fixed daytime schedules on weekdays only. As shown in table 8.1, single mothers were more likely than married mothers to work other than a fixed day shift (25.4 percent and 18.3 percent, respectively) and to work on weekends (39.1 percent and 26.8 percent, respectively).[2]

Comparing the other columns in table 8.1, we see that this low-educated group of mothers (married and single combined) was more likely to work nonstandard schedules, in terms of both hours and days, than its more educated counterparts. The percentage distributions for those with more than a high school education are close to those shown for all employed women with children, regardless of age, and for all employed women, with and without children. Interestingly, being a mother per se does not seem to be as relevant to work schedule behavior as being low-educated.

Occupations and Work Schedules

As we have seen in chapter 2, occupation is a highly relevant source of variation in work schedule behavior. Relatively high percentages of many of those in service occupations work nonstandard hours and weekends. This has special relevance for the female labor force, because women work disproportionately in the service sector and are crowded into relatively few occupations compared with men (Bergmann 1986; Blau et al. 2001). This crowding is particularly evident when we focus on employed women age eighteen to thirty-four with at most a high school education and with children under fourteen years of age. Close to half (45.6 percent) of such women fall into the fifteen occupations listed in table 8.2; indeed, almost one-fourth (22.9 percent) are in the top five occupations. (By comparison, among all employed women age eighteen and over, 41.4 percent fall into the fifteen occupations, and 16.4 percent are in the top five occupations; not shown.)

Exceptionally high proportions of mothers in many of the fifteen occupations listed in table 8.2 work nonstandard schedules, in terms of either hours or weekends. Moreover, one-fifth or more of mothers working in six of these occupations work both nonstandard hours *and* weekends: cashiers; nursing aides, orderlies, and attendants; waitresses; cooks; sales workers, retail and personal services; and hairdressers and cosmetologists. Indeed, about one-third of waitresses and sales workers work both types of nonstandard schedules. Surely these women cannot rely on formal child care arrangements for the care of their children— whether preschool- or school-aged.

Reasons for Working
Nonstandard Hours

It may be argued that women are working these nonstandard hours because they are able to use nonformal child care arrangements. Since such arrangements are generally less expensive than formal child care, this may facilitate the employment of mothers—a consideration especially relevant to women who are in low-paying jobs. However, the data suggest that while this may be a primary motivating factor for many, it is not so for most mothers who work such schedules.

As noted in chapter 2, the CPS asked those working nonstandard hours their main reason for doing so. For all mothers so employed with a child younger than age five, 35.3 percent gave "better child care arrangements" as their main reason; when the youngest child was age five to thirteen, the percentage was 24.5. When we look specifically at low-educated mothers (table 8.3), these percentages are somewhat higher:

37.2 and 29.8, respectively. As would be expected, married mothers are more likely to say their main reason was better child care (38.2 percent) than single mothers (31.3 percent), since many of the former have spouses who provide child care, as shown in the previous chapter. This is a no-cost option, as distinct from relatives, with whom there is often a monetary or exchange cost (Presser 1989b).

Even when considering all personal-familial reasons as a group—that is, combining "better child care arrangements" with "better arrangements for other family members," "allows time for school," and "easier commute"—such considerations remain a minority response among mothers as compared with job constraining reasons, namely "could not get another job," "mandated by employer," and "nature of the job." Although a multiplicity of factors may be relevant when mothers decide to work nonstandard hours, the fact that child care is the main reason for only one-third of them is significant. Other reasons need to be considered when explaining the high prevalence of employment during nonstandard hours among mothers, and many of these may not be a matter of personal preference but rather an accommodation to labor market needs.

Multivariate Analysis: Determinants of Working Nonstandard Schedules

Recognizing that, for some mothers, working a nonstandard schedule fits their personal needs while for others it does not, we turn to the issue of how influential their personal demographic characteristics are as determinants of their work schedule behavior, after controlling for differences in their job characteristics. Table 8.4 presents a multivariate analysis of this issue, distinguishing the determinants of working nonstandard hours, weekends, and both nonstandard hours and weekends—the most complex of all work schedules. The figures in the table are odds ratios derived from logistic regressions; a ratio of unity means equal likelihood relative to the omitted category; less than this means a lower likelihood, and more indicates a greater likelihood.

We see in the first column of table 8.4 that among the personal-demographic characteristics, only the number of children is significantly related to nonstandard work hours for low-educated employed women. Each additional child increases the odds of working nonstandard hours by 20 percent. (Not being a high school graduate also has a high odds ratio, 1.32, but this is only near significance, at <.10). When weekend employment is the dependent variable (same column), being

TABLE 8.2   *Distribution of Nonstandard Work Schedules in Common Occupations of Women Age Eighteen to Thirty-Four with a High School Education or Less and with Children Under Age Fourteen*

Rank	Occupation	Number of Cases	Percentage in Occupation	Nonstandard Hours			Weekends	Both Nonstandard Hours and Weekends
				Fixed Evenings and Nights	Rotating, Irregular Hours	Total		
		1,661	100%	14.8%	6.5%	21.2%	31.9%	12.4%
1	Cashiers	105	6.3	23.0	12.3	35.3	64.9	25.2
2	Secretaries	84	5.1	5.5	3.1	8.6	6.9	2.0
3	Nursing aides, orderlies, and attendants	72	4.3	26.9	3.5	30.4	48.6	21.1
4	Supervisors and proprietors, sales occupations	64	3.9	6.8	6.5	13.3	41.5	7.2
5	Waitresses	55	3.3	29.9	10.0	39.9	67.5	30.5

6	Family child care providers	51	3.1	12.7	2.2	14.9	10.6	5.0
7	Bookkeepers, account- ing, and auditing clerks	48	2.9	3.6	4.7	8.3	11.4	4.4
7	Investigators and adjus- ters	48	2.9	5.5	3.3	8.8	13.4	5.4
9	Cooks	44	2.6	22.2	6.4	28.7	59.3	22.5
10	Sales workers, retail and personal services	38	2.3	12.4	26.4	38.8	54.7	32.3
11	Maids	33	2.0	11.0	0.0	11.0	57.1	7.8
12	Hairdressers and cosme- tologists	31	1.9	7.9	12.8	20.7	69.0	19.8
12	Assemblers	31	1.9	18.5	2.9	21.4	6.5	0.0
14	Janitors and cleaners	27	1.6	30.1	0.8	30.8	23.3	11.6
14	Textile sewing machine operators	27	1.6	14.5	0.0	14.5	3.7	0.0

Source: May 1997 CPS.
Notes: Percentages are weighted; numbers of cases are not weighted. Sample includes only those who have data on both work hours and work days in previous week.

TABLE 8.3   *Distribution of Main Reason Reported for Working Nonstandard Hours for Women Age Eighteen to Thirty-Four with Children Under Age Fourteen, by Age of Youngest Child and by Marital Status*

Main Reason		With High School Education or Less				
	Total	Total	Youngest Child Under Age Five	Youngest Child Age Five to Thirteen	Married	Single
Personal-familial reasons	44.3%	42.7%	42.3%	43.3%	48.2%	37.3%
Better child care arrangements	33.2	34.7	37.2	29.8	38.2	31.3
Better arrangements for care of family members	8.3	6.7	4.7	10.5	9.1	4.3
Allows time for school	2.6	1.0	0.4	2.2	0.4	1.6
Easier commute	0.2	0.3	0.0	0.8	0.6	0.0
Better pay	3.7	4.5	3.9	5.5	3.2	5.7
Job constraining reasons	44.9	45.2	44.8	45.9	41.9	48.4
Could not get any other job	11.2	14.3	14.7	13.6	9.8	18.7
Mandated by employer	5.3	6.3	6.0	6.8	5.3	7.2
Nature of the job	28.4	24.6	24.2	25.5	26.8	22.5
Other reasons	6.9	7.7	9.0	5.2	6.7	8.7
No response/ don't know	0.2	0.0	0.0	0.0	0.0	0.0
Number of cases	576	299	198	101	157	142

Source: May 1997 CPS.
Notes: Percentages are weighted; numbers of cases are not weighted. Sample excludes those with missing data on shift status in the previous week.

married significantly reduces the odds of working Saturday and/or Sunday (.74), and having children significantly increases the odds (1.21). However, when working both nonstandard hours *and* weekends is the dependent variable, only the number of children is statistically significant (1.31).

TABLE 8.4   *Odds Ratios of Working Nonstandard Hours, Weekends, or Both for Employed Women Age Eighteen to Thirty-Four with a High School Education or Less and with Children Under Fourteen Years, According to Selected Characteristics*

Selected Characteristics	Nonstandard Hours	Saturday and/or Sunday	Nonstandard Hours and Weekends
Personal-demographic characteristics			
Married	0.82	0.74*	0.77
Age	0.76	0.74	0.78
Age squared	1.00	1.01	1.00
Not high school graduate	1.32	1.04	1.03
Race and ethnicity			
White	1.00	1.00	1.00
Black	1.08	1.21	1.19
Hispanic	0.72	0.99	0.69
Other	1.03	1.48	1.21
Number of children	1.20*	1.21*	1.31**
Youngest child under age five	1.09	1.03	1.15
Job characteristics			
Part-time	1.38*	0.91	1.16
Has more than one paid job	2.01*	0.89	2.38*
Private sector or self-employed	1.76	1.62	2.02
Industry			
Distributive	1.00	1.00	1.00
Extractive	1.77	3.41	3.24
Transformative	0.88	0.33***	0.51*
Producer	0.49**	0.30***	0.26***
Social	0.60*	0.33***	0.58
Personal	0.80	1.17	0.85
Occupations			
Secretaries	1.00	1.00	1.00
Supervisors and proprietors, sales	1.30	5.34**	2.62
Cashiers	2.94*	9.96***	7.32*
Other technical, sales and administrative support	2.22	4.27**	6.08*
Waitresses	5.24**	13.10***	14.89**
Nursing aides	3.71*	14.86***	8.60*
Family child care providers	1.86	2.45	2.31
Other service	2.39	7.00***	6.07*
All managerial and professional specialties	1.68	4.54**	3.65

TABLE 8.4   *Continued*

Selected Characteristics	Nonstandard Hours	Saturday and/or Sunday	Nonstandard Hours and Weekends
All precision production, craft and repair	0.78	3.84*	2.28
All operators, fabricators and laborers	2.71*	2.64	3.99
Intercept (log odds)	1.74	2.09	0.03
Number of cases	1,649	1,649	1,649

Source: May 1997 CPS.
Note: Omitted categories are women who are: white; not married (including separated); not high school graduates; work full-time; have only one paid job; government workers; employed in a distributive industry; and secretaries.
*p = <0.05; **p = <0.01; ***p = <0.001

In all three models, various job characteristics show significant relationships to work schedule behavior. With regard to nonstandard work hours, the variables that significantly increase the odds of such practice are working part-time (1.38), having a second job (2.01), and being a cashier, waitress, or nursing aide; in these occupations the odds of working nonstandard schedules are 2.94, 5.24, and 3.71 greater, respectively, than they are being a secretary.[3] The job characteristics that significantly decrease the odds of working nonstandard hours are being in the producer or social industries (0.49 and 0.60, respectively, relative to the distributive industry).

Unlike nonstandard work hours, weekend employment is not influenced by part-time status or multiple job holding. All but two of the occupational groups listed are significantly more likely to include mothers who work weekends relative to secretaries: supervisors and proprietors in sales, cashiers, other technical, sales and supportive, waitresses, nursing aides, other services, all managerial and professional specialties, and all precision production, craft and repair. It is the cashiers, waitresses, and nursing aides who are especially likely to work weekends: they are 9.96, 13.10, and 14.86 times more likely, respectively, to work weekends than secretaries.

Overall, this analysis indicates that although the number of children may be a relevant personal-demographic factor influencing the decision to work nonstandard hours and weekends, and that marital status is an additional factor for those working weekends, it is job characteristics—and particularly occupation—that seem to be the strongest determinants. This finding is consistent with the reasons most women give for working other than daytime schedules—that the nature of the job is the compelling factor.

Discussion: Implications for Child Care and Welfare Reform

For those mothers who must seek child care because they are working nonstandard hours, rather than working such a schedule because it allows for a preferred child care arrangement, the minimal availability of formal child care options at such times can be a problem. This may be especially the case if the mothers are in the low-paying jobs characteristic of those with low education. We cannot provide a precise percentage of mothers who fall into this category, but the findings in this chapter suggest that it is substantial. Moreover, we have been looking at mothers who are employed—that is, mothers who have managed to find some child care (or rely on self-care) while they are at work. As we saw in the previous chapter, those working a nonstandard schedule are especially likely to depend on relatives (including husbands, if married) to provide the needed care. One cannot assume that this is the preferred mode of care for many—or most—women, or that it does not generate special stresses on interpersonal relationships as compared with nonrelative care. Clearly, we need more research on this issue.

It is also important to consider mothers who must work for financial reasons but whose job opportunities are limited to those that require working nonstandard hours and who cannot rely on relatives or other informal means of child care. We know from earlier studies that the lack of acceptable child care constrains both the employment of mothers and the number of hours they work. This is the case for all mothers, regardless of educational level or work schedule behavior. Specifically, it is estimated that from 10 to 20 percent of all non-employed mothers with young children do not seek employment because of child care availability and affordability problems. In addition, about 20 to 25 percent of employed mothers report that they would work more hours if they did not experience child care constraints (Presser and Baldwin 1980; Hayes, Palmer, and Zaslow 1990). Although the May 1997 CPS did not ask such questions, these estimates would undoubtedly be higher if we were able to examine this issue specifically for low-educated mothers, and far higher if we were able to do so for low-educated mothers working nonstandard hours.

The lack of such data is telling. We have come a long way in the past decade in documenting the need for expanded child care services and subsidies for the working poor, but the discourse has been primarily about *day* care. Surely, there is much to do on this front. But as the findings of this chapter suggest, the need for expanding care in the evening, at night, and on weekends also requires our attention. This is critical if we are to fully address the needs of low-income working mothers and of non-employed poor mothers who cannot find a daytime job but might be able to get a job at nonstandard hours if there were available (and affordable) child care. As noted at the outset of this chapter, some attempts have been made to meet this need, both privately and publicly, but they have been minimal. At a time when there are problems in expanding the supply (and affordable quality) of day care for low-income women, it may be especially difficult to find providers willing to depart from the eight- to ten-hour daytime range of hours and offer care at variable nondaytime hours. One approach to overcoming this resistance is to offer providers more money to do so. Higher reimbursement rates are offered to providers of care at nonstandard times in special programs funded by some states, but such incentives to date are very limited (Ewen et al. 2002).

Efforts to expand the availability of formal child care during nonstandard hours for low-income mothers have special relevance to the implementation of welfare reform and the effectiveness of employment and child care policies in general. The 1996 Personal Responsibility and Work Opportunity Reconciliation Act (PRWORA) specifically mandates the movement of mothers from welfare to work with certain time limits for subsidies linked to the age of children. The proposed reauthorization of this act under consideration at the time of this writing would extend the mandate from thirty to forty hours a week, which would be especially hard on mothers who work nonstandard hours, given the child care problems discussed here.[4]

We can expect that the kinds of jobs that will be held by mothers moving from welfare to work—and their work schedules—would be similar to the experience of low-educated mothers currently in the labor force. In other words, we can expect two-fifths of these mothers to work nondaytime and/or weekend schedules—one half if they are single mothers. Indeed, these are minimal estimates, since those with little employment experience may have the fewest employment opportunities and be especially likely to work generally undesirable hours. Accordingly, the implementation of welfare reform may be compromised by the poor fit between the temporal nature of job opportunities and the times during which formal child care is available. This undoubtedly puts pressure on relatives, friends, and neighbors to provide child care at nonstandard hours, regardless of their disposition to do so. It may also enhance the likelihood of self-care among children or care by older siblings still too young to assume this responsibility.

Such problems may also be faced by nonwelfare mothers who need paid employment and either have no informal networks to rely on for child care or would prefer formal child care arrangements but cannot afford them. Their only option may be to work nonstandard schedules and rely on their spouse (if married), other relatives, or other informal caregivers to provide child care at low—or no—financial cost and accept the stresses that may ensue from more complex arrangements than from daytime employment with formal child care.

We do not know whether mothers saying that work during nonstandard hours allows for "better child care arrangements" reflects the situation just described, or whether instead they are generally satisfied with these hours, with few if any drawbacks. There surely are some mothers who fit into the latter category. However, we should be cautious not to assume that so many mothers with young children are working nonstandard work schedules because they see this as an ideal or "effective" child care strategy. This position has been deduced from qualitative studies based on small samples (Deutsch 1999; Rubin 1994; Williams 2000; Greenspan with Salmon 2001). Moreover, split-shift child care between parents is sometimes promoted as a way to deal with the child care problem among dual-earners without allowing for potential difficulties (see, for example, Etzioni 1993).[5]

Whatever the reality is—and we surely need more research to better determine this—it is important that work and family policies take into account the late and rotating hours of many of the jobs that mothers with young children hold or are offered when they seek employment. To do so raises many policy-relevant questions yet to be addressed. For example, should mothers in government jobs (local, state, and federal) be given preference over nonmothers for working standard hours if they so desire? Should we increase the reimbursement for all government-supported child care when providers offer such care at nonstandard times? Should we follow Quebec's example—or our own experience during World War II—and experiment with state-supported child care around the clock in major cities?[6]

In conclusion, it is important that we be realistic about the complexity of the work schedules of mothers with young children and those of residing fathers too. Acknowledging this complexity should generate a meaningful dialogue about efforts to improve the fit between work schedules and child care, particularly among the working poor, and lead to more effective ways to enhance the well-being of mothers, children, and family life more generally.

9

Summing Up and Moving Forward

IN THE introduction to this book, I presented a conceptual framework for looking at the process by which factors external to the family—namely, various economic, demographic, and technological factors—affect the timing of employment of family members, and consequently individual and family functioning. In subsequent chapters, I have sought to illuminate this process. Relying on two major data sources, the May 1997 Current Population Survey and two waves of the National Survey of Families and Households (1986 to 1987 and 1992 to 1994), I have focused on documenting the widespread employment of people with nonstandard work schedules, how such persons differ from others, and whether their work schedules matter for family functioning. I have utilized data from these existing data surveys, whose purposes were far more general than the study of nonstandard work schedules and their consequences, to learn as much as possible about this neglected but important topic.

What can we deduce from this analysis? While each of the chapters provides summaries of its findings, in this final chapter I highlight some general findings and offer some conclusions and implications. My objectives are to offer direction for future research and to sensitize policymakers to the special problems faced by families working nonstandard schedules. In this vein, I spell out some of the major voids in our knowledge about such families, as suggested by the present findings. I also discuss my views on the future growth of the twenty-four-hour economy, not just for the United States but for other countries as well. This is clearly a topic that merits more global attention by researchers and policymakers alike.

Conclusions and Implications

With one–fifth of all employed Americans working nonday, variable, or rotating shifts, and one-third working weekends, it is clear that "nonstandard" work schedules are no longer that nonstandard. This fact presents special challenges to the two major types of American families that are on the rise: married dual-earner couples and single-earner mother-only households. In one-fourth of all dual-earner married couples, and one-third of those with children, at least one spouse works other than a fixed day shift. As a result, the "intact" family is often not intact temporally; that is, the family is often not at home together in the evening and at night. Moreover, almost half of dual-earner couples have at least one spouse who works weekends. Single employed mothers are more likely to work nonstandard schedules, both late shifts and weekends, than married employed mothers. The main conclusion here is that *we must rethink the way we view the family in our research and in policy discourse, especially since the proportions of these two types of families have grown remarkably over recent decades and this growth is likely to continue.* A more realistic conception of the "at home" structure of family life is essential.

Why do those who work nonstandard schedules do so? The key reason, of course, is that the jobs are there and people are in need of jobs. But do people agree to accept jobs at odd hours more out of necessity than preference? We cannot answer this question directly, but based on their reported reasons for working nonstandard hours and the distinctive characteristics of such workers, I conclude that *most people who work nonstandard hours do not prefer this schedule to a daytime schedule.* This conclusion is based on the fact that only among mothers with young children was there a substantial minority who reported family rather than job considerations as their primary reason for such employment. Moreover, for the most part, people who work nonstandard schedules appear to have more limited job opportunities, given their human capital and other considerations.

Relatedly, I conclude from their occupations and earnings that *those who work nonstandard schedules are generally more disadvantaged economically than others.* They are mostly serving the local economy in service-related jobs relating to the provision of food, health care, and the sales of commodities, and they receive similar or less pay on average compared with others in the same occupation—at least in most of the big occupations, like cashiers and retail and personal sales. However, it is also important to acknowledge that nonstandard hours of employment are pervasive throughout the occupational hierarchy and that many of the more advantaged participate in the twenty-four-hour economy as well.

What are the consequences of the widespread practice of working nonstandard schedules for American families, particularly married dual-earner couples and single-earner mother-only households? It is evident that *family consequences are complex,* since they depend not only on the type of family but on the particular work schedule, the gender of the person working this schedule, and whether she or he has children; moreover, *there are positive as well as negative family consequences of employment at nonstandard times.*

Nevertheless, *it is primarily negative associations that are evident in the relationships between nonstandard work schedules and both marital quality and marital instability.* Although not always negative for all types of nonstandard schedules, or for both men and women of all family types, the only significant positive relationships are for single-earner households in which the husband is the single earner. The negative associations are evident only with regard to employment at nonstandard hours but not on weekends, and concerning marital quality, only for nontraditional families—that is, where the wife is the single earner, among dual-earner couples, and single-mother households.

The negative associations between nonstandard schedules and the quality and stability of marriages are generally stronger when children are present. The relevance of children is especially evident with regard to marital instability. Only for couples with children do nonstandard work schedules increase the likelihood of marital instability—and then only when the husband or wife works the night shift. It does not appear to be the case that individuals who choose to work late-night hours are especially likely to be in troubled marriages, but rather that working a late-night shift (and experiencing the chronic sleep loss that so often may result) takes a special toll on the marriage.

The functioning as well as the stability of family life appear to be affected by nonstandard work schedules, sometimes positively and sometimes negatively. On the positive side, among dual-earner couples, we see *greater participation of husbands in traditionally female household tasks (such as cooking, cleaning, washing, and ironing) when they and their wives have different work schedules.* But while from a gender equity standpoint this greater male participation may be viewed as positive, we might question whether there is a better way than spouse absence to bring about such equity. (Also, as we have seen, the total amount of household work generally increases when spouses work nonstandard schedules, putting a further burden on the couple.)

As for the effect of nonstandard work schedules on the frequency of parent-child interaction among those with children, it may be positive or negative, depending on the type of interaction under consideration. Of special interest is the effect of these schedules on the extent to which parents eat dinner with their children, which I regard as the most important single daily family ritual. It is clear that *parents eat dinner with children less frequently when they work in the evenings or on rotating shifts,* regardless of the gender of the parent or family type. (Night employment does not have this effect.) *Parents working nonstan-*

dard schedules are more likely, however, to eat breakfast with their children, but which nonstandard schedule has this relationship differs by the gender of the parent and, if female, whether she is a single or married mother.

As for one-on-one parent-child interaction—namely, leisure activities outside the home, work on projects, private talks, and help with homework—there is also a mixed picture of positive and negative relationships. Differences are evident not only by the gender of the parent and the marital status of the mother, but by the type of nonday shift as well as the type of leisure activity.

It is clear that *child care arrangements for preschoolers are more complex when mothers work nonstandard rather than standard schedules;* this too has positive as well as negative implications. Among two-earner couples working different shifts, the heavy reliance on fathers for child care when mothers are employed may be seen as positive; children get to know their fathers better and vice versa. But there may be downsides that have yet to be investigated. Both dual-earner couples and single mothers rely heavily on other relatives as well, especially grandparents, more so than when mothers work daytime schedules. *Insofar as relative care generally saves money (although there is often some economic cost) and may be preferred by parents to nonrelative care, such reliance may be viewed in positive terms. But to the extent that dependence on relative care adds stress to family relationships and may be a burden for those relatives (many of whom have other jobs), this arrangement may be viewed negatively.*

Although there appears to be no research evaluating the effect of multiple caregiving on children's well-being, there is consensus among scholars that the stability of child care arrangements is important for children, and multiple care means multiple opportunities for child care to break down. It is clear from this study that *those working nonstandard schedules are more likely than those on standard schedules to rely on multiple caregiving arrangements.*

School-aged children may benefit from their parents' nonstandard work schedules because of the greater likelihood that a parent will be home when they leave for school and when they return. However, we do not know whether these parents, particularly those in dual-earner and single-mother households, are awake or asleep before and after school. Typically other child care arrangements are made when parents are not present at this time, both when parents work late and during daytime hours. But we do not know whether the small proportions of young children reported to be in self-care before and after school are greatly underestimated because parents who have worked nights are asleep when the child leaves for or returns from school.

217

The finding that those who work nonstandard work schedules tend to be more economically disadvantaged than those who work standard schedules, combined with findings related to the complexity of child care arrangements, points to a major problem for many mothers in the labor force: *mothers in low-paying jobs must put together a patchwork of informal child care arrangements at low cost to hold on to those jobs.* We have seen that about two-fifths of low-educated employed mothers do not work a fixed day schedule on weekdays only. Many others who work during the daytime undoubtedly do so during "shoulder hours"—that is, they begin work very early or end work very late, times when formal child care arrangements are typically not available. This situation has important implications for mothers moving from welfare to work or trying not to fall back into welfare. *Policymakers need to address the misfit between the hours and days of employment they require of these mothers and the availability of affordable formal child care.*

Major Voids and Data Needs

It is clear from the research to date that investigating the social consequences of nonstandard work schedules for American families is not an easy task. There are different work shifts, there is weekend employment, and the cumulative number of hours that people work needs to be taken into account. Other aspects of paid work are also undoubtedly relevant, such as the extent to which people feel they are in control of their work schedules and can change them when necessary (Staines and Pleck 1983). And as we have seen, the consequences may be different for dual-earner and single-earner couples, for single and married women, for families with children and those without children, for families with preschoolers and those with older children, and so on. On top of such considerations are the special problems of low-income parents, particularly single mothers. And there is the question of short-term versus long-term costs and benefits—for example, the benefit to father-child interaction when spouses work split shifts versus the increase in the odds of divorce if one of the spouses works nights.

These issues point to complex situations that need further study, and there are many ways to approach this. I offer my assessment of some important considerations for future research, recognizing that this is not an exhaustive list and that there are multiple approaches to each of the issues proposed.

1. We need to do focused studies on the costs and benefits of working nonstandard schedules As previously noted, most of the research to date on the consequences of working nonstandard schedules has been based on large-scale surveys or on qualitative studies that were not designed with this focus. Thus, we know very little about why people work these schedules, what they think about the trade-offs they have made, and their perception of the impact on their lives and those of family members. For married couples, it would be highly relevant to take a couples perspective and consider the relevance of both spouses' characteristics, including their gender ideologies, in making these trade-offs. It is also important to study possible differences between single and married mothers in the trade-offs made by those who work nonstandard schedules.

2. We need to distinguish different work shifts in studies of the consequences of nonstandard work schedules   As the findings in this book suggest, different nonstandard work shifts can have different effects on family life and on children. To make a more adequate assessment of these effects, we need large-scale (and preferably longitudinal) studies that oversample those working nonstandard shifts so that there are sufficient numbers to make comparisons among those working evenings, nights, and rotating shifts, as well as days.

3. We need to have precise measures of work shifts   Many of the shift work studies based on survey data use ambiguous definitions of work shifts that are often self-categorized by the respondent without clear instruction from the interviewer.[1] It would seem best to ask people the specific hours their work begins and ends (daily or for most days during a reference week) and whether they rotate, then leave the derivation of the day, evening, and night shifts to the investigator, who then reports it with the findings. This approach would also allow investigators to compare different studies by deriving similar definitions of work shifts.[2]

4. We need to study the movement of employees in and out of different work schedules   Studies of shift work have generally been cross-sectional rather than longitudinal, yet there is undoubtedly considerable flow in and out of different work schedules.[3] It is important to know the duration of shift work for employees, and particularly for employed parents, and how movement in and out of nonstandard work shifts relates to family concerns, employer demands, and the lack of alternative daytime job opportunities.

5. We need to explore the effects of nonstandard work schedules on the physical and emotional health of individuals and how these effects on individual well-being interact with the function-ing of family life Given the paucity of knowledge on this interaction, it would seem appropriate to start with intensive qualitative studies of families whose members work late and rotating shifts. It would be especially interesting to explore the extent to which those working such schedules suffer from chronic sleep deprivation and the process by which this may interact with family functioning to affect the quality and stability of marriages as well as the care of children. In the latter regard, it is important to know how well preschool-aged children are being supervised during the day by parents who work nights or rotating shifts.

6. We need more research on married fathers who care for their children during most of the hours that mothers are employed It would be revealing to know how distinctive these fathers are from other fathers and the consequences (both positive and negative) that they per-ceive for themselves of having taken on this responsibility as well as the actual consequences. In the latter context, it would be especially inter-esting to have longitudinal data to assess change over time.

7. We need more intensive research on the reasons for working nonstandard work schedules, particularly those of parents with children To date, we rely on one question in the CPS for our knowl-edge of the reasons Americans work nonstandard hours. Qualitative studies refer to some couples who report either positive or negative con-sequences of shift work, but we have no research that takes a probing look at why substantial numbers of parents have chosen these schedules and what their options were (for example, no job, a lower-paying job, or a less interesting job). In addition to some parents (particularly mothers) preferring to arrange child care by working nonstandard hours, there may be other caregiving reasons that merit exploration, such as being able to make better arrangements for the care of disabled or elderly fam-ily members. Also, it would be good to know what people really mean when they say their main reason for working a nonstandard schedule is that their job requires it, and whether there are gender differences in this meaning.

6. We need more research on the effects of nonstandard work schedules on children, including their development and school achievement Although we have made some important strides over the past decade toward better understanding the effect of child care on child development, we have generally ignored the issue of how the non-standard work schedules of parents, and the more complex child care arrangements these schedules generate, affect child outcomes. This issue calls for studies of the children in addition to the parents, and of both the frequency and quality of parent-child interactions as well as child care quality. Such research would require substantial sample sizes in order to consider children of different ages and the different work schedules of parents, both fathers and mothers. Good measures of child outcomes are also important.

Clearly, employment in a 24/7 economy presents many challenges to American families. The research to date hints at many of these, but we have much more to learn. We should not be turned away by the complexity of the issue. Indeed, I contend that when work and family research does not take into account the nonstandard work schedules of employed family members, it is likely to be missing some important explanatory variables for the outcomes of interest. Moreover, work and family policies cannot continue to ignore the temporal diversity of working families, especially those of low income. Failure to acknowledge such diversity compromises the effectiveness of such policies, as I have stressed in the previous chapter with regard to child care and welfare reform.

Future Expectations and Policy Alternatives

I have argued that the high prevalence of employment around the clock, seven days a week, is the result of various economic, demographic, and technological trends over the past decades. I do not see these trends reversing in the decades ahead. Accordingly, I expect that nonstandard work shifts and weekend employment will be on the rise in the early part of this century. Job growth projections reinforce this prediction; as we have seen, the largest growth over the current decade is expected in big occupations that are high on nonstandard work schedules. Although the speed of this movement cannot be assessed with the data available—and it may well slow down, or even become stalled, because of a weakening economy—there is strong reason to believe that the long-term trend is in an upward direction. Parents as well as nonparents are participating extensively now in the 24/7 economy and undoubtedly will do so in the future.

At the same time, the linkage between marriage and child rearing continues to weaken, resulting in more employed single mothers, and as we have seen, single mothers are more likely to work nonstandard schedules than married mothers. Married couple households with children are increasingly becoming dual-earner households, generating more split-shift couples. Both single-mother and married-couple families will find the temporal diversity in employment schedules a special challenge, particularly if they are of low income. And the job projections suggest that women in low-paying jobs will disproportionately participate in the growth of a 24/7 economy.

On the other hand, this growth may help low-skilled groups by expanding job opportunities, although some might argue that job opportunities at late hours will shift to daytime jobs if restrictive policies limit their expansion. Others might argue that the convenience to consumers is worth the costs to workers, including parents, since employees are presumably free to make their work schedule choice and those least harmed may be selecting in (or staying out). But these considerations do not negate what I believe to be the case: that the net effect of late and rotating work shifts—particularly when one factors in physiological consequences—is generally negative for the functioning of family life and for the well-being of its members, children and parents alike. (I regard weekend employment as more benign.)

"Generally," of course, means that the effects are not negative for all those employed, or for all employed parents. As we have seen, some people cite reasons for working late or rotating shifts that suggest that such a schedule is a matter of preference, and we have seen some positive relationships between parent-child interaction and shift work. The key questions from a policy perspective would seem to be: What can be done to enhance the options of those late and rotating shift workers who would prefer standard daytime schedules but cannot find a comparable or better job at such hours? And how can constraints be eased for those parents who cannot afford child care costs and must rely on split-shift parenting between spouses or relatives while preferring not to do so?

There are two policy options to consider with regard to work hours for those who are on late shifts: enforcing pay premiums without changing the number of hours worked, to better compensate workers for the social and health costs of their schedules; and reducing work hours, without a reduction in pay, to minimize the potential stress of such late schedules on individuals and families. For parents with children, policies related to child care availability are important. Two approaches for specifically helping parents are expanding the availability of evening and night care and providing more child care subsidies to low-income mothers so that they can afford the option of working during the daytime.

With regard to work hours, pay premiums for shift work are generally negotiated by unions. Some unions in the United States and Canada have expanded their approach and negotiated reduced work hours at full-time pay for those working late shifts. For example, the International Brotherhood of Electrical Workers Local 1060 and Thomas Industries agreed on a contract in March 2000 in which maintenance and oiler/cleaner workers could work a "nontraditional shift," Friday through Sunday, for thirty-six hours a week (three twelve-hour days) and receive forty hours of pay; moreover, they are protected from mandatory overtime (Labor Project for Working Families 2001). Similarly, Service Employees International Union Local 616 and the Alameda County Medical Center in 2000 negotiated to allow three twelve-hour shifts in the nursing department with pay and benefits equivalent to those of an employee working forty hours a week, with the same vacation, holiday, and sick leave accruals as full-time employees (Labor Project for Working Families 2000). Reduced work for those working late hours can also be negotiated in terms of more weeks of time off. For example, the Canadian Auto Workers, in their negotiations with Ford, General Motors, and DaimlerChrysler in 2000 (all of which employ many late-shift workers) agreed to two additional weeks of paid time off for all its workers, in addition to standard vacation time (Labor Project for Working Families 2000).

The issue of child care availability in the evenings and nights is a special challenge since it is hard to find providers willing to offer these services. Extra compensation to providers from public sources may be needed. It is also often hard to find sites for such care, since many residential communities are resistant to having busy traffic at late hours when parents would pick up and drop off their children. (This problem came to my attention several years ago when the San Francisco airport was trying to locate a child care center nearby for airline personnel with children, given the around-the-clock hours of such workers.) But hospitals have long provided extended-hour care for their personnel with children, and more recently the military has also begun to offer twenty-four-hour care (Burud, Aschbacher, and McCroskey 1984; M.-A. Lucas 2001), as have companies such as the Ford Motor Company, according to *USA Today* (November 22, 2000). An alternative approach is to provide more child care subsidies to low-income employed mothers so that they have the option of working during the daytime and being able to afford such care. As we have seen, parents who work late shifts rely heavily on multiple child care arrangements with spouses, relatives, and others. Such arrangements for late-hour care may be financially cheaper than center care, but it may be more costly in social terms for all those involved. We clearly need to get a better handle on what these social costs are.

The United States is not alone in the widespread practice of employment at nonstandard times; many other countries seem to be following a similar course. Even in Europe, with its substantial pay premiums for late-hour and weekend employment (sometimes as much as

50 percent higher), there is a movement toward expanding shopkeeping hours (Skuterud 2000).[4] Among European countries there is a diversity of national policies relating to both increased compensation and reduced work hours (Gornick and Meyers 2003). I suspect that many of these policies may not be sustained for long, despite the relatively strong unions in these countries. Employers are calling for more "flexibility" to create new jobs, arguing that employees want this flexibility over the twenty-four-hour day and the seven-day week. One can see this evolution in the growing use of the concept of "flexibilization" in Europe, in both scholarly and public discourse (Garhammer 1995; Rubery, Smith, and Fagan 1998), although it is also interpreted to mean more freedom for employers to lay off workers.

Yet, as we have seen, there is considerable variation in the levels of nonstandard work schedules among European countries. This points to the fact that country context matters—including government policies and union positions regarding the employment of workers at nonstandard times. A better understanding of the contextual reasons for crossnational variations in Europe would be informative as we consider possible directions for the individuals, employers, and governments to take to minimize the negative effects of shift work among families, particularly those with children. Dialogue on this issue is virtually absent in the United States.

The Need for Public Discourse

As I noted in the introduction to this book, as consumers, most Americans like to have stores open around the clock, to know that medical services are always available, to hear live voices on the phone when they make travel reservations at late hours, and so on. As employees, we may benefit from the expansion of job opportunities resulting from a 24/7 economy. But again, this expansion involves risks to our health, to our psychological and social well-being, and to how our families function. At present, these risks are rarely mentioned in the public discourse—indeed, we hear more about the problems of jet lag than the problems of rotating work schedules. Why is this so?

I think the neglect of this issue is due to a combination of the minimal attention given to the negative aspects of late work shifts (by unions, researchers, and policymakers) and the desire of consumers for the convenience of a 24/7 economy. For example, we clearly want nurses and air traffic controllers to be employed around the clock, and we see their parental status as irrelevant. Employers determine who will work when, usually giving priority to seniority over family concerns.

This distancing from the issue is reflected in the fact that legal regulations about night work and other scheduling issues in the United States are minimal, especially compared with other countries (U.S. Congress 1991). The Fair Labor Standards Act deals with minimum-wage and overtime compensation when individuals work more than forty hours a week, but it does not deal explicitly with work shifts. Nor does the restriction of late work shifts seem to be high on the agenda of unions, with their declining membership over recent decades. There is some discourse about the need to reduce the work week from forty to thirty-five hours, without reducing pay (see, for example, Schor 1991), but these discussions treat all hours alike and ignore the work schedule issue. (One could argue that a shorter workweek might especially benefit those working nonstandard schedules, putting them less out of sync with family and friends and perhaps making shift rotation less stressful.)

An important issue that needs to be addressed in public discourse is how to implement work schedule policies that benefit families with children while not encouraging discrimination by employers in hiring parents with young children. This issue has special relevance for women, since they typically bear the primary responsibility for caregiving.[5] Janet Gornick and Marcia Meyers (2003) call for adopting gender-egalitarian protections that disallow employers from forcing parents into nonstandard shifts, in conjunction with extensive child care, so that they can switch out of those shifts if they so desire (but presumably not lose their jobs). They argue that if this is done while also offering pay premiums for working nonstandard schedules, employers could fill these shifts by relying more on nonparents. But another side to this suggestion is that instituting or increasing pay premiums could make these jobs more attractive to parents, especially those of low income, and thus not necessarily lead to a substantial decline in the number of parents working late shifts.

This is clearly a complex matter, especially in light of our movement away from protective legislation in this country and underlying concerns about who is being protected. Indeed, the 1990 decision by the International Labor Organization to remove the recommended restrictions on women working at night in industry, revising the 1948 convention number 89 (International Labor Office 1990), is an outcome of the recognition that this had a discriminatory intent—to save those jobs for men. Similarly, in the United States protective legislation was declared by the courts to be invalidated by the 1964 Civil Rights Act, which outlawed sex discrimination.

Whereas it is debatable as to whether there should be policies that seek to reduce employment at late hours and/or encourage pay premiums, it is more obvious that we need to direct attention to what employers and families can do to minimize the risks of such schedules for workers and their family members. Some employers are concerned about instituting good shift rotation systems that minimize employee fatigue, thereby enhancing productivity and reducing accidents. There has also been employer interest recently in the use of light to control or change the circadian rhythms of those working late hours. But as Donald Tepas, Michael Paley, and Stephen Popkin (1997) note, we need high-quality research to evaluate such efforts. We also need to address the ethical issues that underlie such manipulation, insofar as it puts an employee out of sync with family and friends when off the job and interferes with family functioning. It would also be useful to have more public discourse about the lower wages received by those who work late hours in some occupations relative to the wages of those employed during the day. Such employees undoubtedly have fewer benefits as well—such as, health insurance, sick leave, and vacation time—even among those employed full-time. Improving such benefits would undoubtedly improve family life as well as individual well-being.

As I have stated throughout the book, we need to better understand how employment that is mostly at nonstandard times or rotating around the clock affects America's families—particularly those with children. It is time that we embrace the complexities of this issue by putting it on center stage, both in public discourse and in our research.

Notes

Preface

1. This conference on "Women: A Development Perspective" was sponsored by several institutes within the National Institutes of Health, and was "the first such conference focusing on research concerns to women to be held under the auspices of the NIH." according to Norman Kretchmer, then director of the National Institute of Child Health and Human Development (Berman and Ramey 1982, iii).

Chapter 1

1. The key data sources for national estimates of the hours and days that people work are the May supplements to the Current Population Survey (CPS) conducted by the U.S. Bureau of the Census for the Bureau of Labor Statistics. Although the times employees began and ended work were first collected in 1973, the questions and response categories varied in the supplements after 1980, making comparisons over time difficult. For example, in 1997 the response category "it varies" was added. Also, questions about which days employees worked were not asked until 1991. Further, the CPS sample was redesigned in 1994, adding to comparability problems over time. Using self-designated shift designations (rather than the specific work hours reported), Thomas Beers (2000) found that the percentage working other than fixed daytime shifts increased between 1985 and 1991 and then decreased slightly between 1991 and 1997, but this is shown for full-time wage and salary earners only. (Part-time and self-employed workers were excluded.) Self-designated daytime shifts were supposed to refer only to those in which *all* hours fell between 6:00 A.M. and 6:00 P.M. This instruction was not in the question, however, and Beers (personal communication, September 5, 2000) has indicated that interviewers often did not adhere to it when coding. Thus, when some or most hours, but not all, fell in

this interval, they could have been erroneously classified as daytime self-designated schedules. For a number of reasons—the self-designated shifts are not as precise as those derived from actual work times; the sample design for the CPS changed after 1994; and the response categories for the self-defined shifts changed between 1985 and 1991 (with a new category of "other")—I do not use these data to report the trend.

2. As Jerry Jacobs and Kathleen Gerson (1998) note, the changes in cumulative work time have been essentially in the number of weeks worked per year and the extent of this increase is under considerable debate.

3. These percentages refer to manufacturing and service industries within the goods- and service-producing industries, respectively.

4. National vital statistics data on age at marriage for the United States are not available after 1998.

5. In 1960, 30.5 percent of married women were in the labor force; by 2001 this had doubled to 62.1 percent (U.S. Department of Commerce 1975, table 565; 2002, table 570). The percentage point change is not precise, as several methodological changes were introduced in the Current Population Surveys in January 1994; for further details, see U.S. Department of Commerce (2002).

6. While the focus of this book is on the U.S. labor force, an interesting trend feeding the twenty-four-hour economy at a global level is the increase in the "virtual migration" of foreigners processing information for U.S. companies in their countries. This work arrangement often takes advantage of different time zones but also generates more night work in those countries. For example, Aneesh Aneesh (2001) reports on the rapid growth in the number of informational technology experts in India who provide services to U.S. software firms, allowing for around-the-clock data processing. This arrangement allows for a virtual twenty-four-hour office for U.S. clients, facilitating "just-in-time" labor at low cost relative to employing U.S. programmers. In this context, Aneesh notes, "increased globalization seems at once to also be a process of increasing localization" (363). While these programmers may be maintaining a day shift in their home country, other less-skilled workers are working nights in these countries to respond to daytime 800 phone calls in the United States for travel reservations, catalog ordering, and the like with U.S. firms. (To verify this, make a habit of asking the location of the person with whom you are speaking when making such reservations.) The cheap cost of labor more than offsets the extra expense of out-of-country phone charges.

7. An extreme but relevant demonstration of the demand for night recreation was reported in a June 19, 1995, *International Herald Tribune* headline: "Passionate Golfers No Longer Curse the Dark." The

article was announcing the opening of an all-night golf course in Deer Park, New York. The long waiting times to tee off during the weekends were apparently creating a demand for night golf for those employed in the daytime. To maintain such an enterprise, staff are needed at night. An example of responding to local demand for around-the-clock personal services is the opening in 2003 of the first 24/7 hair salon on the strip in Las Vegas (*National Investors News Update* 2003).

8. Hamermesh (1996) has also studied the prevalence of different kinds of U.S. work schedules using the May 1991 CPS. Because he is interested in comparing the results with German data, he excludes from his sample a large percentage of those who report their work schedules as "irregular," a significant omission when assessing the extent to which Americans work nonstandard hours. For my treatment of this category, see chapter 2.

9. The NSFH does permit analysis of depression in relation to nonstandard work schedules. I did not find a significant relationship.

Chapter 2

1. For an interesting analysis of how night work for a sample of trade union printers in the early 1950s enhanced their socializing with fellow printers because they were not on normal family schedules, see Lipset, Trow, and Coleman (1962). For a more recent discussion of this issue among firefighters, see Chetkovich (1997).

2. A study in England and Wales asked mothers who worked late shifts and weekends whether they preferred to work regular hours and not Saturday or Sunday, and the proportions saying yes were close to half and three-fifths, respectively (La Valle et al. 2002).

3. Often, with seniority, those working nonstandard schedules have more control over the specific hours and days they work. For example, this is the case for most flight attendants.

4. For further details on the sampling frame of the CPS, see the *BLS Handbook of Methods*, chapter 1, "Labor Force, Employment, and Unemployment from the Current Population Survey," available at: www.bls.gov/opub/hom/homch1—itc.htm.

5. Between 1973 and 1980, people were asked the hours they began and ended work most days in the prior week, but there was no question as to whether they were rotators who happened to be on the day shift in the prior week. Since about one-third of those who work other than fixed daytime schedules are rotators, this seriously underestimates the prevalence of nonday shifts. The CPS was changed in 1980 to ask specifically about shift rotation, but the response options on hours work began and ended varied in

other ways in the special CPS supplements on work schedules that followed (1985, 1991, and 1997), presenting comparability problems. As I noted in chapter 1, note 1, I do not believe one can do a rigorous analysis of trends in shift work with these data.

6. Since the writing of this book, the BLS has published very limited data on work schedules for May 2001. Changes in the wording of the questions on the time work began and ended precludes comparison between 1997 and 2001.

7. The interview instructions were to include "anytime between 2:00 P.M. and midnight" as an evening shift, thus permitting someone who worked from 2:00 P.M. to 5:00 P.M. to self-identify as an evening worker. Similarly, those working "anytime around 9:00 P.M. to 8:00 A.M." could self-identify as a night worker, including those working 9:00 P.M. to 11:00 P.M. The person working from 9:00 P.M. to midnight could thus self-identify either as an evening or night worker.

8. It is unfortunate that the BLS added the option of "irregular hours" in 1991, without further specification, since these hours could be all, some, or none worked during the daytime.

9. The BLS used these shift definitions when analyzing only full-time wage and salary workers. I use this designation for all workers, both full- and part-time and both self-employed and wage and salary workers.

10. The question reads: "Which days of the week (do you/does name) work [ON THIS JOB/FOR THIS BUSINESS] [ONLY]? (Check all that apply)."

11. These percentages are based on tabulations with groupings different from those shown for the total column in table 2.1.

12. I restricted the tabulation here to those who, according to my definition, worked evenings, nights, rotating shifts, or varied hours.

13. A study based on the 1996 Medical Expenditure Panel Survey (MEPS) showed a bigger differential than the May 1997 CPS in hourly earnings between those employed on day and nonday shifts: $13.10 and $10.10, respectively (Presser and Altman 2002). This MEPS study was the first national look at the impact of both disability status and the type of shift on hourly earnings. The study showed that employed persons with disabilities work nonday shifts to the same extent as those without such disabilities. A regression analysis controlling for the effects of various job and sociodemographic characteristics revealed that day workers with disabilities have lower hourly wages than nondisabled workers; however, except for employed men with severe disabilities, nonday workers with disabilities have hourly wages similar to those of nonday workers without disabilities.

14. The May 1997 CPS asked two questions about union membership and coverage: "On this job are you a member of a labor union or an employee of an association similar to a union?" and "On this job are you covered by a union or employee association contract?" The percentage of wage and salary earners in the rotation sample who responded yes to either question for the top ten occupations in table 2.4 are as follows: cashiers, 15.5; truck drivers, 22.7; sales workers, 1.8; waiters and waitresses, 0.6; cooks, 5.3; janitors and cleaners, 20.0; sales supervisors and proprietors, 15.9; registered nurses, 21.5; managers, food serving and lodging, 1.5; nursing aides, orderlies, and attendants, 12.2.

15. Charles Brown (1980) tested the theory of equalizing differences, which hypothesizes that workers receive compensating differences when they accept jobs with undesirable nonwage characteristics. Using longitudinal data and controlling for numerous worker characteristics, he did not find substantial compensation.

16. The computer program for grouping the detailed two-digit industries into the six categories was provided by Singlemann (personal communication, 1994). Whereas I excluded those employed in farm occupations from this sample, given the fixed temporal demands of such employment, I did not exclude those in agricultural industries (for example, secretaries or truckers), since they need not be so constrained.

17. Although we have no measures of number of dependents, including those who are ill or disabled, another reason single as well as married persons may work nonstandard schedules is to provide care to these other dependents.

18. When combining children of all ages under fourteen, their presence is associated with a lower prevalence of working nonstandard hours, but the more children the higher the prevalence. The only exception is for men with three or more children, who show the lowest prevalence of working weekend or variable days (26.6 percent) relative to all other men and women (including those with three or more children).

19. Parent's age was categorized in three broad age groups to minimize colinearity with child's age (the latter dichotomized in preschool- and school-aged).

20. Separate regressions were also done for nonmarried men and women. For nonmarried men, there was no significant relationship between parental status and nonstandard work schedules. (Few nonmarried men had children residing with them.) For nonmarried women, relative to those without children, all other parental types showed lower odds of working nonstandard hours. (Three of the five types were statistically significant.) With regard to weekend employment the findings are mixed, although the two significant

relationships show negative effects of children on such employment.

21. As this book was being completed, the U.S. Department of Labor (2002c) released some statistics on work schedules based on the May 2001 CPS, but only for full-time wage and salary earners. The report indicated that the 14.5 percent of full-time wage and salary earners who worked other than a daytime schedule in May 2001 represented a decline over the past decade. This figure was based on the self-report shift designation, which is problematic, as noted earlier (see chapter 1, note 1). With regard to the questions about when work began and ended (which is used in this book), these were changed in the May 2001 CPS and now relate to the "usual" rather than the "last" week worked. This again makes rigorous comparisons over time problematic, biasing the results for 2001 downward, as any given week is more likely to be nonstandard than the average week.

22. Further analysis (not shown) that breaks down the black and Hispanic columns by sex does not change these findings.

23. An important definitional difference is that the Eurostat LFS surveys simply ask respondents whether they usually work evenings or nights; one cannot determine how many hours of the week are worked at these late hours or how often "usually" is. Accordingly, one "usual" hour worked in the evening or at night can be designated as evening or night work, but it does not truly represent a nonday work shift. The work shift definitions for the United States use CPS data to determine whether people work most of their hours in the evening or at night (precisely defined). There is also a difference between the Eurostat LFS and CPS surveys in the way rotating shifts are defined, but an adjustment can be made here. I have classified as day workers those among the LFS respondents who worked two different daytime shifts (for example, morning and afternoon). This is more comparable with the definition of rotating shifts for the CPS (from day to evening or night). To further maximize comparability, I have grouped all nonday shifts together— evening, night, and rotating. For the United States, "nonday" includes work schedules that were too variable to be assigned a shift ("hours vary"). Since some of these workers may have had highly variable day schedules, this is an overestimate, but it compensates somewhat for the more restrictive U.S. definition of nonday work shifts. I am grateful to Janet Gornick for her collaboration in generating the estimates for the European countries.

24. Spain and Portugal are excluded because their Labour Force Surveys did not include the complete set of questions on evening and night work.

25. One should be cautious in interpreting differences in nonday employment among the European countries, since there is variability in the way the Labour Force Surveys defined evening and night work. According to Eurostat (Ana Franco, personal communication, December 7, 1999), the general definition is that evening work is done after the usual hours of working time in the member state but before the usual sleeping hours, and that night work is done during the usual sleeping hours.

Chapter 3

1. For further discussion of this issue and its impact on the interests of men, women, and children, see Presser (1995a).

2. Dual-earner couples are defined here as both spouses age eighteen or over, employed with pay in non-agricultural occupations, and both employed during the previous week except for rotators, who are included if they were employed but not at work in the previous week.

3. This study, focusing on employed mothers age nineteen to twenty-six with children under age five, found that one-third of all grandmothers who care for such children are otherwise employed. The ratio was higher for nonmarried mothers than for married mothers. The 1984 wave of the NLSY is, to my knowledge, the only national survey that includes data on the work schedules of employed grandmothers as well as mothers along with the child care arrangement of children. I had urged this inclusion, but it was not repeated in subsequent waves.

4. Seventeen percent of all nonmarried women aged nineteen to forty-four in 1995 were cohabiting, based on data from the National Survey of Family Growth (Bumpass and Lu 2000). This study also showed that three-fifths of all nonmarital births in 1990 to 1994 were to noncohabiting mothers.

Chapter 4

1. A further issue is the relative earnings of employed husbands and wives. For a discussion of this literature, which has had mixed results, see Sayer and Bianchi (2000).

2. Using the same data source, Paul Kingston and Steven Nock (1985) found among dual-earner couples that there was no strong relationship between the combined *number* of hours couples worked or the amount of time one or both spouses worked and marital or family satisfaction. (This study excluded those who work "irregular hours" and thus presumably excluded rotators.) However, their subsequent analysis of time-diary data from the 1981 Study of

Time Use (STU) showed that dual-earner couples spent less time together in domestic life than other couples, and that this was linked to marital quality—but the direction of the effect was not clear (whether more time increased marital quality or vice versa).

3. The gender of the shift worker was a control variable, however, and not found to be significant.

4. For more information on how the NSFH has been conducted, see the website at: www.ssc.wisc.edu/nsfh/home.htm.

5. The sample sizes of single-earner and dual-earner couples without children are too small for similar separate regression analyses.

6. The sample sizes are too small to do similar analyses for couples with preschoolers and couples with school-aged children separately.

7. The results shown here are different from those previously published (Presser 2000a) in that the sample is limited to married couples with at least one earner rather than including all married couples.

8. An additional demographic control was added, the number of months between the first and second waves of interviews, since this source of variation gave some couples more time at risk of marital disruption than others.

9. The additional variables—multiple job holding and overnight work-related travel—were initially included in these models but were not significant and thus dropped to minimize sample loss due to missing cases on these variables.

10. Duration of marriage was excluded as a control variable in the models distinguishing short and long duration. This permitted the inclusion of age, which was excluded from the regressions for the total sample because it was highly correlated with marital duration.

11. It may be that more egalitarian attitudes are associated with higher income among wives, enabling them to be more able to seek divorce as a viable option. However, one study based on the NSFH (Sayer and Bianchi 2000) found that, controlling for the wife's gender ideology, the wife's higher income *lowered* the odds of divorce.

12. An alternative explanation is that couples who were unhappy in their marriages at wave 1—and thus likely to have separated or divorced by wave 2—reported less quality time together at wave 1 regardless of work schedules. I have excluded other marital quality variables from the models in table 4.6 because of this endogeneity problem.

13. Regressions were also conducted with the further breakdown by whether couples had preschool (under age five) or school-aged chil-

dren (ages five to eighteen). The resulting models generally show similar results for each age group, but because of the smaller numbers in the specific nonday shifts, while high odds ratios obtained, they did not always remain statistically significant, and the validity of some model fits were questionable.

Chapter 5

1. This chapter draws on an earlier analysis of this topic using the NSFH (Presser 1994), although it is more extensive. It considers the relevance of weekend employment as well as work hours and analyzes couples with children separately.

2. Glenna Spitze (1986, 697) critiqued this position by noting: "To suggest that this division [of household labor] is rational rather than based on tradition or power differentials, one would need to show either that women can do these tasks more efficiently (not supported by time budget data) or that men can derive a greater marginal productivity in market work through being relieved of housework than can women."

3. Although the presence and ages of children are considered as constraints on time available for housework, it is never argued that men will do more housework because women do more child care. Rather, women "specialize" in domestic tasks. The nature of the relationship between stage in the life course (including age and family formation variables) and men's participation in family work is contradictory (Pleck 1983; Brubaker and Ade-Ridder 1986; Rexroat and Shehan 1987; Suitor 1991).

4. Richard Berk and Sarah Fenstermaker Berk (1979) found that husbands in dual-earner families participated more in household chores in the evenings than at other times of the day (examining only weekdays). However, their sample was too small to assess the relevance of the husband's—or the wife's—employment schedule.

5. The sample size is smaller than for the earlier study (Presser 1994) based on the NSFH because this study includes weekend employment in the models and there were about two hundred cases with missing values on this variable. The results of the regression models differed only slightly with this omission.

6. The data on hours spent on household tasks for those with excessive hours were capped at eighty-four hours per week for employed persons, while retaining the reported proportional distribution over tasks. This adjustment was necessary for fewer than 3 percent of the respondents and fewer than 2 percent of their spouses.

7. These figures differ from those derived from table 5.2 on hours of overlap in spouses' employment. The former come from a set of

questions on the total number of "usual" work hours, while the latter are derived from the grid on work hours "last week."

8. Methodologically, the level of both spouses' resources *and* the relative differences cannot be controlled, and alternative strategies are inherently problematic because of the high correlation between the husband's and the wife's resources. This analysis examines the effect of the husband's education with and without relative education.

9. Blair and Lichter (1991) used only the respondent's answers to measure both partners' gender role ideologies. I argue that the gender role ideology of each spouse has an independent effect on the hours each spouse spends on traditionally female household tasks, which in turn affects the husband's share of housework. The correlation between the husband's and the wife's gender ideology score for this sample is only .43.

10. These findings are roughly consistent with the CPS estimates reported in chapter 3; the percentages for the latter are 72.2, 10.7, 13.4, and 3.7, respectively. The slightly higher nonday estimates may be due to the fact that "hours vary" is included in nonday shifts when a shift cannot otherwise be determined for the CPS, but this category is not specified for the NSFH.

11. The significant relationships for husband's education obtain for these models when relative education of husbands and wives is omitted, except wife's hours in model 2, husband high school graduate only.

12. Regressions including the wife's earnings (logged) and excluding the husband's earnings and the earnings ratio also found a positive effect on the husband's share of housework, reaffirming the importance of the wife's earnings. High earnings among wives significantly increased husbands' hours of housework and significantly decreased wives' hours in both models.

13. Eligible respondents were asked: "About how many hours in a *typical day* do you spend taking care of [CHILD'S] physical needs, including feeding, bathing, dressing, and putting [him/her] to bed?" Respondents were asked the same question about their spouse's time with this child. Fathers' time with children was derived using both questions.

14. Bergen (1990) analyzed the absolute and relative amounts of time husbands spent in child care using the NSFH data. Neither measure was related to differences in resources, sex role attitudes, or stages in the life cycle.

15. This finding is consistent with Coltrane's (2000, 1219) assessment of the literature: "Studies using measures of men's absolute time spent on all types of household labor identify fewer significant pre-

dictors and explain less variance than studies using women's hours or proportional measures of routine housework."

16. A set of regressions was run for nonparents (not shown). Generally, overlapping hours and work shifts showed similar relationships to husbands' and wives' hours spent on housework. However, there were fewer significant relationships, and the weekend employment of both spouses was not significant for either spouse's hours of housework. Caution should be exercised when comparing these results with those for parents, given that the sample size is only 559 cases for nonparents and thus significance levels are harder to achieve.

17. Kingston and Nock (1987, 396) also argued that work schedules affect spouses' time together rather than vice versa. They noted that workers report little control over their work schedules, and that the one-way direction in which families respond to the demands of jobs "has been a cornerstone of family theory for at least three decades."

18. Scholars have a range of views on this issue. Joseph Pleck (1979), for example, argued over two decades ago that society was in transition with regard to men's roles and that the gender gap in household labor would narrow in the near future; others have been less optimistic or equivocal (Meissner et al. 1975; Huber and Spitze 1983; Goldscheider and Waite 1991).

Chapter 6

1. For a detailed analysis of the different types of parental interaction as they relate to family structure, using the NSFH data, see Acock and Demo (1994).

2. The importance of family dinners has recently been promoted by the National Center on Addiction and Substance Abuse; under the leadership of President Joseph A. Califano, this organization in 2001 launched an annual event—on the fourth Monday in September— called "Family Day—A Day to Eat Dinner with Your Children." The advice columnist Ann Landers endorsed its launching, saying: "What a wonderful idea! The key to helping our children grow up drug-free is communication, and the kitchen table provides the ideal environment. Families should have dinner together as often as possible" (*Washington Post*, September 19, 2001).

3. That dinner is usually provided by women may also be seen as symbolic of the social relations of power and subordination within the family (Charles and Kerr 1988).

4. Putnam (2000, 101) also reports that "contrary to widespread impression, dining out (alone or with others) has increased very little if at all over the last several decades."

5. The effect on the shift worker of missing meals or eating poorly or at the wrong times is another important consideration, although outside the scope of this book. These difficulties are described in a study of chemical workers (Wedderburn 2000, 19): "Morning shift (06.00–14.00) upset lunch time, forcing most workers to delay their meal by 2 or 3 hours, while the afternoon shift (14.00–22.00) had the same effect on dinner time. On the other hand, workers on night shift (22.00–6.00) respected the usual mealtimes, but at the cost of interrupting their morning sleep to eat at midday with other family members." Based on this and other studies, Wedderburn concluded that "digestive problems, including serious ones, are the most clearly established adverse health consequences of shift work" (20).

6. Rarely did employed parents who were at work in the previous week report that they did not have dinner at all with their children during that week. The percentages are fewer than 2 percent of mothers and about 4 percent of fathers.

7. The specific hours at work are determined by examining the hours when work began and ended and by assuming that people were employed during the entire interval. However, some people may not have been at work for several hours in the middle of their shift. We expect the number working split shifts who were absent from work at these precise evening hours to be few, since such splits more typically occur during the daytime. For example, a school bus driver works early-morning and late-afternoon hours but not midday.

8. For single parents who live alone and have one child only, eating meals with that child would also be one-on-one interaction.

9. Households with children under age five are also excluded, but these parent-child interactions were asked about specifically with reference to older children.

Chapter 7

1. A 1990 national child care study (Willer et al. 1991) reported that only 3 percent of centers were open evenings. Family day care providers, both regulated and nonregulated, were more likely to provide care in the evenings (13 percent and 20 percent, respectively). Which hours constitute "evening" in this study is not reported and could be just a few hours after 5:00 P.M.—not much help to those who work most of their hours in the evenings. In contrast to evening care, child care centers were more likely to be open weekends (10 percent) than family day care providers (6 percent). Here too,

data on the number of hours centers were generally open over the weekend are not provided.

2. The NSFH is not the most recent data source that would permit such a detailed analysis, but more recent data sources do not have the data on parent-child interaction and other potential consequences of nonstandard work schedules considered in this book.

3. The inclusion of questions on child care and work shifts on this fertility supplement of the CPS was paid for by NICHD and facilitated by their program officer, Wendy Baldwin, after I and others argued for the need for both types of data on a single survey. About five years earlier, Wendy Baldwin also facilitated NICHD's support of child care questions for the first time on the May 1977 CPS supplement, to study the relationship between child care and the constraints on women's employment (see Presser and Baldwin 1980).

4. Graham Staines and Joseph Pleck (1983), analyzing the 1977 Quality of Employment Survey (QES), found a relationship between informal child care arrangements and split shifts among dual-earner couples with preschool-aged children, but given the small number of cases (eighty-three), this relationship was not statistically significant. Also, as noted in chapter 4, their definition of "nonday" included afternoon employment.

5. An interesting issue not addressed in this chapter is the analytic question of what determines the assumed joint decision of employment at nonstandard times and child care choice, controlling for price. Jean Kimmel and Lisa Powell (2001) present such an analysis based on the 1992 Survey of Income and Program Participation (SIPP). Their simulation model suggests that the joint decision is differentially affected by child care prices, and that standard work schedules are more responsive to this price, implying that employment at nonstandard hours may be the only option for many mothers.

6. Fathers were asked the child care questions only when they were single parents residing with their children. Because the number of such fathers is very small, they are excluded from the analysis.

7. Some of the husbands of dual-earner married couples may have been the child's stepfather rather than father; they are grouped more generally as fathers in the discussion to follow. It is also recognized that some partners not residing in the household may provide child care.

8. A study based on the May 1985 CPS showed that 3.1 percent of all employed women did paid work fully at home (Presser and Bamberger 1993). Among all employed women in the 1986–87 NSFH, 4.67 percent did paid work fully at home.

9. When the same tabulations were computed for mothers with only one child younger than five, very similar results were obtained.

10. These child care issues are also important in relation to fathers' work schedules. However, the questions on child care were asked only in relation to mothers' employment, and the spouse supplement did not ask child care questions in the same format as that used for main respondents.

11. The base in the SIPP data was all children, not all employed mothers.

12. Single fathers living with their children were also asked this question. Given their small number, they are excluded from the analysis (as they were for the child care questions for children under age five).

13. The few children who did not attend school (presumably they were home-schooled) are not included in this analysis.

Chapter 8

1. This analysis updates one that was based on the May 1991 CPS (Presser and Cox 1997). The figures are not directly comparable, since the work schedule questions were asked differently in 1991 and 1997.

2. Among the single, never-married mothers are more likely than previously married mothers to work nonstandard schedules (data not shown). A previous analysis of 1991 CPS data (Cox and Presser 2000) demonstrated that such work schedule differences between never-married, previously married, and married mothers can be attributed in large part to their differences in occupational distribution.

3. Detailed occupations are specified only for those with at least fifty cases; other occupational categories are broad groupings.

4. It has been argued that "the 40-hour requirement would make it harder for states to run effective employment programs; would force states to misallocate limited TANF and child care dollars; ignores the fact that some parents are caring for ill or disabled family members; and does not acknowledge that the average work-week is less than 40 hours for mothers with school-age and younger children" (Greenberg and Rahmanou 2003, 1).

5. Amitai Etzioni (1993, 70) writes: "If both parents work outside the household, it is preferable if they can arrange to work *different shifts*, to increase the all-important parental presence."

6. As reported in *The Globe and Mail* (Toronto) on August 31, 2000, the cost of such care in Quebec is five dollars (Canadian) for a full daily shift.

Chapter 9

1. Time budget studies offer an opportunity to study the precise hours of employment of respondents but are usually based on one day of the workweek and rarely a full week.

2. There is also a need for comparable data over time from the Bureau of Labor Statistics (BLS), as called for by Office of Technology Assessment over a decade ago (U.S. Congress 1991). Despite this call, the BLS has continued to change the response codes to the questions on when work begins and ends. The recent addition of the category "it varies" is especially problematic, as it does not give any indication of what part of the 24-hour clock the person mostly works.

3. Daniel Hamermesh (1996, 93) examined change in the work schedules of people who were in both the May 1977 and May 1978 CPS supplements (rotation groups 1 through 4 and 5 through 8, respectively) and was able to match only 68 percent of them, since many had moved. His study showed considerable movement out of nonstandard work hours over this one year: "Little more than half of the workers who worked at unusual times in 1977 and remained on the same job in 1978 worked at unusual times in the second year." However, this percentage is not very reliable, and not just for the reasons Hamermesh presented relating to matching. An additional problem is that work schedule data from the CPS in these years did not denote shift rotators who may have been working "unusual times" most days during the reference week in 1977 but, while still a rotator, on a day schedule most days during the reference week in 1978. As we saw in chapter 2 for May 1997, rotators and those whose hours vary comprise over one-third of those who do not work fixed days.

4. On March 18, 2003, according to Richard Bernstein of the *New York Times* (March 19, 2003). the German Parliament passed a regulation allowing shopkeepers to extend the time they are open on Saturday by four hours, from 4:00 P.M. until 8:00 P.M. (Bernstein 2003). Protesters have argued that this is contrary to social justice in Germany, but the regulation has not been reversed. In the United Kingdom, where shopkeeping hours are more liberal than in Germany, the *Daily Mail* reported on January 14, 2002, that there is pressure from the business community to further expand the number of hours shops are open on Sunday from the current limit of six.

5. In reporting in the *Washington Post* (February 16, 2003) on a lawsuit against Wal-Mart over sex discrimination in pay and promotion, Steven Greenhouse quoted the company's vice president for communications, Mona Williams, as saying that women had the opportunity of becoming assistant managers, "but they did not want to work the odd shifts, like working all night long, Saturdays or Sundays."

References

Acock, Alan C., and David H. Demo. 1994. *Family Diversity and Well-being.* Thousand Oaks, Calif.: Sage Publications.

Amato, Paul R. 1998. "More Than Money?: Men's Contributions to Their Children's Lives." In *Men in Families: When Do They Get Involved? What Difference Does It Make?,* edited by Alan Booth and Ann C. Crouter. Mahwah, N.J.: Lawrence Erlbaum Associates.

Aneesh, Aneesh. 2001. "Rethinking Migration: On-line Labor Flows from India to the United States." In *The International Migration of the Highly Skilled: Demand, Supply, and Development Consequences in Sending and Receiving Countries,* ed. Wayne A. Cornelius, Thomas J. Espenshade, and Idean Salehyan. La Jolla, Calif.: University of California, Center for Comparative International Studies.

Banks, Olive. 1956. "Continuous Shift Work: The Attitudes of Wives." *Occupational Psychology* 30: 69–84.

Barton, J., Jan M. Aldridge, and Peter A. Smith. 1998. "The Emotional Impact of Shift Work on the Children of Shift Workers." *Scandinavian Journal of Work: Environment and Health* 24(supp. 3): 146–50.

Becker, Gary S. 1973. "A Theory of Marriage: Part I." *Journal of Political Economy* 81: 813–46.

Beers, Thomas M. 2000. "Flexible Schedules and Shift Work: Replacing the 'Nine to Five' Workday?" *Monthly Labor Review* 123(6): 35–40.

Bergen, Elizabeth. 1990. "The Multidimensional Nature of Domestic Labor: An Investigation of Husbands' Participation." Paper presented to the annual meeting of the National Council of Family Relations. Seattle (November).

Berman, Phyllis W., and Estelle R. Ramey, eds. 1982. *Women: A Developmental Perspective.* NIH Publication no. 82–2298. Washington, D.C.: National Institutes of Health.

Bergmann, Barbara R. 1986. *The Economic Emergence of Women.* New York: Basic Books.

Berk, Richard A., and Sarah Fenstermaker Berk. 1979. *Labor and Leisure at Home.* Beverly Hills, Calif.: Sage Publications.

Berk, Sarah Fenstermaker, and Anthony Shih. 1980. "Contributions to

Household Labor: Comparing Wives' and Husbands' Reports." In *Women and Household Labor,* edited by Sarah Fenstermaker Berk. Beverly Hills, Calif.: Sage Publications.

Bianchi, Suzanne M., Melissa A. Milkie, Liana C. Sayer, and John P. Robinson. 2000. "Is Anyone Doing the Housework?: Trends in the Gender Division of Household Labor." *Social Forces* (September): 191–228.

Bird, Gloria W., Gerald A. Bird, and Marguerite Scruggs. 1984. "Determinants of Family Task Sharing: A Study of Husbands and Wives." *Journal of Marriage and the Family* 46: 345–55.

Blair, Sampson Lee. 1993. "Employment, Family, and Perceptions of Marital Quality Among Husbands and Wives." *Journal of Family Issues* 14: 189–212.

Blair, Sampson Lee, and Daniel T. Lichter. 1991. "Measuring the Division of Household Labor." *Journal of Marriage and the Family* 12: 91–113.

Blau, David M. 2001. *The Child Care Problem: An Economic Analysis.* New York: Russell Sage Foundation.

Blau, Francine D. 1998. "Trends in the Well-being of American Women, 1970–1995." *Journal of Economic Literature* 36(1): 112–65.

Blau, Francine D., Marianne A. Ferber, and Anne E. Winkler. 2001. *The Economics of Women, Men, and Work.* 4th ed. Englewood Cliffs, N.J.: Prentice-Hall.

Blood, Robert O., and Donald M. Wolfe. 1960. *The Dynamics of Married Living.* New York: Free Press.

Bogen, Karen, and Pamela Joshi. 2001. "Bad Work or Good Move: The Relationship of Part-time and Nonstandard Work Schedules to Parenting and Child Behavior in Working Poor Families." Paper presented to the Conference on Working Poor Families: Coping as Parents and Workers, National Institutes of Health, Bethesda, Md. (November 13–14).

Boggild, Henrik, and Anders Knutsson. 1999. "Shift Work, Risk Factors, and Cardiovascular Disease." *Scandinavian Journal of Work and Environmental Health* 25(2): 85–99.

Booth, Alan, David R. Johnson, Lynn K. White, and John N. Edwards. 1985. "Predicting Divorce and Permanent Separation." *Journal of Family Issues* 6: 331–46.

Brayfield, April A. 1992. "Employment Resources and Housework in Canada." *Journal of Marriage and the Family* 54: 19–30.

———. 1995. "Juggling Jobs and Kids: The Impact of Employment Schedules on Fathers' Caring for Children." *Journal of Marriage and the Family* 57: 321–32.

Brown, Brett V., Erik A. Michelsen, Tamara G. Halle, and Kristin A. Moore. 2001. "Fathers' Activities with Their Kids." In *Child Trends Research Brief.* Washington, D.C.: Child Trends.

Brown, Charles. 1980. "Equalizing Differences in the Labor Market." *Quarterly Journal of Economics* 94(1): 113–34.

Brown, H. G. 1959. "Some Effects of Shift Work on Social and Domestic Life." Occasional paper 2. Hull, U.K.: Hull College of Higher Education. Cited in *Shift Work: Economic Advantages and Social Costs,* edited by Marc Maurice. Geneva: International Labor Office, 1975.

Brubaker, Timothy H., and Linda Ade-Ridder. 1986. "Husbands' Responsibility for Household Tasks in Older Marriages: Does Living Situation Make a Difference?" In *Men in Families,* edited by Robert A. Lewis and Robert E. Salt. Beverly Hills, Calif.: Sage Publications.

Bumpass, Larry, and Hsien-Hen Lu. 2000. "Trends in Cohabitation and Implications for Children's Family Contexts in the United States." *Population Studies* 54(1): 29–41.

Burud, Sandra L., Pamela R. Aschbacher, and Jacquelyn McCroskey. 1984. *Employer-Supported Child Care: Investing in Human Resources.* Boston: Auburn House.

Cairncross, Frances. 1997. *The Death of Distance.* Cambridge, Mass.: Harvard University Press.

Casper, Lynne M. 1995. "What Does It Cost to Mind Our Preschoolers?" *Current Population Reports,* P70–52. Washington: U.S. Government Printing Office for the U.S. Bureau of the Census (September).

———. 1997. "My Daddy Takes Care of Me!: Fathers as Care Providers." *Current Population Reports,* P70–59. Washington: U.S. Government Printing Office for the U.S. Bureau of the Census (September).

Casper, Lynne M., and Martin O'Connell. 1998. "Work, Income, the Economy, and Married Fathers as Child-Care Providers." *Demography* 35(2): 243–50.

Charles, Nickie, and Marion Kerr. 1988. *Women, Food, and Families.* Manchester, Eng.: Manchester University Press.

Chetkovich, Carol A. 1997. *Real Heat: Gender and Race in the Urban Fire Service.* New Brunswick, N.J.: Rutgers University Press.

Clinton, Angela. 1997. "Flexible Labor: Restructuring the American Work Force." *Monthly Labor Review* 121(8): 3–17.

Collins, Ann M., Jean I. Layzer, J. Lee Kreader, Alan Werner, and Fred B. Glantz. 2000. "National Study of Child Care for Low-Income Families: State and Community Substudy Interim Report." Washington: U.S. Department of Health and Human Services, Administration for Children and Families.

Coltrane, Scott. 2000. "Research on Household Labor: Modeling and Measuring the Social Embeddedness of Routine Family Work." *Journal of Marriage and the Family* 62: 1208–33.

Coverman, Shelley. 1985. "Explaining Husbands' Participation in Domestic Labor." *Sociological Quarterly* 26: 81–97.

Coverman, Shelley, and Alice. A. Kemp. 1987. "The Labor Supply of Female Heads of Household: Comparisons with Male Heads and Wives." *Sociological Inquiry* 57: 32–53.

Cox, Amy G., and Harriet B. Presser. 2000. "Nonstandard Employment Schedules Among American Mothers: The Relevance of Marital Status." In *Work and Family: Research Informing Policy,* edited by Toby L. Parcel and Daniel B. Cornfield. Thousand Oaks, Calif.: Sage Publications.

Darity, William E. 1998. "Evidence on Discrimination: Codes of Color, Codes of Gender." *Journal of Economic Perspectives* 12(2): 63–90.

Deutsch, Francine. 1999. *Halving It All: How Equally Shared Parenting Works.* Cambridge, Mass.: Harvard University Press.

DeVault, Marjorie L. 1991. *Feeding the Family: The Social Organization of Caring as Gendered Work.* Chicago: University of Chicago Press.

Etzioni, Amitai. 1993. *The Spirit of Community.* New York: Crown.

Ewen, Danielle, Helen Blank, Katherine Hart, and Karen Schulman. 2002. *State Developments in Child Care, Early Education, and School-Age Care: 2001.* Washington, D.C.: Children's Defense Fund.

Ferree, Myra Marx. 1984. "Class, Housework, and Happiness: Women's Work and Life Satisfaction." *Sex Roles* 11: 1057–74.

Fields, Jason, and Lynne M. Casper. 2001. "America's Families and Living Conditions." *Current Population Reports,* series P20-537. Washington: U.S. Government Printing Office for U.S. Bureau of the Census (June).

Fried, Mindy, and Kim Clifton. 1998. "Toward Expanding Nontraditional Hour Child Care: Summary of Findings from Employer Interviews." WEIU/PUCC working paper. Boston: Women's Educational and Industrial Union.

Garey, Anita Ilta. 1999. *Weaving Work and Motherhood.* Philadelphia: Temple University Press.

Garhammer, Manfred. 1995. "Changes in Working Hours in Germany." *Time and Society* 4(2): 167–203.

Glenn, Norval D. 1990. "Quantitative Research on Marital Quality in the 1980s: A Critical Review." *Journal of Marriage and the Family* 52: 818–31.

Goldin, Claudia. 1990. *Understanding the Gender Gap: An Economic History of American Women.* New York: Oxford University Press.

Goldscheider, Frances K., and Linda J. Waite. 1991. *New Families, No Families: The Transformation of the American Home.* Berkeley: University of California Press.

Gornick, Janet C., and Marcia K. Meyers. 2003. *Families That Work: Policies for Reconciling Parenthood and Employment.* New York: Russell Sage Foundation.

Greenberg, Mark, and Hedieh Rahmanou. 2003. "Imposing a Forty-Hour Requirement Would Hurt State Welfare Reform Efforts." Unpublished paper. Center for Law and Social Policy, Washington, D.C.

Greenspan, Stanley I., with Jacqueline Salmon. 2001. *The Four-Thirds Solution: Solving the Child-Care Crisis in America Today.* Cambridge, Mass.: Perseus.

Greenstein, Theodore N. 1990. "Marital Disruption and the Employment of Married Women." *Journal of Marriage and the Family* 52: 657–76.

———. 1995. "Gender Ideology, Marital Disruption, and the Employment of Married Women." *Journal of Marriage and the Family* 57: 31–42.

Grosswald, Blanche. 1999. "'I Raised My Kids on the Bus': Transit Shift Workers' Coping Strategies for Parenting." Working paper 10. Berkeley: University of California, Center for Working Families.

Hamermesh, Daniel S. 1996. *Workdays, Workhours, and Work Schedules.* Kalamazoo, Mich.: W.E. Upjohn Institute for Employment Research.

———. 1999a. "The Timing of Work over Time." *Economic Journal* 109(January): 37–66.

———. 1999b. "Changing Inequality in Work Injuries and Work Timing." *Monthly Labor Review* 122(10): 22–30.

Han, Wen-Jui. 2002. "Nonstandard Work Schedules and Child Cognitive Outcomes." Paper prepared for the Family and Work Policies Committee of the National Research Council/Institute of Medicine's Board on Children, Youth, and Families (July 15).

Haskins, Ron. 1988. "What Day Care Crisis?" *AEI Journal on Government and Society* 2: 13–21.

Hattery, Angela J. 2001. "Tag-Team Parenting: Costs and Benefits of Utilizing Non-overlapping Shift Work in Families with Young Children." *Families in Society: The Journal of Contemporary Human Services* 82(4): 419–27.

Hawley, Amos. 1950. *Human Ecology.* New York: Ronald Press.

Hayes, Cheryl D., John L. Palmer, and Martha J. Zaslow, eds. 1990. *Who Cares for America's Children?: Child Care Policy for the 1990s.* Washington, D.C.: National Academy Press.

Hecker, Daniel E. 2001. "Occupational Employment Projections to 2010." *Monthly Labor Review* 124(11): 57–84.

Hedges, Janice N., and Edward S. Sekscenski. 1979. "Workers on Late Shifts in a Changing Economy." *Monthly Labor Review* 102(2): 14–22.

Helburn, Suzanne W., and Barbara R. Bergmann. 2002. *America's Child Care Problem: The Way Out.* New York: Palgrave.

Hertz, Rosanna, and Joy Charlton. 1989. "Making Family Under a Shiftwork Schedule: Air Force Security Guards and Their Wives." *Social Problems* 36(5): 491–507.

Heyman, Jody. 2000. *The Widening Gap: Why America's Working Families Are in Jeopardy and What Can Be Done About It.* New York: Basic Books.

Hinrichs, Karl. 1991. "Working Time Development in West Germany: Departure to a New Stage." In *Working Time in Transition: The Political Economy of Working Hours in Industrialized Nations,* edited by Karl Hinrichs, William Roche, and Carmen Sirianni. Philadelphia: Temple University Press.

Hochschild, Arlie. 1989. *The Second Shift.* New York: Avon Books.

———. 1997. *The Time Bind.* New York: Metropolitan Books.

Hoffman, Lois, and Lise M. Youngblade, with Rebeka Levine Coley, Allison Sidle Fuligni, and Donna Dumm Kovacs. 1999. *Mothers at Work: Effects on Children's Well-being.* New York: Cambridge University Press.

Huber, Joan, and Glenna Spitze. 1983. *Sex Stratification: Children, Housework, and Jobs.* New York: Academic Press.

International Labor Office. 1990. "ILO Acts on Night Work, Chemicals." *ILO Washington Focus* 3(3): 1, 2.

Ishii-Kuntz, Masako, and Scott Coltrane. 1992. "Remarriage, Stepparenting, and Household Labor." *Journal of Family Issues* 13: 215–33.

Jacobs, Jerry A., and Kathleen Gerson. 1998. "Who Are the Overworked Americans?" *Review of Social Economy* 56: 442–59.

Kalleberg, Arne L. 2000. "Evolving Employment Relations in the United States." In *Sourcebook on Labor Markets: Evolving Structures and Processes,* ed. Ivar Berg and Arne L. Kalleberg. New York: Kluwer/ Plenum.

Kamo, Yashinori. 1988. "Determinants of Household Division of Labor: Resources, Power, and Ideology." *Journal of Family Issues* 9: 177–200.

Keller, Suzanne. 1972. "The Future Status of Women in America." In *Demographic and Social Aspects of Population Growth,* vol. 1, edited by Charles F. Westoff and Robert Parke Jr. Washington: U.S. Government Printing Office for Commission on Population Growth and the American Future.

Kimmel, Jean, and Lisa M. Powell. 2001. "Nonstandard Work and Child Care Choices of Married Mothers." Working paper 01–74. Kalamazoo Mich.: W. E. Upjohn Institute for Employment Research (December).

King, Sandra L., and Harry B. Williams. 1985. "Shift Work Differentials and Practices in Manufacturing." *Monthly Labor Review* 108: 26–33.

Kingston, Paul W., and Steven L. Nock. 1985. "Consequences of the Family Work Day." *Journal of Marriage and the Family* 47: 619–29.

———. 1987. "Time Together Among Dual-Earner Couples." *American Sociological Review* 52: 391–400.

Kostiuk, Peter F. 1990. "Compensating Differentials for Shift Work." *Journal of Political Economy* 98(5): 1054–75.

Labor Project for Working Families. 2000. [No title.] *Labor News for Working Families* 8(Winter): 1.

———. 2001. "Unions Respond to Shiftwork." *Labor News for Working Families*: 9(Winter): 3, 4.

La Valle, Ivana, Sue Arthur, Christine Millward, and James Scott, with Marion Clayden. 2002. *Happy Families?: Atypical Work and Its Influence on Family Life.* Bristol, Eng.: Policy Press.

Lipset, Seymour Martin, Martin Trow, and James Coleman. 1962. *Union Democracy.* New York: Anchor Books/Doubleday.

Locksley, Anne. 1980. "On the Effects of Wives' Employment on Marital Adjustment and Companionship." *Journal of Marriage and the Family* 42: 337–46.

Lucas, Margaret-Alice. 2001. "The Military Child Care Connection." *The Future of Children* 11(1): 129–33.

Maasen, Annelies. 1978. The *Family Life of Shiftworkers and the School Career of Their Children.* Leuven, Belgium: Katholiek Universiteit.

Marks, Emily Menlo, Suzy Edelstein, and Doug Turetsky. 1998. "Who's Minding the Kids?: The Need for Around-the-Clock Child Care in New York's Twenty-four-Hour Economy." *Community Concerns* 1(1, occasional series). New York: United Neighborhood Houses.

Mason, Karen Oppenheim, and Karen Kuhlthau. 1992. "The Perceived Impact of Child Care Costs on Women's Labor Supply and Fertility." *Demography* 29(4): 523–43.

Maurice, Marc, and C. Monteil. 1965. "Le Travail continué en équipes successives." *Revue Française du Travail* 18: 5–31. Cited in *Shift Work: Economic Advantages and Social Costs*, edited by Marc Maurice. Geneva: International Labor Office, 1975.

Meisenheimer II, Joseph R. 1998. "The Services Industry in the 'Good' Versus 'Bad' Debate." *Monthly Labor Review* 121(2, February): 22–47.

Meissner, Martin, Elizabeth W. Humphreys, Scott M. Meis, and William J. Scheu. 1975. "No Exit for Wives: Sexual Division of Labor and the Cumulation of Household Demands." *Canadian Review of Sociology and Anthropology* 12: 424–39.

Melbin, Murray. 1978. "Night as Frontier." *American Sociological Review* 43: 3–22.

Mellor, Earl F. 1986. "Shift Work and Flexitime: How Prevalent Are They?" *Monthly Labor Review* 109: 14–21.

Morgan, James N. 1981. "Child Care When Parents Are Employed." In *Five Thousand American Families: Patterns of Economic Progress*, vol. 9, edited by Martha S. Hill, Daniel H. Hill, and James N. Morgan. Ann Arbor: University of Michigan, Institute for Social Research.

Mott, Paul E., Floyd C. Mann, Quain McLoughlin, and Donald P. Warwick. 1965. *Shift Work: The Social, Psychological, and Physical Consequences.* Ann Arbor: University of Michigan Press.

National Investors News Update. 2003. "OTC BB: NBEU Has Increased in Price 200 Percent Last Week" (March).

Nock, Steven, and Paul William Kingston. 1988. "Time with Children: The Impact of Couples' Work Time Commitments." *Social Forces* 67: 59–85.

O'Connell, Martin. 1993. "Where's Papa?: Father's Role in Child Care." Population Trends and Public Policy Report 20. Washington, D.C.: Population Reference Bureau.

Oppenheimer, Valerie Kincade. 1970. *The Female Labor Force in the United States.* Population Monograph Series, no. 5. Berkeley: University of California, Institute of International Studies.

Phillips, Katherin Ross. 2002. "Parent Work and Child Well-being in Low-Income Families." Occasional paper 56. Washington, D.C.: Urban Institute.

Piotrkowski, Chaya S. 1979. *Work and the Family System.* New York: Free Press.

Pleck, Joseph H. 1979. "Men's Family Work: Three Perspectives and Some New Data." *The Family Coordinator* 28: 481–88.

———. 1983. "Husband's Paid Work and Family Roles: Current Issues."

In *Research in the Interweave of Social Roles: Families and Jobs,* edited by Helena Z. Lopata and Joseph H. Pleck. Greenwich, Conn.: JAI Press.

Presser, Harriet B. 1971. "Age Differences Between Spouses." *American Behavioral Scientist* 19: 190–205.

———. 1982. "Working Women and Child Care." In *Women: A Developmental Perspective,* edited by Phyllis W. Berman and Estelle R. Ramey. NIH publication 82–2298. Washington: U.S. Department of Health and Human Services.

———. 1986. "Shift Work Among American Women and Child Care." *Journal of Marriage and the Family* 48: 551–63.

———. 1988. "Shift Work and Child Care Among Young Dual-Earner American Parents." *Journal of Marriage and the Family* 50: 133–48.

———. 1989a. "Can We Make Time for Children?: The Economy, Work Schedules, and Child Care." *Demography* 26: 523–43.

———. 1989b. "Some Economic Complexities of Child Care Provided by Grandmothers." *Journal of Marriage and the Family* 51: 581–91.

———. 1994. "Employment Schedules Among Dual-Earner Spouses and the Division of Household Labor by Gender." *American Sociological Review* 59: 348–64.

———. 1995a. "Are the Interests of Women Inherently at Odds with the Interests of Children? A Viewpoint." In *Gender and Family Change in Industrialized Countries,* edited by Karen O. Mason and An-Magritt Jensen. Oxford, U.K.: Clarendon Press

———. 1995b. "Job, Family, and Gender: Determinants of Nonstandard Work Schedules Among Employed Americans in 1991." *Demography* 32: 577–98.

———. 2000a. "Nonstandard Work Schedules and Marital Instability." *Journal of Marriage and the Family* 62: 93–110.

———. 2000b. "Toward a 24 Hour Economy: Implications for the Temporal Structure and Functioning of Family Life." In *The Social Contract in the Face of Demographic Change,* proceedings of the Second Rencontres Sauvy International Seminar, Montreal (October 4–6).

———. Forthcoming. "Race-Ethnic and Gender Differences in Nonstandard Work Shifts." *Work and Occupations.*

Presser, Harriet B., and Barbara Altman. 2002. "Work Shifts and Disability: A National View." *Monthly Labor Review* (September): 11–24.

Presser, Harriet B., and Wendy Baldwin. 1980. "Child Care as a Constraint on Employment: Prevalence, Correlates, and Bearing on the Work and Fertility Nexus." *American Journal of Sociology* 85(5): 1202–13.

Presser, Harriet B., and Elizabeth Bamberger. 1993. "American Women Who Work at Home for Pay: Distinctions and Determinants." *Social Science Quarterly* 74(4): 815–37.

Presser, Harriet B., and Virginia S. Cain. 1983. "Shift Work Among Dual-Earner Couples with Children." *Science* 219: 876–79.

Presser, Harriet B., and Amy G. Cox. 1997. "The Work Schedules of

Low-Educated Women and Welfare Reform." *Monthly Labor Review* 120(April): 25–34.

Putnam, Robert D. 2000. *Bowling Alone: The Collapse and Revival of American Community.* New York: Simon & Schuster.

Rahman, Azizur, and Sumita Pal. 1993–94. "Subjective Health and Family Life in Rotating Shift Workers." *Bangladesh Journal of Psychology* 14: 49–55.

Reskin, Barbara, and Patricia A. Roos. 1990. *Job Queues, Gender Queues.* Philadelphia: Temple University Press.

Rexroat, Cynthia, and Constance Shehan. 1987. "The Family Life Cycle and Spouses' Time in Housework." *Journal of Marriage and the Family* 49: 737–50.

Robinson, John P., and Geoffrey Godbey. 1997. *Time for Life: The Surprising Way Americans Use Their Time.* University Park: Pennsylvania State University Press.

Rones, Philip L., Randy E. Ilg, and Jennifer M. Gardner. 1997. "Trends in Hours of Work Since the Mid-1970s." *Monthly Labor Review* 120(4): 3–14.

Ross, Catherine E. 1987. "The Division of Labor at Home." *Social Forces* 65: 816–33.

Ross, Heather L., and Isabel V. Sawhill. 1975. *Time of Transition: The Growth of Families Headed by Women.* Washington, D.C.: Urban Institute.

Rubery, Jill, Mark Smith, and Colette Fagan. 1998. "National Working-Time Regimes and Equal Opportunity." *Feminist Economics* 4(1): 71–101.

Rubin, Lillian B. 1994. *Families on the Fault Line.* New York: Harper Perennial.

Sayer, Liana, and Suzanne M. Bianchi. 2000. "Women's Economic Independence and the Probability of Divorce." *Journal of Family Issues* 21: 906–43.

Schernhammer, Eva S., Francine Laden, Frank E. Speizer, Walter C. Willett, David J. Hunter, Irchiro Kawachi, and Graham A. Colditz. 2001. "Rotating Night Shifts and Risk of Breast Cancer in Women Participating in the Nurses' Health Study." *Journal of the National Cancer Institute* 93(20): 1563–68.

Scherrer, Jeffrey. 1981. "Man's Work and Circadian Rhythm Through the Ages." In *Night and Shift Work: Biological and Social Aspects*, ed. Alain Reinberg, Norbert Vieux, and Pierre Andlauer. Oxford: Pergamon Press.

Schor, Juliet. 1991. *The Overworked American.* New York: Basic Books.

Schumacher, Edward J., and Barry T. Hirsch. 1997. "Compensating Differentials and Unmeasured Ability in the Labor Market for Nurses: Why Do Hospitals Pay More?" *Industrial and Labor Relations Review* 50(4): 557–79.

Singlemann, Joachim, and Marta Tienda. 1985. "The Process of Occupational Change in a Service Society: The Case of the United States, 1960–1980." In *New Approaches to Economic Life*, edited by Bryan

Roberts, Ruth Finnegan, and Duncan Gallie. Manchester, Eng.: Manchester University Press.

Skuterud, Mikal. 2000. "The Impact of Sunday Shopping Deregulation on Employment and Hours of Work in the Retail Industry: Evidence from Canada." Unpublished paper. McMaster University, Department of Economics, Hamilton, Ontario (August).

Smith, Kristen. 2000. "Who's Minding the Kids?: Child Care Arrangements: Fall 1995." *Current Population Reports,* series P70-70. Washington: U.S. Government Printing Office for U.S. Bureau of the Census.

Smith, Shirley J. 1986. "The Growing Diversity of Work Schedules." *Monthly Labor Review* 109: 7–13.

Sonenstein, Freya L., Gary J. Gates, Stefanie Schmidt, and Natalya Bolshun. 2002. "Primary Child Care Arrangements of Employed Parents: Findings from the 1999 National Survey of America's Families." Assessing the New Federalism occasional paper 59. Washington, D.C.: Urban Institute.

Spitze, Glenna. 1986. "The Division of Task Responsibility in U.S. Households: Longitudinal Adjustments to Change." *Social Forces* 64: 689–701.

Spitze, Glenna, and Scott J. South. 1985. "Women's Employment, Time Expenditure, and Divorce." *Journal of Family Issues* 6: 307–29.

Staines, Graham L., and Joseph H. Pleck. 1983. *The Impact of Work Schedules on the Family.* Ann Arbor: University of Michigan, Institute for Social Research.

Suitor, J. Jill. 1991. "Marital Quality and Satisfaction with the Division of Household Labor Across the Family Life Cycle." *Journal of Marriage and the Family* 53: 221–30.

Sweet, James, Larry Bumpass, and Vaughn Call. 1988. *The Design and Content of the National Survey of Families and Households.* Madison: University of Wisconsin, Center for Demography and Ecology.

Tepas, Donald I., Michael J. Paley, and Stephen M. Popkin. 1997. "Work Schedules and Sustained Performance." In *Handbook of Human Factors and Ergonomics,* edited by Gavriel Salvendy. New York: John Wiley & Sons.

Tepas, Donald I., and Jana M. Price. 2001. "What Is Stress and What Is Fatigue?" In *Stress, Workload, and Fatigue,* ed. Peter A. Hancock and Paula A. Desmond. Mahwah, N.J.: Lawrence Erlbaum Associates.

Ulich, E. 1957. "Zur Frage der Belstung des Arbeitenden Menschen Durch Nacht-und Schechtarbeit." In *Psychologische Rundschau* (Gottingen). Cited in *Shift Work: Economic Advantages and Social Costs,* edited by Marc Maurice. Geneva: International Labor Office, 1975.

U.S. Congress. Office of Technology Assessment. 1991. *Biological Rhythms: Implications for the Worker,* OTA-BA-463. Washington: U.S. Government Printing Office.

U.S. Department of Commerce. U.S. Bureau of the Census. 1960. "Marital Status and Family Status: March 1960." *Current Population Reports*, series P20-105. Washington: U.S. Government Printing Office.

———. 1975. *Statistical Abstract of the United States: 1975.* 95th ed. Washington: U.S. Government Printing Office.

———. 1998. "Marital Status and Living Arrangements: March 1998." *Current Population Reports*, series P20-514. Washington: U.S. Government Printing Office.

———. 1999. *Statistical Abstract of the United States: 1999.* 119th ed. Washington: U.S. Government Printing Office for the U.S. Bureau of the Census.

———. 2001a. *Statistical Abstract of the United States: 2001*, 121st ed. Washington: U.S. Government Printing Office.

———. 2001b. "America's Families and Living Arrangements: June 2001." *Current Population Reports*, series P20-537. Washington: U.S. Government Printing Office

———. 2002. *Statistical Abstract of the United States: 2001.* 121st ed. Washington: U.S. Government Printing Office.

U.S. Department of Labor. Bureau of Labor Statistics. 1981. "Workers on Late Shifts." Summary 81-13 (September). Washington: U.S. Government Printing Office.

———. 1998. "Workers on Flexible and Shift Schedules." *Labor Force Statistics from the CPS*, USDL98–119. Washington: U.S. Government Printing Office.

———. 2002a. "Labor Force Statistics from the Current Population Survey: Household Data Annual Averages," table 19. Available at: www.bls.gov/cps/cpsaat19.pdf.

———. 2002b. "Current Labor Statistics." *Monthly Labor Review* 125(1): 68–69, table 12.

———. 2002c. "Workers on Flexible and Shift Schedules in 2001." USDL 02-225 (April 18). Available at: www.bls.gov/cps.

U.S. Department of Labor. Women's Bureau. 1995. *Care Around the Clock: Developing Child Care Resources Before Nine and After Five.* Washington: U.S. Department of Labor (April).

Wedderburn, Alexander. 1991. "Compensation for Shiftwork." *Bulletin of Shiftwork Topics.* EF/91/27/EN. Luxembourg: Office for Official Publications of the European Communities. See www.eurofound.ie, website of the European Foundation for the Improvement of Living and Working Conditions.

———, ed. 2000. "Shiftwork and Health." Special issue of *Bulletin of European Studies on Time* (BEST), vol. 1. Luxembourg: Office for Official Publications of the European Communities. Also available at www.eurofound.ie, website of the European Foundation for the Improvement of Living and Working Conditions.

White, Lynn, and Bruce Keith. 1990. "The Effect of Shift Work on the Quality and Stability of Marital Relations." *Journal of Marriage and the Family* 52: 453–62.

Willer, Barbara, Sandra L. Hofferth, Ellen Eliason Kisker, Patricia Divine-Hawkins, Elizabeth Farquhar, and Frederic B. Glantz. 1991. *The Demand and Supply of Child Care in 1990*. Washington, D.C.: National Association for the Education of Young Children.

Williams, Joan. 2000. *Understanding Gender: Why Family and Work Conflict and What To Do About It*. New York: Oxford University Press.

Women's Educational and Industrial Union (WEIU) and Parents United for Child Care (PUCC). 1998. "The Need for Nontraditional Hour Child Care in Greater Boston: Key Findings and Recommendations." Boston: Women's Educational and Industrial Union.

Wyatt, S., and R. Marriott. 1953. "Night Work and Shift Changes." *British Journal of Medicine* 10: 164–72.

Young, Michael, and Peter Willmott. 1973. *The Symmetrical Family: A Study of Work and Leisure in the London Region*. New York: Pantheon Books.

Index

Numbers in **boldface** refer to figures or tables.

ity and quality, 81–89, **90–91,** 100, **102–3,** 105, **106–7,** 108; maternal, and child care, 176, **181,** 182–83; occupation and gender, **21,** 21–25, **23, 24,** 27–31, **28–30, 32, 57;** parent-child interactions, 161, **162–67, 170–71;** paternal employment, **38,** 39, 51–52; preference for, 11, 215, 217*n*2; reasons for nonstandard maternal work, 69–73, **70;** self-employed, **32,** 36; single-earner

households and marriage quality, 89, **91,** 92–96, **93, 95;** single mothers, 68, **69.** *See also* child care

welfare, and nonstandard child care and educational attainment, 200–201, 211–13

whites. *See* race and ethnicity

wives. *See* housework and gender; marriage

Woman's Bureau of BLS, 197, 200

women. *See* gender; mothers